THE LANGUAGE OF SHAKESPEARE

THE LANGUAGE LIBRARY

EDITED BY ERIC PARTRIDGE AND SIMEON POTTER

G. L. Brook

THE LANGUAGE OF
SHAKESPEARE

ANDRE DEUTSCH

First published 1976 by
André Deutsch Limited
105 Great Russell Street London w c1

Copyright © 1976 by G. L. Brook
All rights reserved

Printed in Great Britain by
W & J Mackay Limited, Chatham

ISBN 0 233 96762 1

25780

Contents

🌀🌀🌀🌀🌀🌀

Abbreviated Titles of Shakespeare's Plays and Poems

೫೫೫೫೫೫

Ado	*Much Ado About Nothing*
Ant.	*Antony and Cleopatra*
AW	*All's Well that Ends Well*
AYL	*As You Like It*
Cor.	*Coriolanus*
Cym.	*Cymbeline*
Err.	*The Comedy of Errors*
1H4	*1 King Henry IV*
2H4	*2 King Henry IV*
H5	*King Henry V*
1H6	*1 King Henry VI*
2H6	*2 King Henry VI*
3H6	*3 King Henry VI*
H8	*King Henry VIII*
Ham.	*Hamlet*
JC	*Julius Caesar*
John	*King John*
Lear	*King Lear*
LLL	*Love's Labour's Lost*
Luc.	*The Rape of Lucrece*
Macb.	*Macbeth*
Meas.	*Measure for Measure*
Merch.	*The Merchant of Venice*
MND	*A Midsummer Night's Dream*
MWW	*The Merry Wives of Windsor*
Oth.	*Othello*
Per.	*Pericles*
R2	*King Richard II*
R3	*King Richard III*

Other Abbreviations

🙚🙚🙚🙚🙚🙚

adj.	adjective
AN	Anglo–Norman
CUP	Cambridge University Press
EDD	*English Dialect Dictionary*
F	Folio edition (First Folio 1623)
gen.	genitive
ind.	indicative
JEGP	*Journal of English and Germanic Philology*
ME	Middle English
MnE	Modern English (present day)
MUP	Manchester University Press
OE	Old English
OED	*Oxford English Dictionary*
OF	Old French
ONF	Old North French
OUP	Oxford University Press
pl.	plural
PMLA	*Publications of the Modern Language Association of America*
pred.	predicate
pret.	preterite
Q	Quarto edition
RES	*Review of English Studies*
sb.	substantive
sg.	singular
subj.	subjunctive
s.v.	*sub voce* i.e. 'under the word . . .' in a dictionary
v.	verb

Phonetic Symbols

ᘓᘓᘓᘓᘓᘓ

THE following letters are used as phonetic symbols with their usual values in present-day English: p, b, t, d, k, g, f, v, s, z, h, w, l, r, m, n. Other symbols are used with the values indicated by the italicized letters in the key-words which follow:

CONSONANTS

ʃ	*sh*ip	θ	*th*in
ʒ	plea*s*ure	ð	*th*en
tʃ	*ch*in	ç	German i*ch*
dʒ	*j*u*dg*e	x	Scottish lo*ch*
ŋ	si*ng*	j	*y*es

VOWELS

i	s*i*t	ɑ:	f*a*ther
i:	s*ee*	o	close *o*
e	close *e*	ɔ	open *o* as in *ho*t
ɛ	open *e*	ɔ:	s*aw*
a	f*a*t	u	p*u*t
ə	fath*er*	u:	s*oo*n
ə:	b*ir*d	ʌ	b*u*tter

DIPHTHONGS

ei	d*ay*	ɔi	b*oy*
ou	g*o*	iə	h*ere*
ai	fl*y*	ɛə	th*ere*
au	n*ow*	uə	g*ourd*

Square brackets are used to enclose phonetic symbols. A colon after a phonetic symbol indicates length.

Preface

🪷🪷🪷🪷🪷🪷

EVERY reader of Shakespeare acquires some knowledge of his language by the mere act of reading the plays. This book has been written with the intention of enabling such a reader to build up the scraps of linguistic knowledge that he acquires in this way into a systematic picture. A visitor to London once indicated the journey he wanted to make and asked which bus he ought to take. A Londoner listened with growing consternation and then replied 'Oh, you wouldn't find a bus doing *that*!' The reader, and even more the editor, of Shakespeare can profit from a knowledge of the ways in which the language of Shakespeare, while differing from that of today, follows its own rules which make one reading or interpretation possible while another is virtually inconceivable.

The longest chapter in this book is the one dealing with syntax. Studies of syntax are often long, because of the space taken up by a large number of illustrative examples. I have tried to reduce the length of this chapter by giving references to paragraphs in E. A. Abbott's *A Shakespearian Grammar* (third edition, 1870) and Wilhelm Franz's *Die Sprache Shakespeares* (1939) where further examples may be found.

Reference to Shakespeare's plays are to the line-numbering of the Globe edition and to the first line of the passage quoted. The spelling is that of the First Folio, as reproduced in the thirteen-volume *The First Folio Shakespeare*, edited by Charlotte Porter and H. A. Clarke (Harrap, 1906).

I am indebted to Mrs Beryl Gaffin and Miss Moira Stevenson, who have typed successive drafts of this book with cheerful accuracy. My colleague, Professor John Jump, has allowed me to draw further on my already heavily overdrawn account of indebtedness to him by reading the typescript and allowing me to profit from his judicious comments. Greatest of all is my debt to Professor Simeon Potter, who has edited my text for press and done much more than could be reasonably expected of the general editor of a series to free the book from its grosser shortcomings.

April 1975   G. L. BROOK

CHAPTER I

Introduction

೫೫೫೫೫

1. In his *Apologie for Poetrie* (1595)[1] Sir Philip Sidney defended the English language against two charges: that it is 'a mingled language' and that 'it wanteth grammar'. The reader who has worked his way through the nearly seven hundred closely-printed pages of Wilhelm Franz's *Die Sprache Shakespeares in Vers und Prosa* (Halle, 1939) will readily exonerate the language on the latter charge. The reproach that the English language is mingled simply means that it has drawn its vocabulary from several different sources and, apart from a few eccentrics, most people would regard this as a source of strength and not of weakness.

2. When we study any period in the history of a language, it is important to recognize what varieties of language were current at that time. This reminder is especially necessary when we approach Elizabethan English, because many varieties with which we are familiar today were then taking shape. George Puttenham, in *The Arte of English Poesie* (1589) tells us something about the varieties of English that were in existence when Shakespeare began to write. Some of them are indicated as habits to be avoided. The kind of language which Puttenham regards as suitable for a poet to use must be 'naturall, pure, and the most vsuall of all his countrey'; it is that 'spoken in the kings Court, or in the good townes and Cities within the land'. The poet must avoid the language of 'the marches and frontiers, or in port townes, where straungers haunt for traffike sake', that of the universities 'where Schollers vse much peeuish affectation of words out of the primatiue languages', that used 'in any vplandish village or corner of a Realme, where is no resort but of poore rusticall or vnciuill people', and, finally, he must avoid using 'the speach of a craftes man or carter, or other of the inferiour sort, . . . for such persons doe abuse good speaches

---

1. ed. by Geoffrey Shepherd (MUP, 1973), p. 140.

13

by strange accents or ill shapen soundes, and false ortographie.'[1] All these varieties are found in present-day English and they are all mentioned or exemplified in the plays of Shakespeare, though to varying extents. The language spoken in the king's court is that used in the serious scenes in all the plays; some plays are written wholly in this style. The language of 'the marches and frontiers' may be said to describe the more or less conventional stage dialects of Doctor Caius and Sir Hugh Evans in *The Merry Wives of Windsor* or Jamy and Fluellen in *King Henry V*. The affectations of scholars are admirably illustrated in *Love's Labour's Lost*. Young men who had travelled abroad were fond of imitating French or Italian accents and of introducing loan-words from those languages into English. Pedants were interested in etymology; they used spelling pronunciations and insisted on pronouncing letters which had become silent in ordinary speech. In a few words such as *perfect* and *fault*, they succeeded in persuading the educated classes to follow their example. The speech of rustics is illustrated by Edgar's disguised speech in *King Lear* and by Audrey and William in *As You Like It*. Lastly Puttenham refers to class dialects, of which little had been heard before the time of Shakespeare. We find sub-standard dialects used by the sailors in *Pericles* and by the carters in *1 King Henry IV*, and Prince Hal boasts that he has acquired such a dialect to make himself popular with the drawers at the Boar's Head. Other examples are the speeches, loose in sentence-structure and rich in malapropisms, of characters like Dogberry and Mistress Quickly. Besides the varieties described by Puttenham, there are others, some of which may be literary or dramatic conventions, such as the rhetorical passages which the Players in *Hamlet* provide at Hamlet's request and the inflated stage language parodied by Falstaff when pretending to rebuke Prince Hal (1H4 11.4.438ff) and imitated by Pistol in his quotations of scraps of old plays. Courtiers like Osric and Le Beau and the logic-chopping clowns of the early plays provide further varieties.

There were more permissible variants in Elizabethan pronunciation than there are today. Grammarians writing at the time record pronunciations different from those which they themselves recommend, and phonetic doublets are often fixed by rhyme: *again* rhymes with *vain* and *rain* but also with *men*; *-ly* rhymes with *be*

[1]. George Puttenham *The Arte of English Poesie*, ed. by Gladys Doidge Willcock and Alice Walker (CUP, 1936), p. 144.

and *me* as well as with *eye* and *lie*. There is similar variety in spelling, arising from the mixture of traditional and phonetic spellings. Even today there is not complete uniformity in English spelling or pronunciation, but in Elizabethan times the variety was greater. The existence of variants made the poet's task in scansion and rhyming all the easier. For example, the suffix *-tion* could be pronounced as one syllable or two. In many words long open and close *e* existed side by side. In such words it was usually the form with long close *e* which provided the ancestor for the present-day form, but there are five words (*break, steak, drain, great* and *yea*) whose present-day pronunciation goes back to a sixteenth-century form with long open *e*. Similarly we have *parson* going back to a form in which *er* became *ar* and *servant* from one in which *er* had been preserved or restored. There are some features of Elizabethan English which have affinities with the literary language of today. Like the Elizabethans, we take pleasure in complexity of meaning, and we do not complain of the 'ruggedness or difficulty' which Johnson found in Shakespeare.

3. To study Shakespeare's language it is necessary to go back to the early texts, and the study of language involves a study of textual criticism. An emendation, however ingenious, must be rejected if it is linguistically out of harmony with the language current in Elizabethan England. Some of the most familiar Shakespearean quotations are not from Shakespeare at all, but are the work of eighteenth-century adapters or editors. Did Shakespeare's Richard III ever say 'Off with his head – so much for Buckingham',[1] and did the dying Falstaff babble of green fields? He may have done, and modern studies of Elizabethan handwriting have supported Theobald's famous emendation, but the reading of the First Folio is 'a Table of greene fields' (H5 II.3.19). To study Shakespeare's language it is fortunately not necessary to understand every word he wrote; we often have to admit defeat, but we must avoid drawing conclusions from single occurrences of words or from passages of whose interpretation we cannot feel certain. Ignorance of Elizabethan English or indifference to it has led editors to indulge in emendations that are unjustified; Pope was one of the worst offenders. The use of *his* as a neuter possessive pronoun is normal in Shakespeare, but the fact did not prevent Pope from reading *its* for *his* in the line: That every nice offence

1. The quotation is from Colley Cibber's revision of *Richard III* IV.3.

should beare his Comment. (jc iv.3.8). Pope did not stop short at substituting a different word from the one in the text in order to produce an image that seemed to him an improvement. Polonius advises Laertes how to treat his true friends: 'Grapple them to thy Soule with hoopes of Steele' (Ham. 1.3.63). Pope reads *hooks* for *hoopes*.

4. Lord Evans[1] speaks of the conflict found again and again in Shakespeare's use of language between sumptuous diction and simple and direct statement. It is not altogether a conflict, since one kind of language sets off the other and there is a gain by contrast. It is in *Love's Labour's Lost*, a play known for its extravagant language, that we find simple language used in jest about Hector of Troy:

> The sweet War-man is dead and rotten,
> Sweet chuckes, beat not the bones of the buried:
> When he breathed he was a man (v.2.666)

In Shakespeare's early plays we find a delight in the patterns of language for their own sake, leading to the use of many rhetorical flourishes. In *Love's Labour's Lost* Shakespeare is preoccupied with the mechanics of language, grammar, logic and rhetoric. He wrote at a time when the elaborate rhetorical rules of the Middle Ages were breaking down. The language was changing quickly and there was much linguistic freedom.

5. In Shakespeare's early plays there are many speeches full of easily identified rhetorical devices. In the later plays these rhetorical devices are replaced by more subtle and complicated language. Classical allusions are most common in the early plays. In them we find protracted imagery, where one idea is slowly and carefully compared with another. Later the imagery is more restless and condensed.

The dominant style of the early historical plays is rhetorical, often with a number of comparisons set out one after the other. An outstanding example is John of Gaunt's eulogy of England in *King Richard II*. In the later plays the thought is often so concentrated that comparisons are never fully developed; as soon as a comparison is half-formulated it becomes the basis of a new image.

It is a characteristic of the early plays that every noun should have its adjective, as in Portia's speech:

1. *The Language of Shakespeare's Plays*, p. 2.

How all the other passions fleet to ayre,
As doubtfull thoughts, and rash-imbrac'd despaire:
And shuddring feare, and greene-eyed jealousie.

(Merch. III.2.107)

Devices such as the refrain are more common in the early plays. In the dispute between Portia and Bassanio (Merch. v.1.193–202) nine out of ten lines end with the words 'the Ring'.

A characteristic of the early plays is the piling up of words all performing the same grammatical function. Cupid is:

This wimpled, whyning, purblinde waiward Boy,
This signior Junior, gyant-dwarfe, don *Cupid*,   (LLL III.1.181)

In the same speech Berowne says 'Well, I will love, write, sigh, pray, sue and groan'. Holofernes, with his love of synonyms, readily conforms to this practice:

after his undressed, unpolished, uneducated, unpruned, untrained, or rather unlettered, or ratherest unconfirmed fashion.

(LLL IV.2.16)

Such piling-up is especially useful to express strong emotion in the use of terms of abuse, as when Berowne is annoyed at the disclosure of his plot:

Some carry-tale, some please-man, some slight Zanie,
Some mumble-news, some trencher-knight, som Dick,
That smiles his cheeke in yeares, and knowes the trick
To make my Lady laugh, when she's dispos'd.   (LLL V.2.463)

The piling-up becomes more striking when the units are phrases rather than words, as when Holofernes says of Don Armado:

His humour is lofty, his discourse peremptorie: his tongue filed, his eye ambitious, his gait majesticall, and his generall behaviour vaine, ridiculous, and thrasonicall. He is too picked, too spruce, too affected, too odde, as it were, too peregrinat, as I may call it.

(LLL V.1.42)

6. There are several famous passages in the plays which analyse or extol the appeal of literature and the arts: Theseus on the poet in *A Midsummer Night's Dream*, Lorenzo and Jessica on music in *The Merchant of Venice*, and Hamlet's advice to the Players. The

17

first two of these do not give much detailed criticism, but Hamlet gives sound practical advice. Criticism of language takes two forms. It may be direct, with characters in the plays commenting on what seem to them to be the linguistic shortcomings of other characters, or it may be indirect. If a particular word or phrase is used mainly or exclusively by foolish characters, we may suspect a satirical intention.

The number of characters who indulge in linguistic criticism is large and they belong to a surprisingly wide range of social classes. There is nothing surprising in such comments from Berowne, Mercutio, Falstaff, Prince Hal, Hotspur, Hamlet and Polonius, but the critics include also Costard and Doll Tearsheet. Costard's comment on Sir Nathaniel's failure as Alexander is essentially sound:

> He is a marvellous good neighbour in sooth, and a verie good Bowler: but for Alisander, alas you see, how 'tis a little ore-parted.   (LLL V.2.585)

There is sometimes a suggestion that plain men should not try to imitate the language of their betters. In *King John* a citizen of Angiers makes a speech full of hyperbolical rhetoric, and the Bastard derides it:

> Our eares are cudgel'd . . . I was never so bethumpt with words. Since I first cal'd my brothers father Dad.   (II.1.464)

There may be some class feeling here. What business has a mere citizen to use the figures of rhetoric? There are other plays where characters show signs of impatience with the language used by other characters, and the comment often anticipates the criticism of a modern reader. The dying John of Gaunt puns on his name for ten lines and King Richard makes the reasonable comment: Can sicke men play so nicely with their names? (R2 II.1.84). In *The Merchant of Venice* Lorenzo grows tired of Launcelot's quibbling:

> How everie foole can play upon the word, I thinke the best grace of witte will shortly turne into silence, and discourse grow commendable in none onely but Parrats: (Merch. III.5.49)

When Launcelot refuses to take the hint, Lorenzo bursts out: Yet more quarrelling with occasion.

The characters in *The Merry Wives of Windsor* are very language-conscious, and correct one another freely. It adds to the jest if the corrector himself uses eccentric English. Slender's 'that I am freely dissolved, and dissolutely' earns a rebuke from Sir Hugh Evans: 'It is a fery discretion-answer; save the fall is in the 'ord, dissolutely' (MWW 1.1.261). Page calls the Host 'my ranting-Host of the Garter' (II.1.196) and the Host justifies the description by calling Page *Bully-Rooke* and *Cavaleiro-Justice* (II.1.200).

The characters in *Twelfth Night* are all conscious of nuances in the use of words. Feste describes himself as Olivia's 'corrupter of words' (III.1.39) and he is very ready to play on words. When he is tired of quibbling, he anticipates any protest: wordes are growne so false, I am loath to prove reason with them (III.1.29). He protests against the use of a vogue word: 'who you are, and what you would are out of my welkin, I might say Element, but the word is over-worne' (III.1.64). He is equally critical of Sebastian's use of the words 'vent thy folly':

> Vent my folly: He has heard that word of some great man, and now applyes it to a foole, . . . I prethee now ungird thy strange-nes, and tell me what I shall vent to my Lady? Shall I vent to hir that thou art comming? (IV.1.13)

Hamlet is the play with most criticism. Hamlet is a very sensitive critic of language both in his comments on the speech of other characters in the play and in his general reflections on the way in which language is used. He realizes that language is a much more complicated matter than a mere statement of fact. In asking for a pledge of secrecy from his friends, he mentions some of the ways in which information can be conveyed by hints. He asks for a promise:

> That you at such time seeing me, never shall
> With Armes encombred thus, or thus head-shake;
> Or by pronouncing of some doubtfull Phrase;
> As well, we know, or we could and if we would,
> Or if we list to speake; or there be and if there might,
> Or such ambiguous giving out to note,
> That you know ought of me; (I.5.171)

His advice to the Players at the beginning of III.2 is a plea for natural delivery on the part of actors without ranting or excessive use of gestures. It is clear that the style of acting which Hamlet attacks was even then coming to be regarded as old-fashioned. The First Player does not claim that the charges are without foundation; he expresses the hope that they are no longer true.

As a dramatic critic Hamlet has a rival in Polonius. His praise of Hamlet's delivery, 'well spoken, with good accent, and good discretion' (II.2.488), has the vagueness of a courtier, and his comment on the Player's continuation, 'This is too long', provokes Hamlet to the contemptuous protest: 'He's for a Jigge, or a tale of Baudry, or hee sleepes' (II.2.522). Polonius is not a man to take such a rebuke lying down, so Hamlet's protest about 'the mobled Queene' brings Polonius to its defence: 'That's good: Mobled Queene is good'. He has earlier criticized Hamlet's use of words: 'beautified is a vilde Phrase' (II.2.111), and he has himself been the subject of the Queen's censure for his long-winded playing with words: 'More matter, with lesse Arte' (II.2.95). Hamlet's interest in language is shown especially in his treatment of Osric:

> He did Complie with his Dugge before hee suck't it: thus had he and many more of the same Beavy that I know the drossie age dotes on; only got the tune of the time, and outward habite of encounter, a kinde of yesty collection, which carries them through & through the most fond and winnowed opinions; and doe but blow them to their tryalls: the Bubbles are out.
>
> (V.2.195)

Other examples of linguistic criticism in the plays include the scornful comment of Jaques to Orlando: 'You are ful of prety answers' (AYL III.2.289), and Benedick's opinion that falling in love has had a bad effect on Claudio:

> he was wont to speake plaine & to the purpose (like an honest man & a souldier) and now is he turn'd orthography, his words are a very fantasticall banquet, just so many strange dishes:
>
> (Ado II.3.17)

7. Characters criticize themselves by implication when there is a noticeable gap between promise and performance. Berowne in *Love's Labour's Lost* forswears the use of fine language in words that provide a good example of the kind of language that he is promising to forswear:

> Taffata phrases, silken termes precise,
> Three-pil'd Hyperboles, spruce affection;

> Figures pedanticall, these summer flies,
> Have blowne me full of maggot ostentation.
>
> (v.2.406)

Hotspur represents the point of view of the plain man who has no use for poetry: I had rather be a Kitten, and cry mew, then one of these same Meeter Ballad-mongers (1H4 III.1.128). But he rails against poetry with such poetic eloquence that we are left wondering whether he is insensitive to poetry or whether he just doesn't like Glendower:

> he angers me,
> With telling me of the Moldwarpe and the Ant,
> Of the Dreamer *Merlin*, and his Prophecies;
> And of a Dragon, and a finne-lesse Fish,
> A clip-wing'd Griffin, and a moulten Raven,
> A couching Lyon, and a ramping Cat,
> And such a deale of skimble-skamble Stuffe,
> As puts me from my Faith. (III.1.148)

8. Criticism is not always adverse. When Holofernes describes Armado as 'Peregrinat', Nathaniel's admiration is so great as to cause him to draw out his table-book to make a note of the word for his own future use. Similarly Armado's reference to 'the *posteriors* of this day, which the rude multitude call the after-noone' arouses the admiration of Holofernes:

> The *posterior* of the day, most generous sir, is liable, congruent, and measurable for the afternoone: the word is well culd, chose, sweet, and apt I doe assure you sir, I doe assure. (LLL v.1.96)

In *Twelfth Night* Sir Andrew is impressed by Viola's extravagant language, which amuses Olivia:

> That youth's a rare Courtier, raine odours, wel . . . Odours pregnant and vouchsafed: Ile get 'em all three already'
>
> (III.1.98)

Criticism is here used to portray the character of the critic. Similarly in *The Merry Wives of Windsor* Nym announces in a foolish speech that Falstaff loves Mistress Ford. Page comments 'I never heard such a drawling-affecting rogue' (II.1.145). Ford, on the other hand, approves of Nym because he provides confirmation of his jealousy, and says: 'Twas a good sensible fellow: well. (II.1.151).

Justice Shallow and Bardolph are agreed on the excellence of the word 'accommodated':

Bardolph Sir, pardon: a Souldier is better accommodated, then with a Wife.

Shallow It is well said, Sir; and it is well said indeede, too: Better accommodated? it is good, yea indeede is it: good phrases are surely, and every where very commendable . . .

Bardolph . . . I will maintaine the word with my Sword, to bee a Souldier-like Word, and a Word of exceeding good Command.
(2H4 III.2.72)

9. Parody is frequently used with the purpose of mockery or criticism. An example is to be found in Touchstone's verses in *As You Like It*, beginning:

If a Hart do lacke a Hinde,
Let him seeke out Rosalinde: (III.2.107)

Another example is in *Othello*. The Duke tries to comfort Brabantio with a series of sententious platitudes in rhymed couplets, to which Brabantio replies in bitter mockery with a series of comments in the same metre, then breaks off impatiently with a line of prose: 'I humbly beseech you proceed to th'Affaires of State' (I.3.220). In *Twelfth Night* Olivia makes fun of the inventory of beauty of the romantic lover: Item two lippes indifferent redde (I.5.265), and Feste, as Sir Topas, parodies the use of pedantic jargon (IV.2.40). Falstaff and Prince Hal parody Lyly's Euphuism and the old drama (1H4 II.4.435). Falstaff's soliloquy on honour is a parody of the old question and answer type of debate that Lyly had taken over from the schoolroom (1H4 V.1.128). Armado and other affected characters make frequent use of such debate. The scene where Hamlet leaps into Ophelia's grave is full of old-fashioned rhetoric, and Hamlet calls attention to it himself:

Nay, and thou'lt mouth,
Ile rant as well as thou.   (V.1.306)

When Silvius in *As You Like It* has recited the feelings of a true lover, Touchstone parodies them:

> I remember when I was in love, I broke my sword upon a stone, and bid him take that for comming a night to *Jane Smile*
>
> (II.4.47)

Dogberry parodies the methods of logical exposition when he enumerates offences that are all really the same offence:

> Marrie sir, they have committed false report, moreover they have spoken untruths, secondarily they are slanders, sixt and lastly, they have belyed a Ladie, thirdly, they have verified unjust things, and to conclude, they are lying knaves.

Don Pedro parodies this parody by replying under the same heads, and again each supposedly separate question is really the same:

> First I aske thee what they have done, thirdlie I aske thee what's their offence, sixt and lastlie why they are committed, and to conclude, what you lay to their charge. (Ado v.1.225)

Hamlet parodies Osric's affectations in such questions as 'What imports the nomination of this gentleman?' (v.2.132). Osric is too dull-witted to recognize parody, so Hamlet has to resort to direct criticism:

> *Ham.* What call you the Carriages?
> *Osric* The Carriages Sir, are the hangers.
> *Ham.* The phrase would bee more Germaine to the matter:
>   If we could carry Cannon by our sides; I would it might
>   be Hangers till then; (v.2.160)

When Kent has been rebuked for rudeness, he retaliates by addressing Cornwall in a parody of the language that would be used by a flattering courtier:

> *Kent* Sir, in good faith, in sincere verity,
>   Under th' allowance of your great aspect,
>   Whose influence like the wreath of radiant fire
>   On flicking *Phoebus* front. (Lear II.2.111)

In *Troilus and Cressida* Thersites parodies Cressida's insincere couplets in a couplet in similar metre and style which sums up the speaker's opinion of her speech:

> A proofe of strength she could not publish more;
> Unless she say, my minde is now turn'd whore. (v.2.113)

10. Beside the parody of the speech of characters in the plays, there are several passages which parody prevailing literary fashions, or, more often, fashions which were just ceasing to prevail. Such passages often occur in a play within a play. The most famous examples are the speech about 'the rugged Pyrrhus' and 'The Mousetrap' in *Hamlet*, and the play produced by the rude mechanicals in *A Midsummer Night's Dream*. Another example occurs in the second part of *King Henry IV*, where Pistol's rhetoric is a parody of the ranting passages in old historical plays.

11. Another form of criticism is the rhetorical figure *tapinosis*, the repetition of a word to ridicule it. When Thersites overhears Hector saying 'Goodnight, sweet Lord *Menelaus*', he is moved to ridicule: Sweet draught: sweet quoth–a ? sweet sinke, sweet sure (Troil. v.1.83). In *The Merry Wives of Windsor* Mistress Quickly says 'Shall I vouch-safe your worship a word, or two?' and Falstaff comments on the stilted word by replying 'ile vouchsafe thee the hearing' (11.2.42).

A word may be ridiculed by repetition in apparent agreement. When Hamlet's mother tries to console him by reminding him that death is common, he seems to be holding himself in when he agrees 'I Madam, it is common'. The Queen, encouraged by this agreement, goes on to ask 'If it be; Why seemes it so particular with thee?' Hamlet again replies by repeating one word used by the Queen, but this time his angry disagreement is obvious: Seemes, Madam? Nay, it is: I know not Seemes: (1.2.74).

The word held up to ridicule is generally used by another character, but sometimes a speaker seems to be parodying only himself, as when Pandarus says:

Faire be to you my Lord, and to all this faire company: faire desires in all faire measure fairely guide them, especially to you faire Queene, faire thoughts be your faire pillow.

(Troil. iii.1.46)

Criticism may be expressed by the preservation of another speaker's imagery, sometimes with the addition of a comment. Pandarus says 'I will make a complementall assault upon him, for my businesse seethes', and a servant replies 'Sodden businesse, there's a stewed phrase indeede.' (Troil. iii.1.41).

12. When a character in a play uses an unusual word, another character is liable to comment on it derisively or to make a mis-

taken guess at its meaning. Hamlet says to Osric: why is this impon'd as you call it? (v.2.170). In *The Winter's Tale* the Clown explains an unfamiliar word to his father: 'Advocate's the Courtword for a Pheasant' (IV.4.768). Casca refuses to understand Cassius when he says that they both have the falling sickness: I know not what you meane by that, but I am sure *Cæsar* fell downe (JC 1.2.259). Shopkeepers were satirized for their mild oaths. Falstaff, refused credit by a shopkeeper, describes him as 'a Rascally-yea-forsooth-knave' (2H4 1.2.42).

13. It is not only words that are criticized. In *Love's Labour's Lost* there is criticism of pronunciation and the use of Latin. One of the most famous passages of phonetic criticism in Shakespeare, interesting because it is so explicit, is that by Holofernes of the pronunciation of Don Armado:

> I abhor such phinaticall phantasims, such insociable and poynt devise companions, such rackers of ortagriphie, as to speake dout fine, when he should say doubt; det, when he shold pronounce debt; d e b t not d e t: he clepeth a Calf, caufe: halfe, haufe: neighbour *vocatur* nebour; neigh abreviated 'ne': this is abhominable, which he would call abhominable: (LLL V.1.20)

Holofernes is equally vigilant and equally wrong-headed as a critic of Latin. He comments on Sir Nathaniel's Latin reply with the words: '*prescian*, a little scratcht, 'twil serve' (v.1.31). It is shortly after this that Moth utters his often-quoted comment 'They have beene at a great feast of Languages, and stolne the scraps', and Costard, with unexpected erudition, quotes the medieval jest of the longest known word: honorificabilitudinitatibus.

CHAPTER 2

Words and their Meanings

🙰🙰🙰🙰🙰🙰

14. Precision in describing the extent of the vocabulary of any author is impossible, because there is room for difference of opinion how far derivatives are distinct words, but we may accept the view that Shakespeare's vocabulary is of the order of twenty thousand words. There is no contradiction between this figure and the figure of fifty thousand or so that the average man may find from a random check of a dictionary to be his own vocabulary. The number of words known is always larger than the number actually used in published writings.

One of the characteristics of Shakespeare's vocabulary is its exuberance. Some of the characters in *1 King Henry IV* show great skill in the piling-up of terms of abuse of the kind that we find in Nashe. Gadshill says:

> I am joyned with no Foot-land-Rakers, no Long-staffe six-penny strikers, none of these mad Mustachio-purple-hu'd-Maltwormes, but with Nobility, and Tranquilitie; Bourgomasters, and great Oneyers, such as can holde in, such as will strike sooner then speake, and speake sooner then drinke, and drinke sooner then pray: (II.1.78)

The exuberance of Shakespearean vocabulary is sometimes heightened by contrast. When Kent meets Oswald in *King Lear*, he is at first pointedly taciturn, making replies like 'T'th'myre' and 'I love thee not'. After a few exchanges of this kind, Oswald's question 'What do'st thou know me for?' opens the floodgates, and Kent replies:

> A knave, a Rascall, an eater of broken meates; a base, proud, shallow, beggerly, three-suited-hundred-pound, filthy woosted-stocking knave, a Lilly-livered, action-taking, whoreson, glasse-gazing super-serviceable finicall Rogue, one Trunke-inheriting slave, one that woulds't be a Baud in way of good service, and

26

art nothing but the composition of a Knave, Begger, Coward, Pandar, and the Sonne and Heire of a Mungrill Bitch, one whom I will beate into clamours whining, if thou deny'st the least sillable of thy addition. (II.2.15)

15. Shakespeare's vocabulary shows an interesting mixture of old and new. There are some words, strange to a modern reader, which cause no difficulty to one familiar with Middle English poetry. Side by side with these archaisms, there are many neologisms, some of which have since become well established, while others have never really taken root in the language. Archaisms tend to occur especially in plays within a play, in the language of Gower as Prologue in *Pericles*, and in the speech of certain characters, such as Pistol. Tags, which often had little meaning, were a feature of Middle English poetry. One such tag was *more and less*, which is used in Shakespeare in the sense 'persons of all ranks' as at *2 King Henry 4* 1.1.209 and *Macbeth* v.4.9. Another was the comparison 'white as whalebone'. A fourteenth-century poet began a lyric in praise of his lady with the words 'A wayle whyt ase whalles bon'.[1] Berowne, in *Love's Labour's Lost* speaks of a flower 'that smiles on everie one, To shew his teeth as white as Whales bone' (v.2.331).

Words which are now obsolete, but which survived, sometimes as archaisms, in Shakespeare's day include: *brook* 'endure', *clepe* 'call', *cote* 'cottage', *dole* 'sorrow', *eke* 'also', *ging* 'gang, set', *hardiment* 'valour', *hie* 'hasten', *hight* 'is called', *leman* 'sweetheart', *perdy* 'by God, certainly', *targe* 'light shield', *tristful* 'sad', *wight* 'person', *yare* 'ready, nimble, brisk'.

16. Some Shakespearean characters, such as Don Armado and Pistol, go out of their way to coin new words and others, such as Osric, like to use familiar words in unfamiliar senses. Don Armado is described as a man fond of neologisms: 'A man of fire, new words, fashions owne Knight' (LLL I. 1.179), and Sir Nathaniel takes a pride in the piling up of synonyms: 'I did converse this *quondam* day with a companion of Kings, who is intituled, nominated, or called Don Adriano de Armatho.' (LLL v.1.6).

There are many English words whose earliest recorded occurrence is in Shakespeare's plays. One reason for this is that Shakespeare's vocabulary has been studied very thoroughly, but the chief

1. *The Harley Lyrics* ed. by G. L. Brook (MUP, 1948), 9.1.

reason is that he was in fact an innovator. Some of his innovations are now so familiar that we have no idea that Shakespeare was the first to use them. Such words are *assassination*, *barefaced*, *countless*, *courtship*, *dwindle* and *laughable*. Others are words so rare that the Shakespearean use is the last, as well as the first, recorded occurrence in English, but such words are generally loan-words, made up of such familiar elements that their meaning is obvious. Words first used in English by Shakespeare which have never really taken root in the language include *appertainments*, *conflux*, *embrasures*, *tortive*, *unplausive*, *abruption*, *persistive*, *protractive* and *soilure*, all from *Troilus and Cressida*. Other examples are *cadent*, *questrist*, *vastidity*, *ungenitured*, *circummur'd* and *exsufflicate*. Shakespeare made very effective use of compounds made up of short familiar elements, such as *fretful*, *eventful*, *dog-weary*, *fancy-free*, *crop-ear*, *ill-got*, and *lack-lustre*. He had no fear of hybrids, like *bodement*, *exteriorly*, and *increaseful*. Another group consists of poetic compounds made up of two adjectives like *deep-contemplative* (AYL II.7.31) and *wilful-negligent* (WT I.2.255). There are compounds made up of two elements which resemble each other except for the initial consonant or the stem-vowel. Some of these are very expressive words like *skimble-skamble* 'nonsensical', *kickie-wickie* 'wife' and *hugger-mugger* 'secrecy'. Another group of compound words which have not taken root in the language consists of nouns prefixed by adverbs which normally follow the noun. Such are *my here-remain* (Macb. IV.3.148), *my hence-departure* (WT I.2.450), *thy here approach* (Macb. IV.3.133). Some new words are formed by the addition of affixes which seem to have no effect on the meaning of a word but which serve a metrical purpose in avoiding the juxtaposition of two strongly-stressed syllables:

I can call Spirits from the vastie Deepe   (1H4 III.1.53)

Most brisky Juvenall, and eke most lovely Jew   (MND III.1.97)

The occurrence in Shakespeare of a large number of nonce-words leads one to wonder how many such words have been emended out of existence on the assumption that they were mistakes for more familiar words. It is a principle of textual criticism that when different texts give different readings the less familiar reading, other things being equal, is more likely to be the true one because a scribe or a compositor, unfamiliar with the form, is more likely to treat it as a mistake. In *Othello* 1.2.21 the Quarto has *provulgate* while the Folios have the more common word *promulgate*. *Provul-*

gate 'to make public' makes reasonable sense, though this is the only occurrence of the word. Another example occurs in the same scene. At line 41, the First Folio refers to 'a dozen sequent messengers', while the Quarto reads *frequent*. *Sequent* is a rarer word than *frequent*, though it is found elsewhere in Shakespeare and the compound *consequent* is common enough. The meaning 'following upon one another' arises naturally from the etymology and gives excellent sense in the context.

17. Some words are over-used by particular characters, like *humour*, which Nym introduces into nearly every speech he makes in *Henry V* and *The Merry Wives of Windsor*. We know from the plays of Ben Jonson that this was a particularly popular vogue word of the time. *Accommodation* is included by Ben Jonson among 'the perfumed termes of the time'[1] and Bardolph's use of the word (2H4 III.2.75) arouses Shallow's admiration.

18. Some words and phrases owe their wide currency today to the accident that Shakespeare used them, and his use has often had an effect on their meaning. Examples are *beetle* v., *it beggars all description, coign of vantage, fitful, a foregone conclusion, gouts of blood, head and front, hoist with his own petard, lush, in my mind's eye, the very pink of courtesy, that way madness lies, metal more attractive, weird* as an adjective. When Holinshed speaks of the Weird Sisters, he is probably using *weird* as a noun; its use as an adjective arises from a misunderstanding of the description *Weird Sisters* in *Macbeth*. Some of these phrases are used today in senses different from the Shakespearean sense. *Single blessedness* is now ironical but was not so used in *A Midsummer Night's Dream* (1.1.78).

19. Shakespeare cannot be closely associated with any of the plans for enriching the language put forward by Elizabethan rhetoricians, such as the use of inkhorn terms, archaisms and dialect words, though it is possible to find some examples in each category. F. P. Wilson points out[2] that such terms would have been out of place in an Elizabethan playhouse. Shakespeare was less fond than some of his contemporaries of 'showing off'. He can portray Autolycus without making him use much of the cony-catching vocabulary.

1. *Discoveries* 1.2275 in *Ben Jonson*, ed. by C. H. Herford, Percy and Evelyn Simpson, Vol. 8 (OUP, 1947), p. 632.
2. 'Shakespeare and the Diction of Common Life' *Proceedings of the British Academy* 27 (1941), p. 169.

Examples of learned loan-words include: *accite* v. 'to summon', *evitate* 'to avoid', *facinerious* 'vile', *festinately* 'quickly', *mure* 'wall', *operant* 'active', *peregrinate* 'having the air of one who has travelled abroad', *phantasime* 'fantastic being', *rigol* 'crown', *sequent* 'follower'.

Some learned loan-words are only rarely used and they are therefore liable to diverge in form or meaning from their etymons. *Intrinsicate* 'intricate (applied to a knot)' (Ant. v.2.307) is from Italian *intrinsecato* but has been confused in sense with *intricate* (OED). It occurs in the abbreviated form *intrince* in Lear ii.2.81. In the same way the verb *reverbe* 'to re-echo' (Lear i.1.156) has been shortened from *reverberate*.

Of the many Latin verbs that came into English during the sixteenth century, many were adopted first in the past participle, without the addition of the native *-ed* ending, as in *the king had depopulate the country*. Today such forms are normally employed only as adjectives. Henry Bradley points out[1] that the reason why these participles, down to the end of the sixteenth century or later, were not felt to be un-English in form was that many native verbs ending in *t* could still form their past participle without the addition of *-ed*. This mode of conjugation is now confined to a very few verbs, such as *cast*, *put* and *set*, but as late as the Elizabethan period it was permissible in many other words such as *acquit(ted)*, *heat(ed)*. Hence a past participle ending in *-ate* did not sound irregular to an English ear. All that was required to make it normal was the assumption that it belonged to a verb of the same form. Hence the large number of English infinitives, such as *accelerate* and *depopulate*, formed from Latin past participles. In Shakespeare's time the forms in *-ed* were usual except in poetry.

The use of long words of foreign origin is often satirized, as in the speeches of Osric. Some Latin loan-words are used comically in some plays, but seriously in others. *Remuneration* and *festinately* are used comically in *Love's Labour's Lost* but *remuneration* is used seriously in *Troilus and Cressida*, as is *festinate* in *King Lear*. It may be that such words had come to be accepted between the date of the early play and that of the later play.

20. Technical terms in Shakespeare come both singly and in groups. We find occasional passages where technical terms from one sphere of activity come thick and fast, like the legal terms used by Hamlet when the Gravedigger unearths a skull. After describ-

1. 'Shakespeare's English' in *Shakespeare's England* (OUP, 1916), ii.562.

ing the blow of the shovel against the skull as an action of battery, Hamlet says:

> This fellow might be in's time a great buyer of Land, with his Statutes, his Recognizances, his Fines, his double Vouchers, his Recoveries: is this the fine of his Fines, and the recovery of his Recoveries, to have his fine Pate full of fine Dirt? will his Vouchers vouch him no more of his Purchases, and double ones too, then the length and breadth of a paire of Indentures? the very Conveyances of his Lands will hardly lye in this Boxe; and must the Inheritor himselfe have no more?   (Ham. v.1.113)

Names of coins occur frequently. Pistol says that he will have a tester in his pouch (NWW 1.3.96). A tester was a coin of small value. Onions describes *testrill* (TN 11.3.34) as a 'fanciful' form of *tester*. The coin names *angel* and *noble* provided a constant temptation to make puns. A knowledge of the technical language of now almost-forgotten card games is necessary if the reader of today is to understand the exact meaning of Shakespeare's fashionable young men, though most readers are content to get along without this exact knowledge. In talking to Parolles, the Clown describes Lafew as 'a purre of Fortunes' (AW v.2.21), an allusion to the card game of post and pair. Helena urges the King to set up his rest against remedy (AW 11.1.138), an allusion to the card game primero, where the *rest* described the stakes kept in reserve. 'To set up one's rest' thus meant 'to stake one's all'. The phrase comes to mean 'to be resolved or determined'. Juliet's Nurse sees the phrase as the opportunity for a pun:

> Sleepe for a weeke; for the next night I warrant
> The Countie *Paris* hath set up his rest,
> That you shall rest but little, God forgive me: (RJ IV.5.5)

21. In all Shakespeare's plays we find, side by side with passages of magnificent rhetoric, passages which make their effect by the use of very simple language. Such passages are especially frequent in *As You Like It*:

> when I was at home I was in a better place   (11.4.16)

> I thinke of as many matters as he, but I give Heaven thankes, and make no boast of them   (11.5.37)

what though you hav no beauty
As by my faith, I see no more in you
Then without Candle may goe darke to bed: (III.5.37)

men have died from time to time, and wormes have eaten them,
but not for love, (IV.1.108)

In any of the plays we are liable suddenly to come across a homely
simile like 'They'l take suggestion, as a Cat laps milke' (Temp.
II.1.286). Even in *Love's Labour's Lost*, enriched as it is with the
Latinate vocabulary of Armado and Holofernes, we find Boyet
describing the king's friends as his 'book-mates', a compound that
would have appealed to William Barnes.

22. In comic scenes there are several different kinds of appropriate language. The speakers are not necessarily low-life. In the
sub-plot of *Twelfth Night* all the characters are upper-class, but the
words they use are of a kind that would never be found in serious
scenes. They include such words, slang in themselves or in their
application, as *tillyvally, testril, sneck up, scab, brock, sowter, bawcock,
chuck, Biddy, collier* and *bum-baily*. Some low-life characters, like
Dogberry and Mistress Quickly, are held up to ridicule for their
failure to cope with the difficulties of the English language. There
are other characters, like the fishermen in *Pericles*, who use substandard language without any very marked comic effect (II.1).
They use common but obscure oaths like 'with a wanion', which
seems to mean 'with a vengeance', 'with a curse to you'. A more
easily understandable oath is 'bots on't', since bots are worms that
breed in cattle. To protest against Pericles' hint that he might die,
they say 'Die, ke-tha', equivalent to 'Die, did you say?' When they
ask for a reward they use *condolements* in a unique sense as equivalent to 'vails', perhaps confusing the word with *dole* 'share'. Their
contraction 'Do'e' for 'Do you' is substandard.

In the tavern scenes of *1* and *2 King Henry IV* there are heavy
demands on the vocabulary of abuse, and sometimes this vocabulary is enriched by the creation of new high-sounding words.
Falstaff's page calls Mistress Quickly a scullion, a rampallian and a
fustillirian (2H4 II.1.63). *Scullion* is easy enough; it is used frequently to describe a domestic servant of the lowest rank. *Rampallian* is not found earlier than Elizabethan times; it is a term of
abuse generally applied to men, but sometimes to women. Onions

suggests that *fustillirian* is a comic formation based on *fustilugs* 'a fat frowzy woman'.

Low-life characters show a lack of self-confidence, which leads them to make frequent use of apologetic phrases like Costard's 'under correction', which he uses twice in arguing with Berowne about whether three threes are nine (LLL v.2.491).

The Elizabethans had a robust interest in bawdy. The language of bawdy changes so quickly that many allusions of this kind are now lost. It seems clear that the apparently innocent cry 'Tailor' had some indecent associations, and the rage caused by references to *Ajax* suggests that it is often a pun on 'a jakes', as at LLL v.2.580. References to venereal disease were always good for a laugh, and there are frequent allusions to 'French crowns', denoting the baldness associated with the disease. Stewed prunes were a staple dish in bawdy houses, and they are therefore often mentioned in comic scenes. The horns which a cuckold was supposed to wear are often mentioned, and it was assumed that everybody would understand the allusion.

23. It is not always easy to recognize colloquial language in literature that was written three or four centuries ago, for the colloquial language of one century may be the formal language of the next. The context is the best guide, expecially if a word or a construction occurs frequently. If it occurs many times in informal contexts and never on formal occasions, we are probably safe in assuming it to be colloquial. Jokes, especially if they are not very good ones, are a useful pointer to possible colloquialisms, since such pleasantries are commonly used on informal occasions. In the first scene of *Hamlet*, Horatio's reply to Barnardo's question asking if he is there is a pleasantry of this kind: 'A peece of him' (l.22), and in the same scene Horatio expresses his scepticism by the colloquial 'Tush, tush' (l.30). Marcellus and Hamlet greet each other in a colloquial style:

Mar. Illo, ho, ho, my Lord!
Ham. Hillo, ho, ho, boy; come, bird, come.   (1.5.117),

and Hamlet addresses the Ghost in an unexpectedly colloquial style: 'Ah ha boy! sayest thou so. Art thou there truepenny?' (1.5.149). Hamlet's welcome of Rosencrantz and Guildenstern, before he has learnt to distrust them, is expressed in a cordial colloquial style: good Lads: How doe ye both? (II.2.229). He uses a less friendly colloquialism in reply to Polonius's announcement of the arrival of the actors: Buzze, buzze (II.2.411), an exclamation used when anyone began a story that was already generally known. A more recent equivalent would be 'Queen Anne's dead'.

It is to be expected that the Clowns in the grave-digging scene should use colloquial language. *Whoreson* as an intensive expletive is a substandard colloquialism: your horson dead body (V.1.190). One expression used by the gravediggers that was no doubt in Shakespeare's day a colloquial vulgarism has now become literary simply because, as a quotation from Shakespeare, it has become respectable: Cudgell thy braines (v.1.64).

Certain features of accidence and syntax can be regarded as colloquialisms. Examples are the use of *a* for *he* and of the possessive adjective *your* to show that the subject under discussion is one in which the person addressed takes an interest:

There are more things in Heaven and Earth, *Horatio*,
Then are dream't of in your philosophy.

(Ham. 1.5.167, Quarto reading)

There are phrases which, besides their obvious meaning, have a secondary meaning which would be at once obvious to an Elizabethan audience. *To carry coals* (RJ 1.1.1) is dirty work and the phrase therefore comes to mean 'to put up with an insult'. Similarly, *Will you take Egges for Money?* (WT 1.2.161) seems to be used proverbially, an egg being regarded as a type of a worthless thing. Leontes' comment on his son's negative reply, 'why happy man be's dole' has a proverbial ring, but we have always to be prepared for the transition of idioms to proverbs as a result of their Shakespearean use. To burn candles by day is obviously wasteful, so the expression *We burn daylight* comes to mean 'We are wasting time', and it is so used by Mercutio (RJ 1.4.43). Some colloquial phrases current in Elizabethan English had a wide currency both before and after that period: *Bought and sold* 'tricked, betrayed' (Err. 111.1.72) occurs in a political poem in the fourteenth-century MS. Harley 2253, and *In good time* 'Indeed' (Err. 11.2.57) was one of Mrs Thrale's favourite exclamations. *Sir reverence*, a corruption of 'save your reverence' (Err. 111.2.92), is a phrase of apology for introducing an offensive remark.

Juliet's Nurse uses colloquial language. Her description of Count Paris as 'a Lovely Gentleman' could be paralleled in the class dialects of today, as could her comment 'Romeos a dish-clout to him' (RJ III.5.222). Nym in *King Henry V* twice uses *shog* 'to go away' which Onions says survives in Midland dialects. Pistol uses colloquial forms of address, such as 'Good Bawcock . . . sweet Chuck' (H5 III.2.26).

Beside its modern sense, *old* is used colloquially to mean 'plentiful, abundant', as in 'an old abusing of Gods patience and the Kings English' (MWW 1.4.5). Romeo is not thinking of his age when he says of Juliet 'Doth not she thinke me an old Murtherer' (RJ III.3.95).

24. We know more about the familiar speech of the Elizabethan period than we do of that of any earlier time, thanks especially to the comic scenes of the dramatists. Of one of the varieties of non-literary English of the sixteenth century – the cryptic jargon of thieves and vagrants – we know a great deal from such sources as Robert Greene's *Cony-Catching Pamphlets*. There are not many examples of it in Shakespeare. One of the few examples is *prig* 'thief' (WT IV.3.108). One or two words, such as *filch* and *rogue*, which were originally thieves' cant, had become literary English before Shakespeare began to write. *To cog*, which denoted some mode of cheating at dice, is now little used, but Shakespeare uses it several times. Poins describes Bardolph as a *setter* (1H4 II.2.53); this is thieves' cant for a decoy.

Beside the secret jargon of the disreputable classes is the slang of general society or of particular sections of society, which has its origin in a feeling of impatience with the restraints of convention in language. One such expression is *Poor John* 'salted hake', used as a type of poor fare (RJ I.1.36). It is clear from the reference in *The Tempest* (II.2.28) that salt was not always an adequate preservative.

Noteworthy also is the very extensive vocabulary of profane oaths and substitutes for them. The Act of Parliament of 1606, which forbade the profane use of the names of God or Christ in any stage play, did much to discourage the use of blasphemous slang. There are many corruptions of *God*, adopted in an attempt to avoid profanity: *By cock, By cock and pie, By gogs-wouns, Swounds, Zounds, Od's me, By gar, 'Sdeath, 'Sblood, 'Slid, 'Slight, Perdie*. The meaning of most of these oaths is self-evident, but sometimes explanation is needed, as in *cock and pie* (MWW 1.1.319), where *pie* is generally taken to mean 'directory of divine service'. *Marry*, originally the name of the Virgin Mary, is very common in the sense 'indeed' and we also find *By'r lady* and *By'r lakin. What the Dickens* is at least as old as Shakespeare: 'I cannot tell what (the dickens) his name is my husband had him of', (MWW III.2.20).

Many familiar terms of endearment and abuse which belonged to the everyday speech of the Elizabethan age, now survive, if at all, chiefly as literary archaisms. *Bully* was a familiar term of endearment used by low-life characters either as an adjective or as a noun. It is often prefixed to a proper name, as in 'O sweet bully *Bottome*' (MND IV.2.20). Other examples include *bully monster, bully Hercules, bully doctor*, and *the lovely bully*. Other terms of affection in Shakespeare's time, such as *sweeting* and *chuck*, are now obsolete. The language of the sixteenth century had a rich store of vituperative words that have not survived, such as *coystrill, cullion, mome, hilding*. On the other hand, *scoundrel*, a word of obscure etymology which first appears in the late sixteenth century, is still current English, and has come to have a stronger sense than it had in Elizabethan times.

In view of the evanescent nature of slang, it can present difficulties when it is preserved in literature to be read by later generations. What are we to make of Nym's remark to Slender: 'I will say marry trap with you, if you runne the nut-hooks humor on me' (MWW I.1.170)? *Nuthook* occurs as a name for a beadle in 2H4 V.4.8. It was used of someone who hooked down nuts and hence, since *poll* and *nut* were both used for 'head', a *nuthook* was a catchpoll. 'If you run the nuthook's humour on me' probably means 'If you try to behave like a catchpoll with me'. *Trap* was the name applied to a popular game, *marry* was an interjection joined to many retorts, and 'I will say "marry trap" with you' probably means 'I will retaliate and outwit you'. In the same scene Bardolph says that Slender had been 'casheerd' while 'fap' (l.183). It is clear from the context that *fap* is one of the large number of synonyms for 'drunk', though only one other example of the word, dated 1818, is quoted by OED (s.v. Fap, *a*). *Casheerd* probably derives its meaning from a pun on *cash* and means 'deprived of cash'.

25. A knowledge of Elizabethan proverbs is a help to a student of Shakespeare's language. The popularity of proverbs was not confined to England. Sancho Panza is a match for any Shakespearean character in his fondness for proverbs and in his habit of maltreating words in the manner of Mrs Malaprop. Proverbs come thick and fast in the scene in the inn yard at Rochester (1H4 II.1).

The carriers use proverbs as repartee. The reply to an inconvenient request is 'I know a trick worth two of that' or the less common 'I, when, canst tell?' The Second Carrier is indignant at the request for the loan of his lantern and replies by holding the question up to ridicule; 'Lend mee thy Lanthorne (quoth-a)'. This is followed by a reply that has remained in use until the present day. 'Ile see thee hang'd first'. Countrymen do not very much like answering questions, and there are many proverbial devices to avoid giving a direct reply. In reply to the question 'What time do you mean to come to London?' the Second Carrier replies 'Time enough to goe to bed with a Candle'. The chamberlain replies to a summons in another idiomatic sentence: 'At hand, quoth Pick-purse'. This is equivalent to the modern 'Ready, as the pick-purse said'.

Proverbial language is very common in *The Merry Wives of Windsor*, especially in the speech of Mrs Quickly. If the proverbs are quoted in full, they usually cause little difficulty, as when Ford says 'for they say, if money goe before, all waies doe lye open' (II.2.174) or when Mistress Quickly says 'ile nere put my finger in the fire' (1.4.88) or 'an honest maid as ever broke bread' (1.4.157). Slender can misunderstand even an easy proverb, as when he says that, though there be no great love in the beginning between himself and Anne Page, he hopes that 'upon familiarity will grow more content' (1.1.260).

Proverbs may be used for the sake of courtesy. When Slender's servant is asked if his name is not Peter Simple, he feels that a simple affirmative would be too brusque, so he replies 'I: for fault of a better' (MWW 1.4.16). He goes on to use proverbial expressions for the sake of emphasis. To praise his master he says that he is 'as tall a man of his hands, as any is betweene this and his head' (MWW 1.4.25).

A succession of brief proverbs may be used to express dark hints in a style similar to that of gnomic verses, as when Nym speaks of his relations with Pistol:

> I cannot tell, Things must be as they may: men may sleepe, and they may have their throats about them at that time, and some say, knives have edges: It must be as it may, though patience be a tyred mare, yet shee will plodde, there must be Conclusions. Well, I cannot tell. (H5 II.1.22)

Fondness for proverbs is a trait of character; it reveals a sententious person, full of homely wisdom but without much profundity; one who does not think for himself, but relies on clichés. A proverb may reveal conventional piety, even when the speaker is worldly. Mistress Quickly replies to Fenton's anxious questions about his chances of success in his wooing of Ann Page with a pious 'Troth Sir, all is in his hands above:' (MWW 1.4.151).

Proverbs are generally associated with low-life characters, but they are not confined to them. On occasion courtiers can use proverbs and vie with one another in capping them, as in the verbal contest between Orleans and the Constable of France in *King Henry V* (III.7.123).

Coriolanus pours scorn on the use of proverbs by the plebeians by the simple device of putting the proverbs into indirect speech:

> They said they were an-hungry, sigh'd forth Proverbes
> That Hunger broke stone wals: that dogges must eate
> That meate was made for mouths. That the gods sent not
> Corne for the Richmen onely: With these shreds
> They vented their Complainings,   (I.1.209)

We can often guess the meaning of a proverb, as when Falstaff asks 'Whose Mare's dead?' i.e. 'What is all the fuss about?' (2H4 II.1.42). Slender's 'come cut and long-taile' (MWW III.4.46) is more obscure, but it seems to mean 'no matter who comes'. Some proverbial expressions have little meaning to discover. Like the modern 'Well, for running round the houses', they derive what meaning they have from the context, as when Mistress Quickly says 'what the good-jer' (1.4.126).

What makes familiarity with proverbial lore necessary for the reader of Shakespeare is his habit of taking familiarity with a proverb for granted and alluding to it. There are several passages which make sense only when we have identified the underlying proverb, which may not itself be quoted. The most famous allusion to a proverb in Shakespeare takes a knowledge of the proverb for granted and refers merely to the poor cat in the adage. When Ford thinks that he is about to prove his wife's guilt by opening a basket of dirty linen, he says 'Now shall the divel be sham'd' (MWW IV.2.127). He means 'Now will the truth be revealed', alluding to the proverb 'Truth will shame the Devil'. Some forgotten proverb may explain phrases that are apparently nonsense, like Ophelia's 'They say the Owle was a Bakers daughter' (Ham. IV.5.42), and proverbs form the basis of some pathetic passages. The Fool's last speech in *King Lear* is an allusion to the proverb 'You would make me go to bed at noon'.

26. Catch-phrases and clichés have much in common with proverbs. All three forms appeal to conventional wisdom as a substitute for thought. An example is Mistress Quickly's 'but let that pass', used when events are getting too difficult for her. Some of these tags have remained in colloquial use until the present day, like Mistress Quickly's 'that's neither heere nor there' (MWW 1.4.111). Catch-phrases are generally associated with comic characters and their excessive use is a frequent source of humour. Nym is fond of 'That's the humour of it', and in *King Henry V* he adds another: It must be as it may. Pompey, in *Measure for Measure*, has his own favourite phrase:

> As I say, this Mistris *Elbow*, being (as I say) with childe, and being great bellied, and longing (as I said) for prewyns: and having but two in the dish (as I said) . . . (II.1.100).

Catch-phrases often seem to have little meaning. Then as now, to quote the latest fashionable phrase was in itself considered a bit of smart repartee, whatever the context.

27. On the stage the words of the author are reinforced by gestures at the discretion of the actor. As a rule we cannot tell with what gestures Elizabethan actors heightened the meaning of the words they used, but occasionally a gesture is described. Samson, one of Capulet's servants, says 'I will bite my Thumb at them, which is a disgrace to them, if they beare it' (RJ 1.1.47). This is one variety of the gesture known as 'the Figge of Spaine' (H5 III.6.61), a contemptuous, bawdy gesture made by thrusting the thumb between two of the closed fingers or into the mouth. *Figge* is used as a verb, meaning 'to insult', at 2H4 v.3.23. The Spanish origin of the phrase is preserved in the variant *figo*: Figo for thy friendship (2H4 III.6.59).

28. The real difficulty in understanding Shakespeare is not presented by words that are obviously unusual, like *miching mallecho*, or by words in senses strikingly different from those current today. It is presented by words which make sense if we give them their modern meaning but which were used in Elizabethan English in a slightly different sense. A word like *do* can have meanings not current today, as when Portia says 'I could not

doe withall' (Merch. III.4.72), meaning 'I could not help it' (OED Do, vb 54). Although gross misunderstandings may be rare, the reader of Elizabethan literature is constantly liable to fail to appreciate the precise shade of meaning with which a word is used or the precise tone of feeling which it implies. Commentators and the compilers of dictionaries cannot do much for us here; the attempt to point out every subtle distinction between the modern and the earlier use of words would appear very tedious and pedantic. The remedy is wide and careful reading of Elizabethan texts, not merely the plays of Shakespeare.

Among the changes of meaning which cause most difficulty to the reader without much knowledge of the English language are those affecting certain adverbs which originally expressed an easily definable meaning but which have come to be used as mere particles, whose chief function is to modify the meaning or relationship of other words. In the sixteenth century these adverbs had already acquired a weakened sense, but the sense today has been still further weakened. Sometimes it is the Shakespearean sense that is the more general. *Simply* is used as an intensive by Orleans in an attempt at 'piling it on': He is simply the most active Gentleman of France (H5 III.7.106). The sense here is roughly equivalent to 'indeed'. *Even* originally meant 'on a level, equally'. In Shakespeare it means 'exactly, quite'. In the Authorized Version of the Bible it is often used in the sense 'that is to say'. Today it is used to emphasize the statement of an extreme case, as in 'Even his best friends admitted it'. *Still* in Shakespeare usually means 'always' as when Corin explains why a courtier's hands are greasy: we are still handling our Ewes (AYL III.2.54). *Along* is used adverbially in the sense 'at full length', as when Celia says that she has seen Orlando under a tree: 'There lay hee stretch'd along like a Wounded knight' (AYL III.2.253). In Shakespeare we often find common words, of both native and foreign origin, used in senses that are now obsolete. Horatio's estimate of the duration of the Ghost's visit is: While one with moderate hast might tell a hundred (Ham. 1.2.237), where *tell* is used in the sense 'count'. *Round* is used today both as adjective and adverb in a literal sense to refer to circular shape or motion, but *round* and the derived adverb *roundly* are frequently used in Shakespeare to describe anything that is plain and straightforward, unceremonious and outspoken. Othello says that he will 'a round un-varnish'd Tale deliver' (Oth. 1.3.90). *Tonight* is an everyday word used by Shakespeare in a sense not current today, though the context generally prevents misunderstanding. In Shakespeare it often means 'last night': For I did dreame of money bags to night (Merch. II.5.20). We are in danger of seeing the irony of understatement in 'Perplexed in the extreme' (Oth. v. 2.346) and 'these unluckie deeds' (Oth. v.2.341). *Perplexed* and *unlucky* were stronger then than they are today.

29. When we try to discover the meaning of a word in Shakespeare, the first problem is to identify the word in question. The problem is made more difficult by our habit of adding several suffixes to a stem, each of which may modify its meaning for a time. When Hamlet explains that the play within the play gets its name *The Mousetrap* 'tropically' (III.2.247), our first response is to associate the adverb with the tropics. This gives no sense at all in the context, but if we derive the word from *trope* the meaning becomes clear: 'figuratively'. Sometimes the suffix that we use today differs from that current in Elizabethan times. There is a bar to our understanding if the Elizabethan suffix survives today with a different meaning. Hamlet says: Thus Conscience does make Cowards of us all (III.1.83). None of the present-day meanings of *conscience* fits the context, but a change of suffix gives the meaning: 'consciousness', i.e. 'reflection'. The loss of a prefix may cause a Shakespearean word to become identical in form with another word of different meaning. *Motion* is often used in the sense 'emotion' or 'desire', as when Orsino says to Viola that all true lovers are 'Unstaid and skittish in all motions else' (TN II.4.18). It is often possible to arrive at the meaning of a Shakespearean word by thinking of the meaning of some derivative of the word in present-day English. The usual meaning of the verb *affect* in Shakespeare is 'to be fond of', as in the first line of *King Lear*: I thought the king had more affected the Duke of *Albany*, then *Cornwall*. Today *affect* has quite a different meaning, but the Shakespearean sense is preserved in the noun *affection* and the adjective *affectionate*. *Expedience* has two meanings in Shakespeare. In *Richard II* II.1.287 Northumberland says that Bolingbroke is on his way 'with all due expedience', i.e. 'speed'; in *1 King Henry IV* I.1.33 the king describes his projected Crusade as 'this deere expedience', i.e. 'this noble enterprise'. The first of these meanings can be linked with *expeditious*, the second with *expedition*. In *Julius*

Cæsar Portia says: Is Brutus sicke? And is it Physicall to walke unbraced, and sucke up the humours Of the danke Morning? (II.1.261). The sense of *physical* is close to that of *physician*, i.e. 'remedial, likely to act as a cure'.

The meaning of an unfamiliar word may be understood from some more familiar derivative. *Debile* (Cor. I.9.51) is not a common word, but it is clear from the noun *debility* that it means 'weak'. Sometimes the meaning is preserved today in a comparatively rare meaning of the word in question. Gloucester, reflecting on the foolishness of King Lear in giving away his kingdom, says that the King is now 'Confin'd to exhibition' (Lear I.2.25). The usual modern meaning of *exhibition* makes no sense here, but the word *exhibitioner*, as applied to an undergraduate, provides a clue. An exhibition is an allowance of money for a person's support, and the meaning of the phrase is that Lear is now restricted to an allowance.

The difficulty of identifying a word becomes greater when the two words between which a choice has to be made are not equally common or when one of them is obsolete. Antonio says to Bassanio:

Then doe but say to me what I should doe
That in your knowledge may by me be done,
And I am prest unto it: (Merch. I.1.158)

Prest may at first seem to be the past participle of *press*, and Antonio may mean that his affection for Bassanio will exert pressure on him. But we remember that French *prêt* 'ready' presupposes an earlier *prest*, and this is the word, borrowed into English, that Antonio is using. Hamlet's warning to his friends who try to prevent him from following the Ghost is: Unhand me Gentlemen: By Heav'n, Ile make a Ghost of him that lets me! (I.4.84). This is not an example of startling sense-development of the word *let*. Hamlet is using the verb *let* 'hinder' (OE *lettan*) whereas the Modern English *let* 'allow' is from OE *lætan*, with which *lettan* has often been confused. We are used to thinking of a *target* as the point at which one aims, but it occurs frequently in Shakespeare as a variant of *targe* in the sense 'light shield'. Falstaff, describing the attack of the four men in buckram, says 'I made no more adoe, but tooke all their seven points in my Targuet', (1H4 II.4.223).

Beside the verb *earn* 'to gain as recompense' there is another verb, often spelt in the same way, meaning 'to grieve'. The latter verb, sometimes spelt *yearn*, is used by Pistol: Boy, brissle thy Courage up: for Falstaffe hee is dead, and wee must erne therefore (H5 II.3.4). The form *yernes* occurs at H5 IV.3.26. When Kent speaks of 'one selfe mate and make' (Lear IV.3.36), *make* has nothing to do with the common verb; it is an obsolete noun meaning 'mate, husband or wife'. A messenger in *Antony and Cleopatra* says:

> *Menacrates* and *Menas* famous Pyrates
> Makes the Sea serve them, which they eare and wound
> With keeles of every kinde.   (1.4.48)

Ear has nothing to do with the familiar noun; it is a verb meaning 'to plough' (OE *erian*).

30. Sometimes the spelling of the First Folio can help in the understanding of the text, but occasionally it can be misleading. In *Cymbeline* a Senator says that Lucius remains in Gallia:

> With those Legions
> Which I have spoke of, whereunto your levie
> Must be suppliant: (III.7.14)

The familiar word *suppliant* 'one who entreats' makes no sense in the context, but Capell, followed by many modern editors, helps the reader to identify the word by altering the spelling to *supplyant* i.e. 'auxiliary'. Another example of a word whose identity is concealed by unfamiliar spelling is the word which is today spelt *oeillades*. In the First Folio this is spelt *illiads* in MWW 1.3.68 and *Eliads* in Lear IV.5.25.

Identification may become more difficult by reason of mispronunciation. In *Love's Labour's Lost* Dull describes himself as 'his graces Tharborough' (1.1.186). The Quarto has 'farborough'. Neither form is easy for a modern reader, but the Quarto reading is at one remove more difficult because the *f* is due to Dull's mispronunciation of *th*. *Tharborough* is a form of *thirdborough* 'constable'.

The problem of identification is made more difficult by the Elizabethan fondness for playing on words. Morton, trying to console Northumberland after the death of his son, says: It was your presurmize, That in the dole of blowes your Son might drop (2H4 1.1.169). *Dole* is a native English word meaning 'dealing out', and its resemblance in form to *dole* 'grief' is entirely accidental. We cannot be sure, however, that this identity of form was not present in the minds of the speaker and the hearer, to contribute something to the meaning of the word.

31. Familiarity with the modern meaning of a word may stand in the way of an understanding of the Shakespearean meaning. *Lottery* (Ant. II.2.247) has much the same meaning as *allottery* (AYL I.1.77) 'portion, that which falls to one by lot', but the reader of the first word is more likely to know what a lottery is, whereas *allottery*, being unfamiliar, forces a reader to think of its etymology, when association with *allot* puts him on the right track. We need to be constantly on the alert for the use of a familiar word with an unfamiliar meaning. We think that we know the meaning of *laughter*, and we are liable to be taken aback when we find it used in the sense 'a sitting of eggs' in Temp. II.1.32.

32. It is not only the modern reader who has difficulty in identifying words in Shakespeare's plays; some of the humour in the plays is provided by characters who have a similar difficulty. Apart from frequent malapropisms, we find some characters using high-sounding words with little attention to their meaning, and others who obviously do not understand the words they hear. The misunderstanding is often satirical. If it is feigned, the satire is that of the speaker; if it is real, the satire is the author's. Armado rewards Costard for carrying a letter and says: There is remuneration. Costard opens his palm and says: Now will I looke to his remuneration. Remuneration, O, that's the Latine word for three-farthings: Three-farthings remuneration. (LLL III.1.138). Costard's mistake calls attention to the contrast between the grandiloquence of the word and the meagreness, even by Elizabethan values, of the reward. Berowne shows a similar fondness for high-flown words but a more generous idea of the rate for the job in rewarding Costard by giving him a shilling with the words 'Ther's thy guerdon: goe', and Costard shows his appreciation: Gardon, O sweete gardon, better then remuneration, a levenpence-farthing better: (III.1.172). Sir Andrew Aguecheek has particular difficulty with words. He demands an explanation of Maria's flowery language: What's your Metaphor? (TN I.3.75), and he is puzzled by Sir Toby's French: What is *purquoy*? Do, or not do? (I.96). The two Middle English verbs *leren* (OE *lǣran*) 'to teach' and *lernen* (OE *leornian*) 'to learn' were confused in view of their resemblance

44

in form and meaning. This confusion is found in dialect speech today and it is found in Shakespeare. Caliban says: the red-plague rid you For learning me your language. (Temp. 1.2.365).

33. The practice of memorizing passages from Shakespeare divorced from their context has tended to blur the meaning of certain words. Misunderstanding is frequent since the quotations are used by people whose knowledge of them is derived from their everyday use, not directly from the play. A familiar example is 'The quality of mercy is not strain'd' (Merch. IV.1.184), where *strain'd* 'forced, constrained' is a direct reply to Shylock's question 'On what compulsion must I? tell me that'. Experiment has shown that a large number of people who knew the speech by heart thought that the line simply meant 'Mercy is a desirable quality'. Another familiar quotation is Hamlet's 'a Custome More honour'd in the breach, then the observance' (Ham. 1.4.16). This quotation is often misused to mean that a rule is often broken, but this interpretation ignores the context and the meaning of the word 'honoured'. Hamlet means that the custom of using the kettle-drum and the trumpet to proclaim that the king is having a drink is one that would be better abandoned.

34. A knowledge of Shakespearean usage can protect an editor from making unnecessary emendations. Prospero questions Miranda:

> Canst thou remember
> A time before we came unto this Cell?
> I doe not thinke thou canst, for then thou was't not
> Out three yeeres old.   (Temp. 1.2.36)

An editor may be tempted to emend *out* to *but* 'only', but *out* can have the meaning 'fully, quite', as in: Thou hast beate mee out Twelve severall times. (Cor. IV.5.127). Another example occurs in *As You Like It*. After Oliver's quarrel with Orlando, he addresses his departing brother with the words: 'Is it even so, begin you to grow upon me?' (1.1.90). Collier emended *grow* to *growl*, but there are passages in Shakespeare which show that *grow on* could mean 'to increase so as to become more troublesome to'. In *Julius Cæsar* we have: the Sunne arises, Which is a great way growing on the South (II.1.106). Oliver means 'Are you beginning to take liberties with me?' In the Quarto of *Love's Labour's Lost* there are many examples at the beginning of a speech of a superfluous 'O' that does not occur in the Folios. An example is 'O, you are welcome, sir' (II.1.211). It has been suggested that Shakespeare may have been caricaturing some contemporary trick of speech, but Dover Wilson, following Aldis Wright, points out that the superfluous 'O' occurs especially in the speeches of Berowne and that it may well be the last letter of the speech-heading 'Bero' which has crept into the text. This example illustrates the importance of having access to editions which preserve the eccentricities of the early texts, since in most modern editions both *Ber.* and *Bero.* would be silently expanded. An uncommon word may sometimes provide an editor with a parallel that will justify him in emending a more common word occurring elsewhere. *Shent* is a past participle meaning 'blamed, rebuked' that occurs, for example, in: I am shent for speaking to you (TN IV.2.112). It suggested to Theobald the emendation of the Folio reading *sent* to *shent* when Agamemnon says of Achilles: 'He sent our Messengers' (Troil. II.3.86).

35. We encounter polysemy at every stage of the history of a language, and when we speak of a word having a different meaning in Shakespeare's day from that current today, we must always be prepared to find the modern meanings of the word occurring in Shakespeare side by side with others now obsolete. *Censure* is used as a noun by Polonius in the sense 'opinion, not necessarily unfavourable' (Ham. 1.3.69), but it is used as a verb by Lucio to mean 'to pass sentence upon' (Meas. 1.4.73), a sense even narrower than that current today, and it is used by the Duke in its normal present-day meaning 'unfavourable opinion' (Meas. III.2.197).

In semantics there are differences arising from the literal and metaphorical meanings of certain words. Shakespeare uses many Latin loan-words literally while we use them metaphorically, often with some restriction of meaning. Thus *metaphysical* meant 'supernatural', and *fantastical* could mean 'imagined' and could be applied to a murder. *Exorbitant* meant 'uncommon', not merely 'uncommonly expensive'. *Speculation* meant 'the power of seeing'. *Advertise* meant 'inform' or 'warn'. The restriction of meaning has taken place because there were already English words expressing the wider ideas. The same principle applies to French loan-words. *Travail*, finding its work performed by *work* or *labour*, had to find a narrower meaning.

The imagery of a passage may make it clear that a word is to have more than one meaning, often with a play on words. Polonius advises Ophelia to beware of Hamlet: Doe not beleeve his vowes; for they are Broakers, Not of the eye, which their Investments show. (Ham. 1.3.127). Here *Investments* is used in its modern sense of 'money investments', in which sense it is properly linked with *Broakers*, but if the reading 'that dye' of most of the Quartos is correct, it also has the sense 'vestments', which it has in 2H4 IV.1.45, where Westmorland addresses the Archbishop of York as one 'Whose white Investments figure Innocence'.

36. There are innumerable examples of the use of words in Shakespeare in an etymological sense. In their modern senses neither *extravagant* nor *erring* is a very suitable adjective to apply to a ghost, but Horatio's use of the adjectives (Ham. 1.1.154) is very natural if we remember that the literal meaning of *extravagant* is 'wandering out of bounds' and that *erring* earlier meant 'wandering'. Horatio says that the disappearance of the Ghost of Hamlet's father 'made probation' (l.156) of the truth of this belief, i.e. it put it to the test (Latin *probare* 'to test'). Pitfalls caused to the modern reader by the use of words in an etymological sense are least serious when they are most striking. When Rosencrantz tells Hamlet that his behaviour has struck his mother 'into amazement, and admiration' (Ham. III.2.337), only the most inattentive reader will give *admiration* its modern sense. The word clearly has its older sense 'wonder, astonishment'. The words that cause trouble are those where the present-day meaning differs in some subtle shade from the Elizabethan. Portia's comment on Nerissa's conventional moralizing is: Good sentences, and well pronounc'd (Merch. 1.2.10). This remark makes adequate sense if we give *sentences* its modern meaning, but most of the point of the comment is lost unless we remember that Portia is using the word in a pejorative sense (Latin *sententiae*), which is preserved in the adjective *sententious*.

Most of the words that cause trouble by being used in an older sense are Latin loan-words, but there are examples among more familiar words of native or French origin. After the battle with the Romans in *Cymbeline* a Captain speaks of 'a fourth man, in a silly habit' (v.3.87). *Silly* (from OE *sælig* 'blessed') means here 'simple, homely' and *habit* means 'dress, garment'. The difference between this use of *silly* and that current today reflects two different attitudes towards the simple life.

37. A knowledge of etymology can help us to recognize the

THE LANGUAGE OF SHAKESPEARE

meaning of a familiar word used by Shakespeare in an unusual sense. King Henry dismisses Worcester from his presence because he is offended by 'The moody Frontier of a servant brow' (1H4 1.3.19). The associations of a hostile frontier between states may have influenced the meaning here, but the primary meaning of *frontier* in this context is 'forehead', which is both obsolete and rare. French *front* 'forehead' gives a pointer to this meaning. *Collection* is used in two senses in *Hamlet*. At one occurrence (V.2.199) it has a sense not unlike the usual modern sense: 'assortment (of extracts)'. The other occurrence (IV.5.9) is in the Gentleman's account of the mad Ophelia. Her uncontrolled utterances 'move The hearers to Collection'. Latin *collectio* was a term of rhetoric meaning 'deduction, inference'. Ophelia's words are causing people to wonder what is behind them. Touchstone, speaking of horns, says: the noblest Deere hath them as huge as the Rascall (AYL III.3.51). We think of *rascal* as a vague term of abuse, but the sense here is more technical: a young deer, lean and out of season.

38. To understand Shakespeare it is necessary to study not only the history of words but also the history of ideas which words describe. Doctors no longer explain the health of a patient in terms of the four humours, but an Elizabethan audience would take such an explanation for granted. The primary meaning of *humour* was 'moisture', and we find this meaning in: sucke up the humours Of the danke Morning (JC II.1.262). The word obtained a much wider currency from its use in medieval physiology, where it was thought that a man's physical and mental qualities were determined by the relative proportions of the four chief fluids or 'cardinal humours' in the human body: blood, phlegm, choler and melancholy. In Shakespeare we find allusions to 'the blacke oppressing humour' (LLL 1.1.234). From this use it was an easy step to the meaning 'mental disposition, temperament' as in 'His humour is lofty' (LLL V.1.9). It could be applied to a temporary state of mind, and we still speak of someone being in a good humour. Any temporary state of mind is liable to seem capricious to those who dislike change, and hence *humour* came to mean 'whim, caprice': let it be as humors and conceits shall governe. (Merch. III.5.65). A further development was to 'inclination, desire (to do something)', as in: I have an humor to knocke you indifferently well (H5 II.1.56). From the noun was derived the verb *to humour*, not found earlier

than Shakespeare, which still survives in its usual Elizabethan sense 'to indulge someone by complying with his inclinations', but the verb was used, like the noun, inappropriately by Nym:

I like not the humor of lying: hee hath wronged mee in some humors: I should have borne the humour'd Letter to her.

(MWW II.1.131)

The adjective *humorous* shows a similar development from 'moist, damp', as in 'the Humerous night' (RJ II.1.31) to 'capricious, whimsical' or 'moody'. Berowne says that he has been 'a verie Beadle to a humerous sigh' (LLL III.1.177).

We still think of the brain and heart in connexion with our emotions, but not of the liver, except when we use *liverish* in the sense 'ill-tempered'. For Orsino the liver is coupled with the brain and the heart as 'soveraigne thrones' (TN I.1.38), and cowards are frequently described as *milk-livered* or *lily-livered*. *Stomach* now means a part of the body, but in Shakespeare it could also have the abstract meaning 'courage', as when we are told that Douglas 'Gan vaile his stomacke' i.e. 'began to abate his courage' (2H4 I.1.129). In astronomy the Ptolemaic system is taken for granted, and Olivia says to Viola:

But would you undertake another suite
I had rather heare you, to solicit that,
Then Musicke from the spheares.   (TN III.1.118)

The adjective *jovial* is used in Shakespeare in both its etymological and derived senses. When Imogen mistakes the body of Cloten for that of her husband, she says she can recognize 'his Joviall face', and the meaning she gives to *Joviall* is clear since she also mentions 'His Foote Mercuriall: his martiall Thigh' (Cym. IV.2.310). The etymological sense is even more clear when, in the same play, Jupiter speaks of 'Our Joviall Starre' (V.4.105). When Lady Macbeth urges her husband 'Be bright and Joviall among your Guests to Night' (Macb. III.2.28), she is giving the word its modern sense 'merry, jolly', a sense derived from the astrological use of the word, since Jupiter as a natal planet was regarded as the source of happiness.

39. A play on words may show that the etymological meaning of a word has to be taken into account as well as a later meaning. Touchstone says to Audrey 'I am heere with thee, and the Goats,

as the most capricious Poet honest *Ovid* was among the Gothes.'
(AYL III.3.5). By *capricious* Touchstone means 'characterized by
play of wit or fancy, fantastic', and he is also obviously alluding to
the Latin *capra* 'goat', from which the word was thought to be
derived, thus reinforcing the pun on *goats* and *Goths*. In the same
play Oliver asks Charles 'what's the new newes at the new Court?'
(I.I.103). It is clear that the etymological sense of *news* has been
blurred or forgotten. Since *news* has acquired a meaning different
from the etymological sense of 'things which are new', *new news*
seems not so much tautology as a play on words.

40. The following are examples of words used by Shakespeare
in etymological senses:

Allow normally means 'to approve, sanction', as in 'an allow'd
foole' (TN I.5.101), but it has the sense 'praise' when Ford says to
Falstaff: 'you are . . . generally allow'd for your many war-like,
court-like, and learned preparations' (MWW II.2.234).

Approbation is used in its modern sense, but it is also used with
the meaning 'probation, novitiate':

This day, my sister should the Cloyster enter,
And there receive her approbation. (Meas. I.2.182)

Atone is today generally used in a religious sense, but it is a
compound of *at* and *one*, and hence 'agree' is a natural meaning.
The word is used in this sense in *Coriolanus*:

He, and *Auffidius* can no more attone
Then violent'st Contrariety. (IV.6.72)

Capitulate is used in a sense directly opposite to the meaning
current today. King Henry says to Prince Hal:

Percy, *Northumberland*,
The Arch-bishops Grace of Yorke, *Dowglas, Mortimer*,
Capitulate against us, and are up. (IH4 III.2.118)

Capitulate here has no suggestion of surrender; it means 'to draw
up articles of agreement'. Far from surrendering, Northumberland
and the rest have joined the rebels.

Charm, both as verb and noun, keeps a strong element of the
original meaning of enchantment running through its various
figurative uses. The original meaning of the noun 'magic spell' is

found in Temp. 1.2.231, where Ariel uses the word to describe how he has put the royal party to sleep. *To charm the tongue* was a common idiom meaning 'to silence', as in: To tame a shrew and charme her chattering tongue (Shrew IV.2.58), and *charm* is used in the sense 'to entreat, conjure, as if by an invocation': I charme you, by my once commended Beauty (JC II.1.271).

Conceit. The exact meaning of the noun *conceit* in Shakespeare is often difficult to determine, but most of the senses arise naturally from the idea of conception. The primary sense is 'what is conceived in the mind; idea, thought'. Adriana says that she is 'prest downe with conceit' (Err. IV.2.68). Another common meaning is 'faculty of conceiving, mental capacity' as in: a Gentleman of good conceit (AYL V.2.58). A sense near to one of the present-day meanings of the word is 'fanciful device or thing' as in 'rings, gawdes, conceits' (MND I.1.33). *Conceited* is used in the sense 'possessed of an idea', as when Fabian says that Viola, in her fear of Sir Andrew, 'is as horribly conceited of him: and pants, & lookes pale, as if a Beare were at his heeles' (TN III.4.326).

Crescent. Laertes says that 'nature cressant does not grow alone, In thewes and Bulke:' (Ham. 1.3.11). *Cressant* here means 'growing' (Latin *crescere* 'to grow').

Defend is used in the sense 'forbid', usually in *God defend*: And Heaven defend, but still I should stand so. (1H4 IV.3.38).

Defy. Beside the modern sense 'set at defiance', *defy* has in Shakespeare the meaning 'reject, despise', a sense close to that of its etymon, French *défier* 'distrust'. This sense is found in Hotspur's: I defie The Tongues of Soothers. (1H4 IV.1.6).

Exhale is generally used in the sense 'draw forth' of the sun drawing up vapours. Pistol, always in search of linguistic eccentricities, uses the word in its literal sense with reference to drawing a sword (H5 II.1.63).

Mystery. Othello, accusing Emilia of being a bawd, urges her to perform her 'Mystery', i.e. her trade or occupation (IV.2.29). *Mystery* (from Med. Latin *ministerium*) is cognate with French *métier*, and is the word used when we speak of the medieval mystery plays.

Owe often has the modern meaning 'to be indebted or under an obligation', but nearly as common as this is the sense 'to possess, own', and this was the original meaning of the verb. Ferdinand, after hearing Ariel's song 'Full fathom five', says:

> This is no mortall business, nor no sound
> That the earth owes!   (Temp. 1.2.406)

Proper is used in Shakespeare with its modern meaning 'suitable', but it is also used frequently in the sense 'one's own'. King Henry IV refers to Prince Hal as 'my proper Sonne' (2H4 v.2.109). It is also frequently used as a term of praise, 'excellent' or 'handsome': as proper a man as ever went on foure legs (Temp. II.2.64).

Rival. When Barnardo describes Horatio and Marcellus as the 'Rivals' of his watch (Ham. I.I.12) there is no suggestion of hostility or competition. He simply means that they are partners. The word is ultimately from Latin *rivalis* 'sharing the same stream'. It is easy to see how disputes over water rights could lead to the development of hostility that is found in the present-day use of the word.

Solicitor. Desdemona says:

> Therefore be merry *Cassio*,
> For thy Solicitor shall rather dye,
> Then give thy cause away.   (Oth. III.3.26)

She describes herself as a solicitor because she intends to solicit or intercede with Othello on behalf of Cassio.

Speed has a sense close to that of OE *spēd* 'success'. It is frequently used in expressions invoking the assistance of a protector, as when Rosalind encourages Orlando before his wrestling-match: Now Hercules, be thy speede yong man. (AYL 1.2.222). It then comes to mean 'fortune, fate', not necessarily happy, as when Mamilius dies 'with meere conceit, and feare Of the Queenes speed' (WT III.2.147).

Sympathy has the meaning 'agreement, conformity, correspondence'. Aumerle seeks to provoke a challenge from a man of high rank, and Fitzwater answers him with a sneer: If that thy valour stand on sympathize: There is my Gage, (R2 IV.1.33). He is using *sympathize* for *sympathy* in the sense 'correspondence in rank'.

Thrift. The modern sense is found occasionally in Shakespeare, as when Hamlet says bitterly that it was thrift that caused his mother's wedding to follow so closely on his father's funeral because it provided a use for the funeral baked meats (1.2.180). The usual meaning of *thrift* in Shakespeare, however, is 'gain, profit' and it is useful to remember that it is the noun derived from *thrive*. This is the sense of the word when Hamlet says:

No, let the Candied tongue lick (F like) absurd pompe,
And crooke the pregnant Hindges of the knee,
Where thrift may follow faining.   (III.2.65)

Tributary. Marullus, speaking of Caesar, asks: What Tributaries
follow him to Rome, To grace in Captive bonds his Chariot
Wheeles? (JC I.1.38). The usual modern meaning of *tributary* is a
metaphor. In Shakespeare we have the original sense: a tributary
is one who pays tribute.

Undertaker is now used chiefly in the specialized sense 'funeral
director', but it is used by Shakespeare in the wider etymological
meaning 'one who takes a task upon himself'. There is an implication that such a man is meddling when Antonio, coming to the
defence of Viola, says: Nay, if you be an undertaker, I am for you
(TN III.4.348).

Seminar. Those who are familiar with the academic sense of the
word may be puzzled by Cleopatra's use of *unseminar'd* to describe
a eunuch (Ant. I.5.12). She is assuming the etymological meaning
of *semen* from which *seminar* is derived; *unseminar'd* means 'without
seed'.

41. *Extension and Restriction.* Many words are used by Shakespeare with meanings wider than those current today, and a smaller
number are used with narrower meanings. Examples of words
whose meanings have been restricted since the time of Shakespeare
are:

Accident. Prince Hal says that 'nothing pleaseth but rare accidents', (IH4 I.2.231), using *accidents* to refer to an unexpected
occurrence without any suggestion that the occurrence involves
misfortune.

Bonnet means a man's cap or hat of any kind. The adjective
unbonnetted meant 'uncovered', hence 'on equal terms' (Oth. I.2.23).

Condign. When we use the word *condign* today it is nearly always
coupled with *punishment*, and the word is so used in 2H6 III.1.130.
Onions points out that this use originated in the phraseology of
Tudor acts of parliament and that the meaning is 'appropriate'.
The word could be used in Shakespeare in the sense 'worthily
deserved' without any pejorative associations. Moth says 'Speake
you this in my praise Master?' and Armado replies 'In thy condigne
praise' (LLL I.2.25).

Deer. In *King Lear* Edgar says: But Mice, and Rats, and such small Deare, Have bin Toms food, for seven long yeare (III.4.142). *Deer* clearly has a wider sense than it has today, whether we take it to mean 'animals hunted to be eaten' or in the still wider sense 'animals'.

Dunghill is used in apposition with another noun as a vague term of abuse. Gloucester describes the Warders who refuse him admission to the Tower as 'dunghill Groomes' (1H6 1.3.11).

Envy. Brutus says that to kill Antony as well as Caesar would seem 'Like Wrath in death, and Envy afterwards' (JC II.1.164). *Envy* here means 'malice, hatred'. Similarly, the adjective *envious* generally means 'malicious, spiteful', as when the Queen speaks of the 'envious sliver' that caused Ophelia's death (Ham. IV.7.174).

Fearful is today most often used in the subjective sense 'timorous, apprehensive', but in Shakespeare the objective sense is almost equally common: 'dreadful, terrible'. When Miranda tells her father that Ferdinand is 'gentle, and not fearfull' (Temp. I.2.470), she means that he is not to be feared.

Four. In present-day English certain numbers, such as *fifty* or *a dozen*, are often used in an indefinite sense to mean 'a fairly large number'. So in Shakespeare the numeral *four* is sometimes used vaguely with *hours* and *days* to denote fairly long periods of time. Polonius says of Hamlet: You know sometimes He walkes foure houres together, heere In the Lobby (II.2.160). In WT v.2.149 we have 'any time these foure houres' and in Cor. 1.2.6 ''tis not foure dayes gone'. A knowledge of this use of *four* can preserve an editor from an unnecessary emendation, since editors sometimes emend *four* to *for*. *Twice and once* is used as a general expression of frequency to mean 'several times'. Silence boasts 'I have beene merry twice and once, ere now' (2H4 V.3.41).

Furniture. Prince Henry promises to send Falstaff's recruits 'Money and Order for their Furniture' (1H4 III.3.226). *Furniture* means 'equipment' i.e. that with which they are furnished. The meaning has now been specialized.

Happily has today been restricted to refer only to fortunate events, but its original sense is wider, and in the early texts of Shakespeare *happily* varies with *haply* to mean 'by chance, perhaps'. Othello would have been even more angry than he was if he had given the modern meaning to Iago's hint that Desdemona might 'happily repent' of her marriage (Oth. III.3.236).

Hope is today used to refer to something that is both expected and desired; in Shakespeare it could refer to something expected without the implication that it is also desired. Prince Hal, soliloquizing about his future reformation, says: By how much better than my word I am, By so much shall I falsifie mens hopes (1H4 1.2.200).

Malign, as a verb, is now used only of speaking evil; in Shakespeare it could be used to mean 'to treat malignantly'. Marina says: though wayward fortune did maligne my state, my derivation was from ancestors, who stood equivalent with mightie Kings, (Per. v.1.88).

Orchard is from OE *ort-geard* 'an enclosed piece of ground used for horticulture'. In Shakespeare it means 'garden' without the modern restriction to mean a garden containing fruit trees. Brutus is in his orchard in JC II.1 and Hamlet's father was poisoned as he took his customary afternoon sleep in his orchard (1.5.35).

Portly in Shakespeare's day had already begun to acquire its modern meaning indicating size, as when Hector speaks of the 'large and portly size' of Achilles (Troil. IV.5.162). It is, however, sometimes used without this association, as a term of praise to mean 'dignified, bearing oneself well'. Old Capulet is praising Romeo when he says: A beares him like a portly Gentleman: (RJ 1.5.68).

Succeed in Shakespeare meant 'to come to pass' without necessarily implying that the outcome was favourable. The wider sense is found in 'the effects he writes of, succeede unhappily' (Lear 1.2.156). Similarly, the noun *success*, although it usually had the modern sense of 'favourable outcome', could also have the wider sense 'outcome', the nature of the outcome being indicated by the addition of an adjective, as in *such vilde successe* (Oth. III.3.222).

Warp today has pejorative associations, whether it is applied to wood or character. It has a wider range of meanings in Elizabethan English, which develop naturally from its Old English etymon *weorpan* 'to throw'. The usual Shakespearean meaning is 'to change the aspect of something, usually, but not necessarily, for the worse'. Polixenes says 'My favor here begins to warpe' (WT 1.2.364), and in Amiens' song in AYL II.7.186 the bitter sky is said to warp the waters by freezing them.

42. Words whose meanings have been extended since the time of Shakespeare are often used by him in a sense close to the etymological sense. In course of time the etymology has been

forgotten and the sense has become wider. Such extension has taken place with quite common words. The verb *to go* in Early English had the meaning 'to walk' as well as the more general sense current today, and this sense is preserved when the Fool in *King Lear* says 'Ride more then thou goest' (1.4.134). *Moiety* in Shakespeare generally means 'half', as does the French *moitié*, from which it is derived, but it can mean 'share' in a more general sense; and Hotspur, having claimed one-third of King Henry's kingdom, describes his share as a 'Moity' (1H4 III.1.96). Today the process of extension has been carried further and, when the word is used at all, it means 'a (small) part'. Other examples of words which have a narrower sense in Shakespeare than today are *decimation*, used of the killing of one in ten (Tim. V.4.31), *preposterous* applied to someone who puts music before philosophy (Shrew III.1.9), *triumph* in the sense 'public rejoicing' (MND I.1.19), and *civil* in the sense 'belonging to citizens' (RJ Prol. 4).

Some suffixes could be either active or passive: *unexpressive* is applied to a woman whose praises cannot be expressed. *Plausibly* is used actively to mean 'with applause'.

43. *Euphemism and Dysphemism.* It is well known that for most familiar ideas it is possible to find three terms, one dispassionate, one implying praise and one implying blame. The different attitudes of Shylock and Antonio towards lending money at interest are illustrated by the words they use to describe the practice. Shylock speaks of 'my well-worne thrift, Which he cals interrest' (Merch. 1.3.50), and in the same scene (l.71) he calls it 'advantage'. Antonio calls it 'excess' (1.3.63) and 'A breede of barraine mettall' (1.3.134).

Pistol and his friends make plentiful use of euphemisms. The Boy says of them: They will steale any thing, and call it Purchase (H5 III.2.46) and Pistol objects to the use of the word 'steal': Convay: the wise it call (MWW 1.3.32). There are the familiar euphemisms for death, as when Macbeth speaks of the 'taking off' of Duncan (1.7.20). A servant, telling Leontes that his son is dead, says that he is 'gone' (WT III.2.145); and Horatio, speaking of the death of Rosencrantz and Guildenstern, says that they 'go too't' (Ham. V.2.56).

There are many euphemisms dealing with sex in the plays. Many of these pass unnoticed today because of changes in linguistic fashion. A *double entendre* is something added to the normal straightforward meaning of a word and, if the reader misses the point, there is nothing to tell him that he has done so. As Hilda Hulme points out, in the detection of such matters 'what might be regarded as an adolescent alertness to sex innuendo is more valuable than a high academic seriousness'.[1] Some of the veiled allusions recur so frequently that even the most innocent reader will in time come to recognize them. *Tailor* is sometimes used in the sense 'buttocks', as in Puck's *tailour* (MND II.1.54), but in Elizabethan English the meaning often seems to be 'organ of generation'. This sense occurs in 'Yet a Tailor might scratch her where ere she did itch' (Temp. II.2.55) and Falstaff's 'But if he had beene a mans Taylor, he would have prick'd you' (2H4 III.2.165). No additional meaning of *tailor* is required to make sense of Kent's taunt to Oswald: A Taylor made thee (Lear II.2.56), but if the obscene meaning is established from other sources, it makes the taunt more offensive.

The brothel-scene in *Pericles* (IV.6) is full of euphemisms. The bawd is a 'hearbe-woman'; Marina is expected to 'doe the deedes of darknes'; we are told that 'shees not pac'ste yet', and she is said to 'doe for Clyents her fitment'. In other plays there are several euphemisms for prostitutes of varying degrees of social standing: *customer* (Oth. IV.1.119), *doxy* (WT IV.3.2), and *aunt* (WT IV.3.11). *Pagan* is used by Prince Hal of Doll Tearsheet (2H4 II.2.168). This is the earliest example in OED of the sense 'harlot'. Another slang word for a harlot is *road*, again used by Prince Hal: This *Doll Teare-sheet* should be some Rode (2H4 II.2.181). Falstaff mentions the 'huswives' with whom Shallow had consorted when a young man (2H4 III.2.340). It is easier to recognize this as a euphemism for 'whores' when we remember that *hussy* is derived from the same word. Another euphemism for 'whore' found in the same play is *bona-Roba* (III.2.28), a term used to describe whores of more showy appearance. Leontes imagines that people are calling him a cuckold, but he cannot bring himself to use the word, so he claims that they are saying 'Sicilia is a so-forth' (WT I.2.217).

'Dead men's fingers' does not at first glance seem to be very euphemistic, but there is a clear suggestion that it is so used in the Queen's speech about the dead Ophelia:

> long Purples,
> That liberall Shepheards give a grosser name;

---

1. *Explorations in Shakespeare's Language* (Longman, 1962), pp. 108f.

But our cold Maids doe Dead Mens Fingers call them:
(Ham. IV.7.170)

In his *Shakespeare Glossary* Onions identifies the plant as the early purple orchis, *Orchis mascula*.

44. Euphemism is liable to occur in any scene of any play, but only in a few plays, such as *Troilus and Cressida* or *1* and *2 Henry IV* is dysphemism at all common. When Falstaff and Prince Hal are together, the tradition of the medieval *flyting* is continued, and they vie with each other in coining picturesque terms of abuse:

Prince   This sanguine Coward, this Bed-presser, this Hors-back-breaker, this huge Hill of Flesh.

Falstaff   Away you Starveling, you Elfe-skin, you dried Neats tongue, Bulles-pissell, you stocke-fish: O for breth to utter, What is like thee? You Tailors yard, you sheath, you Bow-case, you vile standing tucke.

Prince   Well, breath a-while, and then to't againe: (1H4 II.4.270)

The Falstaff of *The Merry Wives of Windsor* does not indulge in such sustained abusive language, but he can manage an occasional pungent phrase, as when he refuses eggs as *Pullet-Sperme* (III.5.31) and describes Ford as a 'mechanicall-salt-butter rogue' (II.2.291). Glendower, provoked by his daughter's insistence on accompanying her husband to the war, describes her as 'a peevish, selfe-will'd Harlotry' (1H4 III.1.201), and Capulet uses the same phrase to describe Juliet (RJ IV.2.14). There is no suggestion of sexual transgression; the expression means more or less 'silly girl'. *Harlotry* is used as a term of contempt meaning 'worthless' in *these harlotry Players* (1H4 II.4.438).

45. *Pejorative and Ameliorative Development.* The various kinds of semantic change are not mutually exclusive. A term of praise of one generation may become a term of abuse for the next, and in changing, it may provide an example of restriction or extension or the use of a word with varying degrees of consciousness of its etymology. The following are examples of words which in Shakespeare have pejorative associations which they have generally lost today.

Companion is often used as a term of contempt, much as we might use *fellow*, which has in some respects had a parallel semantic development, though we may notice that Malvolio is flattered when Olivia describes him as a fellow: Fellow? not *Malvolio*, nor after my degree, but Fellow (TN III.4.85). *Fellow* is often linked with the adjective *scurvy*, as in *Othello* IV.2.140.

Compassionate is today a term of praise, but it is used in Shakespeare in a distinctly pejorative sense. King Richard II replies unsympathetically to Mowbray's protest at his banishment: It boots thee not to be compassionate (R2 1.3.174). *Compassionate* here means 'sorry for oneself, full of self-pity'.

An *emulator* is today someone who is spurred on by the good deeds of others to try to imitate them; in Shakespeare the word is used pejoratively of one who disparages them. Oliver describes Orlando as 'an envious emulator of every mans good parts' (AYL 1.1.151). The related adjective *emulous* is used in both a good and a bad sense. In Troil. IV.1.28 it means 'ambitious' in a good sense; in Troil. II.3.79 it means 'envious' and is coupled with 'factions'.

We think of a *mountaineer* as a hardy, admirable man, but to Guiderius it is a fighting word. Coupled with other insults, it is enough to make him kill Cloten (Cym. IV.2.120).

Even today *politician* is not often used as a term of praise, but in Shakespeare it is even more derogatory; it nearly always involves scheming. Sir Andrew Aguecheek says 'I had as liefe be a Brownist, as a Politician' (TN III.2.36).

Secure in Shakespeare as today means 'safe', but there is often a suggestion that the feeling of safety is without foundation. Ford describes Page as 'a secure Asse' (MWW II.2.316). Similarly *security* describes a consciousness of safety that leads a man to neglect precautions: Security Is Mortals chiefest Enemie (Macb. III.5.32).

Shrewd in Shakespeare nearly always has a pejorative sense which it has since lost. It sometimes means 'mischievous'; Puck is 'that shrew'd and knavish spirit' (MND II.1.33). It also means 'shrewish, sharp-tongued': when she's angry, she is keene and shrewd (MND III.2.323). The next stage is that *shrewd* joins the large number of adjectives that have become merely vague terms of abuse meaning 'evil, unpleasant': There are some shrewd contents in yond same Paper. (Merch. III.2.244). The adverb *shrewdly* means 'sharply', either mentally or physically, as when Hamlet says 'the Ayre bites shrewdly' (1.4.1). It then comes to be used as an intensive 'intensely, very much' as in the phrase *shrewdly vext* (AW III.5.91).

Suggestion had much more sinister associations than it has today. Now it is rather a diffident word – just a suggestion. In Shakespeare it usually means 'prompting or urging to evil, temptation', as in 'thy suggestion, plot, and damned practise' (Lear II.1.75), and Sir Walter Blunt speaks to Hotspur about those 'mis-led, by your suggestion' (1H4 IV.3.52).

Taxation is used in a different pejorative sense from the one current today. Rosalind warns Touchstone 'you'l be whipt for taxation one of these daies' (AYL 1.2.87). The word is used here in the sense 'fault-finding', a sense that we keep today when we speak of taxing somebody with an offence.

46. Words used in Shakespeare without the pejorative associations that they have today include the following words:

Accomplice is used in the sense 'colleague, assistant'. A Scout greets Charles the Dauphin with the words: Successe unto our valiant Generall, And happinesse to his accomplices. (1H6 V.2.9).

In *Twelfth Night* Maria is described as Olivia's 'chamber-maid' (1.3.54). It is clear from the play that her duties are of a more exalted kind than those that would be undertaken by a chambermaid in more recent times. Olivia calls her 'my Gentlewoman' (1.5.171), and her marriage to Sir Toby arouses little comment. It is clear that the word then described a companion to a lady of rank.

King Henry describes Sir Walter Blunt as 'a deere and true industrious friend' (1H4 1.1.62). The word *industrious* has been spoilt for a reader of today by its disparaging use in phrases like *an industrious apprentice*; we think of an industrious man as a hard-working dullard. King Henry's use of the word is wholly laudatory; he means that Sir Walter is loyal and zealous.

Remorse is today used of regret for something that one has done wrong. In Shakespeare the usual sense is 'pity, compassion', but the word is used in the sense 'solemn obligation', as in: to obey shall be in me remorse (Oth. III.3.469).

In spite of its etymology, which links the word with Latin *sanctus* 'holy', *sanctimonious* is today a term of abuse: 'pretending to be holy'. Prospero uses it without any disparagement in the sense 'holy'; he describes the sacrament of marriage as 'All sanctimonious ceremonies' (Temp. IV.1.16).

Today *sirrah*, if used at all, is archaic and disrespectful. In Shakespeare it could be used without offence to an equal or a superior. Poins uses it to Prince Hal (1H4 1.2.200) and Rosalind, disguised as Ganymede, to Oliver (AYL IV.3.166).

Underhand is now always used pejoratively; we achieve our wicked aims by underhand means. In Shakespeare it simply means 'indirect' with no suggestion of dishonesty. Oliver, when appealing for the sympathy of Charles the wrestler, says: I had my selfe notice of my Brothers purpose heerein, and have by under-hand meanes laboured to disswade him from it. (AYL I.I.147).

Terms of abuse are often used as terms of endearment. Editors who have emended 'Excellent wretch' to 'Excellent wench' in Oth. III.3.90, failed to notice the similar use of *wretch* in RJ 1.3.44 and Ant. V.2.306. Similarly, there is affection rather than contempt in Hermione's words to the women in attendance on her: Doe not weepe (good Fooles) (WT II.1.118). Doll Tearsheet's language of affection is rich in words that might be regarded as terms of abuse. She addresses Falstaff as 'you whorson little valiant Villaine', 'you sweet little Rogue', 'poore Ape', 'you whorson Chops', 'Rogue', 'Villaine' (2H4 II.4.223–40).

47. Some words that are today used only in trivial contexts are used in Shakespeare with a stronger meaning.

Annoy, like *naughty*, has been trivialized in English of the present day. Cassius says of Antony: his meanes, If he improve them, may well stretch so farre As to annoy us all: (JC II.1.158). The meaning of *annoy* is 'harm, injure'.

Apparent is found in Shakespeare with the modern meaning of something which seems to be true, but the most usual sense is 'evident, manifest', a sense which survives to the present day in *heir apparent*. The Bishop of Carlisle, speaking in defence of the absent King Richard, says: Theeves are not judg'd, but are by to heare, Although apparent guilt be seene in them: (R2 IV.1.123).

Convenient. When Portia sends Balthazar with a message, she urges him to waste no time in words but to go on his way. He replies: Madam, I goe with all convenient speed (Merch. III.4.56). Such a reply would today be discourteous and it would suggest procrastination. The meaning of the word in this context is 'appropriate'.

Mere is today a disparaging or apologetic word, but in Elizabethan times it still kept something of its original force (Latin *merus* 'unmixed') and meant 'absolute, complete'. In *Othello* II.2.3 a proclamation refers to 'the meere perdition of the Turkish Fleete'. Bassanio describes Shylock as Antonio's 'meere enemie' (Merch. III.2.265). Here *mere* means 'unqualified, outstanding', a sense much stronger than that current today. A similar change has affected the adverb *merely*, which in Shakespeare means 'absolutely, entirely'.

Rosalind tells Orlando that, by her capricious behaviour, she drove a lover 'to forsweare the ful stream of the world, and to live in a nooke meerly Monastic' (AYL III.2.439).

Naughty is now usually applied to the peccadilloes of children, but etymologically it is the adjective derived from *naught*. In the opening scene of *Julius Caesar* the Tribune Marullus, annoyed by a cobbler's refusal to give a direct answer to his question, addresses him as 'Thou naughty knave' (l.16). Shylock rebukes the gaoler for allowing Antonio too much freedom and calls him 'Thou naughty Jaylor' (Merch. III.3.9).

Presently in Shakespeare nearly always means 'immediately', as when Prospero replies to Ariel's question 'Presently' with the words 'I: with a twincke' (Temp. IV.1.42), but we always have to be prepared for occasional examples of the modern sense, as when Iago says to Roderigo: Do thou meet me presently at the Harbour (Oth. II.1.217).

The adjective *willing* now indicates acquiescence without enthusiasm, but the meaning in Shakespeare is stronger. Sebastian says to Antonio: I perceive in you so excellent a touch of modestie, that you will not extort from me, what I am willing to keepe in: (TN II.1.12). Something of the Elizabethan sense is preserved when we say of anyone that he has a strong will.

48. Some words have a weaker meaning in Shakespeare than they have today. The verb *heave* (OE *hebban* 'to lift') is today used in connexion with lifting heavy weights; in using it we tend to think of coal. In Shakespeare there is no such restriction, and when Iachimo says that he wishes that the food which he 'heav'd to head' had been poisoned (Cym. V.5.157), he does not necessarily mean that he has had a heavy meal. *Once* is used to mean 'at least on this occasion' where we should say 'for once': once in my dayes Ile be a mad-cap. (1H4 1.2.163). Hence it comes to be used merely to strengthen an imperative: Oh, once tell true (MND III.2.68).

Some difficulty is caused by words which vary in strength from one century to another. It is well known that a misleading impression may be made if French *demander* is translated by 'demand', since the English word has imperative overtones not present in the French. Similar misunderstanding may be caused by the use of *require*, which today has a stronger meaning than it had in Elizabethan times. Antony sends an ambassador to Octavius to say: Lord of his Fortunes he salutes thee, and Requires to live in Egypt

(Ant. III.12.12). *Requires* here means no more than 'requests'.

49. The status of a word can change very considerably in the course of a century or so. We find it hard to understand the contempt which Shakespearean characters feel for some words which we regard as commonplace. Mercutio finds fault with the excessive use of *very*:

> The Pox of such antique lisping affecting phantacies, these new tuners of accent: By Jesu a very good blade, a very tall man, a very good whore. (RJ II.4.31)

Often a word falls into disrepute as a result of its use with sexual associations. *Occupy* was used in the sense 'to have to do with carnally', and, as a result of its use in this sense, the verb was not much used in literature in the seventeenth and eighteenth centuries. Doll Tearsheet, in her indignation at hearing Pistol addressed as Captain, resorts to an unexpected linguistic comparison. After protesting against Pistol's claim to the rank of Captain, she says 'A Captaine? These Villaines will make the word Captaine odious:' The Quarto adds: as the word occupy, which was an excellent good worde before it was ill sorted (2H4 II.4.159).

We can learn about the status of words in Elizabethan English, partly by the comments of other characters upon them ('Mobled queen is good') and, with less certainty, by noticing the characters who use them. For this kind of evidence to be useful it is necessary that the word in question should be neither very common nor very rare. If it is very common, it is unlikely to be restricted to any one category of speakers; if it is rare, its use by a particular character may be accidental. *Very* is not the only adverb to be frowned upon in Shakespeare. Jespersen calls attention to a number of words which seem to have been held in low esteem.[1] *Nowadays* is used only by Bottom, the gravedigger in *Hamlet*, and a fisherman in *Pericles*. *Eke*, which is now archaic or poetical, seems to have been regarded as comic in Shakespeare; it is found only three times, the speakers being the Host and Pistol in *The Merry Wives of Windsor* and Flute in *A Midsummer Night's Dream*. *Also* is used twenty-two times, nearly always by vulgar characters like Dogberry and foreigners like Sir Hugh Evans and affected characters, represented by various Second Lords. Falstaff uses the word twice in his euphuistic impersonation of the King (1H4 II.4.440–66).

1. *Growth and Structure of the English Language* (Fifth edition, Blackwell, 1927), § 220.

Accommodate is rare in Shakespeare and seems to have been regarded as affected. *Wag* was free from its present trivial associations, and could be used without incongruity in a serious passage, as in 'Untill my eielids will no longer wag' (Ham. v.1.290). The use of *imp* for 'child' seems to involve playfulness or affectation. Armado calls Moth 'deare impe' (LLL 1.2.5) and Holofernes describes him as 'this Impe' (v.2.591). Pistol addresses Prince Hal, on his accession to the throne, as 'most royall Impe of Fame' (2H4 v.5.45). *Perpend* is a word which is used by characters who are not to be taken very seriously, such as Pistol, Polonius, Feste and Touchstone. *La* is primarily a feminine exclamation and is used by Mistress Quickly and Cressida. When it is used by men it generally, but not always, indicates a speaker who is foolishly effeminate, like Slender in MWW 1.1.322. *Ergo* 'therefore', with its variants *argo* and *argal*, is used only by low-life characters: *Grumio* 'Ergo thou best Shrew' (Shrew iv.3.126), *Dromio of S* 'Ergo, light wenches will burn' (Err. iv.3.52), *Launcelot* 'Ergo, old man' (Merch. ii.2.51), *Clown* 'Ergo, he that kisses my wife is my friend' (AW 1.3.47), *Bevis (a workman)* 'Argo, their thread of life is spun' (2H6 iv.2.28), *Gravedigger* 'Argal, she drowned herself wittingly' (Ham. v.1.12; cf. ll.19, 48).

CHAPTER 3

Syntax

𝔊𝔊𝔊𝔊𝔊𝔊

50. Many of the differences between Elizabethan syntax and that of the present day can be explained if we remember that the Elizabethans preferred vigour to logic. The double negative and double comparative are regarded as perfectly natural ways of achieving emphasis. Shakespeare was writing for an audience, not a reader, and hence such features as false concord and mixed constructions are common in the First Folio, which reflects the familiar and spontaneous style of the spoken language. Thanks to editorial intervention, the Second Folio is more studied and formal and corrects many of the examples of false concord in the First Folio.[1]

CONCORD

51. False concord can arise easily in the spoken language especially when sentences are long. The following are some of the chief causes of lack of concord:

(a) A plural subject, consisting of two components, may express a single idea, especially when the subject is abstract. Such a subject often takes a singular verb: Sorrow, and griefe of heart Makes him speake fondly, (R2 III.3.184).

(b) Collective nouns can take a singular or a plural verb according to whether the noun refers to a group that can act as a single body or as a number of separate individuals. The subject, though plural in form, may be one that can be regarded as singular in meaning, like *manners* in: Which very manners urges (Lear v.3.234). Phrases like *a sort of men*, meaning 'men of a certain sort' generally take a plural verb: There are a sort of men, whose visages Do creame and mantle like a standing pond, (Merch. 1.1.88).

(c) The verb may precede its subject, with the result that, when

---

1. See G. Alphonso Smith 'The Chief Differences between the First and Second Folios of Shakespeare' *Englische Studien* 30 (1902), 1–20.

the verb is used, it is uncertain whether the subject is going to be singular or plural: Hath all his ventures faild, (Merch. III.2.270; Rowe, followed by the Globe edition, reads *have* for *hath*); That Spirit, upon whose spirit depends and rests The lives of many, (Ham. III.3.14); Is there not wars? Is there not imployment? (2H4 I.2.84); there lives not three good men unhang'd in England, (1H4 II.4.145).

(d) The writer may fail to identify the true subject of a sentence. The verb is said to be 'attracted' to the person or number of some word in the sentence which is not the true subject of the verb, but which happens to be near to it: The very thought of my Revenges that way Recoyle upon me: (WT II.3.18); I hope in no place so unsanctified, Where such as thou may'st finde him. (Macb. IV.2.81); The posture of your blowes are yet unknowne; (JC V.1.33). Attraction is always liable to take place when the logical subject of a sentence is not the same as the grammatical subject. In the following passage the grammatical subject is in the third person but the real subject is the person addressed, i.e. Puck:

> Are you not hee,
> That frights the maidens of the Villagree,
> Skim milke, and sometimes labour in the querne,
> And bootlesse make the breathlesse huswife cherne,
>
> (MND II.1.34)

When a singular noun is followed by an *of*-genitive in the plural, the verb is often attracted into the plural: How oft the sight of meanes to do ill deeds, Make deeds ill done? (John IV.2.219; some editors emend *make* to *makes*).

(e) When a verb has two subjects linked by *and*, it may agree with only one of these subjects: how doost thou and thy Master agree, (Merch. II.2.106); for the which, my selfe and them Bend their best studies, (John IV.2.50). [Franz 677]

(f) Because the relative pronoun is not fully inflected, there is often a lack of concord between its antecedent and the following verb: So, so, so, so: they laugh, that winnes. (Oth. IV.1.125); *Caska*, you are the first that reares your hand. (JC III.1.30). Here there is confusion between *that rears his* and *to rear your*. [Abbott 247]

(g) Some apparent false concord may arise from the use of an *s*-ending in a plural verbal form. Such plurals passed out of use in the written language during the course of the seventeenth century

but they have remained in some regional dialects. In Shakespeare
they occur especially in rhyme: Whiles I threat, he lives: Words to
the heat of deedes too cold breath gives. (Macb. II.1.60).[1]

WORD-ORDER

52. The normal word-order in an English sentence is for the subject to precede the verb while the object follows it. The most common reason for departing from this order is a desire for emphasis.
If the object precedes the verb, it becomes more emphatic: there is
Vertue in that *Falstaffe*: him keepe with, the rest banish. (1H4
II.4.472). Pistol is fond of this device. Two examples from his
speeches are: I thee command (H5 II.3.62) and: Convay: the wise
it call (NWW 1.3.29). Inversion of pronoun and verb is especially
common in verse: I might not this beleeve (Ham. I.1.56). Another
way of obtaining emphasis is to put the pronominal object at the
very end of a sentence, after an adverb:

Feste I say againe, take her away.
Olivia Sir, I bad them take away you.   (TN 1.5.58)

Cassius *Cinna*, where haste you so?
Cinna To finde out you: (JC 1.3.132)

53. As a result of French influence, an adjective sometimes follows its noun. Legal terms like *fee-simple* (MWW IV.2.222) and *Heire
apparant* (1H4 II.4.398) are borrowed from French, and the phrase
a gentleman born (WT V.2.143) clearly has a special appeal for the
Clown because he thinks that it is a legal term which conveys
special status. Touchstone's phrases like *Quip-modest, reply Churlish
and Counterchecke quarrelsome* (AYL V.4.99) may be parodies of legal
formulas. [Franz 685]

54. When an adjective is followed by an adverbial phrase, the
two are often separated by a noun: Nor scarre that whiter skin of
hers, then Snow, (Oth. V.2.4); As any the most vulgar thing to
sence, (Ham 1.2.99). [Abbott 419a]

55. An indefinite article sometimes splits the two elements of a
compound adjective or an adjective preceded by an adverb: Or

1. See George O. Curme, *A Grammar of the English Language*: *Parts of Speech and
Accidence* (D. C. Heath, 1935), p. 240, George O. Curme, *A Grammar of the English
Language*: *Syntax* (D. C. Heath, 1931), p. 53, C. A. Smith, 'Shakespeare's Present
Indicative *s*-endings with Plural Subjects', *PMLA* xi (1896), 362–376.

having sworne too hard a keeping oath Studie to breake it, (LLL
1.1.65); I would have beene much more a fresher man, (Troil.
v.6.20). [Abbott 422]

56. The group genitive had become established by the time of
Shakespeare. We find *the Duke of Norfolkes Seignories* (2H4 IV.1.111)
and *my Lord of Yorkes Armor* (2H6 1.3.195) beside the older construction *the Arch-bishops Grace of Yorke* (1H4 III.2.119) [Franz 684b]

57. If two genitives, linked by *and*, both precede a noun, the *-s*
ending is added only to the second of them: my Wife and Childrens
Ghosts will haunt me still: (Macb. v.7.16); Yet am I *Suffolke* and
the Cardinalls Broker, (2H6 1.2.101). This rule does not apply if one
or both of the genitives is a personal pronoun. Then both genitives
have an indication of their case: at the very instant of *Falstaffes* and
our meeting, (MWW v.3.17); In yours, and my discharge. (Temp.
II.1.255). [Franz 684 d and e]

58. When a noun in the genitive is in apposition to another
noun, it normally precedes the noun on which it depends while the
noun in apposition follows the noun, often without a genitive
ending: this same Scull sir, was *Yoricks* Scull, the Kings Jester.
(Ham. v.1.197); who beares hard His Brothers death at *Bristow*, the
Lord *Scroope*. (1H4 1.3.270). [Franz 684a]

59. There were two ways of asking a question. The older
method was by inversion of the usual position of subject and verb;
the newer method was by the use of the auxiliary *do*. In general,
inversion is preferred in tragedy and high style; the use of *do* is
preferred in everyday colloquial style. Examples of inversion are:
Ride you this afternoone? (Macb. III.1.19); How goes the world
Sir, now? (Macb. II.4.21). [Franz 706a]

ELLIPSIS

60. Elizabethan love of brevity tolerated almost any ellipsis provided that the missing words could be understood from the context. The following are among the most common types of ellipsis:

(a) When there is no doubt what is the subject of a sentence it
is sometimes omitted: They call him *Doricles*, and boasts himselfe
To have a worthy Feeding; (WT IV.4.168). [Abbott 399–401]

(b) In antithetical sentences the words that are not contrasted
are often not repeated: She was belov'd, she lov'd; she is, and
dooth; (Troil. IV.5.293); What most he should dislike, seemes

pleasant to him; What like, offensive. (Lear IV.2.10) [Abbott 395].

(c) In relative clauses a preposition is often not repeated, and the relative pronoun itself may be understood: To dye upon the bed my father dy'de, (WT IV.4.466); As well appeareth by the cause you come (R2 1.1.26); Most ignorant of what he's most assur'd (Meas. II.2.119). The *of* is overworked. [Abbott 394]

(d) The infinitive of a verb of motion is often understood when *shall* or *will* is followed by a preposition: Ile to him, (RJ III.2.141); And he to England shall along with you: (Ham. III.3.4). [Abbott 405]

(e) A verb that has to be understood may be the negative of one actually used:

I heard you say, that you had rather refuse
The offer of an hundred thousand Crownes,
Then *Bullingbrookes* returne to England; (R2 IV.1.15)

Some verb like *endure* is to be understood after *then*. [Abbott 390]

FUNCTIONAL SHIFT

61. A feature of Elizabethan syntax which is found to a lesser extent in the English of today is that known as functional shift, which allows one part of speech to be used for another. By the time of Shakespeare the decay of inflexional endings had produced a large number of verbs identical in form with nouns of similar meaning. It was very easy for such verbs to be used as nouns, sometimes as nonce usages: *accuse* 'accusation', *amaze* 'astonishment', *impose* 'injunction', *prepare* 'preparation'. Adjectives were freely used as verbs, usually transitive. An adjective used as a verb generally has the sense 'to make (that adjective)', as in *happies* 'makes happy' (Sonnet 6.6), *bolds* 'emboldens' (Lear V.1.26), *gentle* 'to ennoble' (H5 IV.3.63), *pale* 'to make pale' (Ham. 1.5.90), *plaine* 'to explain' (Per. 111, Prol. 14). A new group of verbs was created by adding the prefix *un-* to an adjective to make a verb: *unfaire* 'to deface' (Sonnet 5.4), *undeafe* 'to cure the deafness of' (R2 11.1.16). When nouns were used as verbs, there was more variety in the relationship of meaning between the noun and the verb. The verb could mean 'apply (the noun) to', as in: such stuffe as Madmen Tongue, and braine not: (Cym. v.4.147). Other examples are *knee* 'kneel' (Cor. v.1.5), *skaling* 'weighing' (Cor. 11.3.257). The verb

could mean 'treat as', as in: He godded me (Cor. v.3.11); They have heere propertied me: (TN IV.2.99). Sometimes the meaning of the new verb is very compressed, as in: Still Virginalling Upon his Palme? (WR 1.2.125), where *virginal* means to touch as though playing upon the virginal. Another group of nouns used as verbs has the meaning 'to change into'; Why, what reade you there, That have so cowarded and chac'd your blood (H5 11.2.75).

Functional shift is used to avoid the use of the verb *make*. *Safe* is used in *Antony and Cleopatra* in the sense 'to make safe' (1.3.55) or 'to conduct safely': I tell you true: Best you saf't the bringer out of the hoast, (Ant. IV.6.26).

A concrete noun may be used in place of an abstract verb to make the meaning more vivid or disgusting. *To lip* is more emotive than *to kiss*: To lip a wanton in a secure Cowch; (Oth. IV.1.73).

It is not always easy to distinguish between a noun used in apposition with another noun and one used adjectivally, but in the following quotation the use of *so* makes it clear that *flood-gate* is an adjective: For my particular griefe, Is of so flood-gate, and ore-bearing Nature, That it engluts, and swallowes other sorrowes, (Oth. 1.3.55).

62. In present-day English we often turn a noun into a verb by the addition of a prefix, as in *befriend* or *bewitch*. In Shakespeare nouns could be used as verbs without any prefix: Disorder that hath spoyl'd us, friend us now, (H5 IV.5.20); And witch the World with Noble Horsemanship (1H4 IV.1.110).

63. A common type of derisive repartee is the use as a verb of some other part of speech that has just been used by someone else: Tut, tut, Grace me no Grace, nor Unckle me, [no unckle] (R2 II.3.82; the bracketed words are from Q1–4). Thanke me no thankings, nor proud me no prouds, (RJ III.5.153).

MIXED CONSTRUCTIONS

64. Mixed constructions are especially common in the spoken language. They are more common in Shakespeare than today because liveliness and vigour so often overrode formal reasoning in the daily conversation of the Elizabethans. Examples are: Why I do trifle thus with his dispaire, Is done to cure it. (Lear IV.6.33); The Battaile done, and they within our power, Shall never see his pardon: (Lear V.1.67); Rather proclaime it (Westmerland) through

my Hoast, That he which hath no stomack to this fight, Let him depart, (H5 IV.3.34). [Abbott 411, Franz 690]

65. Verbs of hearing, seeing or knowing may take a noun (or pronoun) or a noun clause as a direct object. Sometimes we find both, the clause serving as an explanation of the noun or pronoun: I see you what you are, you are too proud: (TN 1.5.268); Wee'l heare him what he sayes, (Ant. v.1.51). [Abbott 414, Franz 304]

66. False concord is common in relative clauses, as the result of a mixture of two constructions: I beseech you heare me, who professes My selfe your loyall Servant, (WT II.3.53). This is a mixture of *who profess myself* and *who professes himself*. When a relative follows two pronouns, there is room for variety in a single sentence: Are not you hee, That frights the maidens of the Villagree, Skim milke, and sometimes labour in the querne, (MND II.1.34). *Frights* agrees with *hee*, while *skim* and *labour* agree with *you*. [Franz 677]

67. Confusion of a relative clause with an accusative and infinitive construction sometimes leads to the use of *whom* where we should expect *who*: Yong *Ferdinand* (whom they suppose is droun'd) (Temp. III.3.92); Of *Arthur*, whom they say is kill'd to night, (John IV.2.165). [Abbott 410]

68. A common type of mixed construction arises from two different ways of expressing the superlative. 'A greater error than all the rest' and 'the greatest error of all' combine to produce: This is the greatest error of all the rest; (MND V.1.249). There is a similar accidental exclusion of the person compared in: Of all men else I have avoyded thee: (Macb. v.8.4). [Abbott 409]

69. Beside the confusion of constructions within a single sentence, we sometimes find a lack of correspondence between question and answer. The person who answers has assumed the question to be in a slightly different form from the one actually used:

King How now good *Blunt*? thy Lookes are full of speed,
Blunt So hath the Businesse that I come to speake of.

(1H4 III.2.162)

In this exchange *are* and *hath* do not correspond. [Franz 695]

NOUNS

70. Old English grammatical gender did not survive until the time of Shakespeare, but Shakespeare made free use of personification. The influence of classical mythology sometimes determined the

gender of nouns; the sun (Apollo) is masculine while the moon (Luna) is feminine. Countries and towns are usually feminine but sometimes neuter, and the gender can change within a single sentence: this deere-deere Land, Deere for her reputation through the world, . . . Hath made a shamefull conquest of it selfe. (R2 II.1.57). Rivers are sometimes feminine: Have you not made an Universall shout, That Tyber trembled underneath her bankes (JC 1.1.49). [Abbott 229, Franz 203]

71. In present-day English, nouns that refer to inanimate objects generally form their genitive by means of an *of*-phrase; in Shakespeare the genitive in -*s* is commonly used: this Ages yoake (JC 1.2.61); on the houses top (Ham. III.4.193). We sometimes find two successive genitives in -*s*: Caesars deaths houre (JC III.1.154); your Husbands Brothers wife. (Ham. III.4.15). [Franz 279–80]

PRONOUNS
Personal

72. Objective forms of personal pronouns are often used instead of subjective, especially when they follow the verb: That's mee I warrant you. (TN II.5.87); A man no mightier then thy selfe, or me, (JC 1.3.76); And damn'd be him, that first cries hold, enough. (Macb. V.8.34). The use of *thee* for *thou* is especially common after an imperative: But far thee well (Merch. II.3.4); but heare thee Gratiano, (Merch. II.2.190). This usage may be due to the influence of reflexive verbs as in: Hast thee for thy life. (Lear V.3.251). [Franz 283]

73. Just as a pronoun following a verb is liable to be in the objective case whatever its function in the sentence, so a pronoun preceding the verb which governs it is liable to be in the subjective case: And he, my husband best of all affects: (MWW IV.4.87). Subjective pronouns are particularly liable to be used for objective when they stand at some distance from the governing verb or preposition, with the result that the speaker and the hearer lose sight of the construction of the sentence: Your Majestie, and wee that have free soules, it touches us not: (Ham. III.2.250). Another cause of the use of a subjective for an objective pronoun is the linking of the pronoun by *and* with a noun which precedes it. The case of the noun is not clear from its form and this uncertainty leads to a similar doubt about the case of the pronoun: I never saw

SYNTAX

a woman But onely *Sycorax* my Dam, and she; (Temp. III.2.108).
There is a similar confusion when the pronoun in question is
linked with a pronoun like *you* which has the same form in subjective and objective cases: all debts are cleerd betweene you and I,
(Merch. III.2.320). The substitution is liable to take place when the
logical subject of a sentence is not the same as the grammatical: let
no man abide this deede, But we the Doers. (JC III.1.93). *We* is
grammatically the object of *let*, but logically it is the subject of the
sentence.

74. *Shall* was sometimes regarded as an impersonal verb, and it
may consequently be followed by *'s* for *us*: Shal's to the Capitoll?
(Cor. IV.6.148); Say, where shall's lay him? (Cym. IV.2.235).
[Abbott 215, Franz 285]

75. In Old English the noun *wā* 'woe' is often used with the
dative of the pronoun, and this is the construction that has survived in *Oh woe is me*, (Ham. III.1.167). In *woe is my heart* (Cym. V.5.2)
the cases of the two nouns cannot be deduced from their forms,
and such constructions led to others where *woe* was clearly regarded
as an adjective with the pronoun in the subjective case: I am woe
for't, Sir (Temp. V.1.139). Similarly the old construction *me were
better* becomes *I were better* through the intermediate stage of such
constructions as *you were best* (JC III.3.13), where the case of the
pronoun is not obvious from its form. Hence we have: Poor Lady,
she were better love a dreame: (TN II.2.27). [Abbott 230]

76. There are several tendencies which affect the use of *thou* and
you. Together they result in a complicated situation because they
sometimes cut across each other. *You* is the usual pronoun used
by upper-class speakers to one another. *Thou* is used in various
special situations:

(a) It is used by lower-class characters in speaking to other
members of the same social class: Samson and Gregory in *Romeo
and Juliet*, Launce and Speed in *The Two Gentlemen of Verona*,
Stephano and Trinculo in *The Tempest*.

(b) It expresses any emotion, either friendly or hostile, and it is
used between friends as a mark of affection, which may vary with
changing moods. At the beginning of *The Two Gentlemen of Verona*
Proteus and Valentine use *thou*, but after a long separation they at
first use the colder *you* (II.4.122). Fathers address their sons as *thou*,
but sons speaking to fathers use the more respectful *you*, as in the
scene between Prince Hal and his father (1H4 III.2). A wife

73

addressing her husband varies between *thou* and *you*. Lady Percy to Hotspur nearly always uses *you*, but in a long and earnest appeal she uses *thou* (1H4 III.3.39–67) and again in the playfully familiar threat: Indeede Ile breake thy little finger *Harry*, (II.3.88). Hotspur generally uses *thou* to his wife, but when he becomes serious, *thou* gives way to *you*. In *Julius Cæsar* Portia and Brutus use *you*, not rising to the declamatory or falling to the familiar, for both of which styles *thou* would be appropriate. There is a special interest in scenes where there is an apparent inconsistency in the use of the two pronouns, for the transition from one to the other often indicates an important change of mood. Polonius, scolding Laertes, uses *you* at the beginning and end of his speech; in the middle, while giving him fatherly advice, he uses *thou*. Prospero to Miranda begins with *you* but, as he becomes more affectionate, he uses *thou*. The Queen, reproaching Hamlet, begins with an affectionate *thou* but, finding him unresponsive, she turns to the less affectionate *you*. Deeply moved by fear, she uses the more emotional *thou*: thou wilt not murther me? (III.4.21). Capulet uses *thou* to Tybalt until he becomes annoyed with him, when *thou* gives place to *you*. Bianca, trying to conciliate her elder sister Katherine, uses the respectful *you*, whereas Katherine uses the impatient *thou*. Lovers generally begin with *you* but pass on to *thou* when they become more sure of each other's affection. It is in keeping with Romeo's passionate nature that he addresses Juliet as *thou* from the first. Ferdinand and Miranda keep to *you*; they have not known each other very long.

(c) *Thou* is used to express good-humoured superiority to servants. When a master is finding fault with a servant, he calls him *you*. In *The Two Gentlemen of Verona* Proteus, after addressing the newly-engaged servant Julia as *thou*, turns to Launce: How now you whor-son pezant, Where have you bin these two dayes loytering? (IV.4.48).

(d) The easy assumption that familiarity will be welcomed makes *thou* an insult when addressed to a stranger. Prospero, treating Ferdinand as an impostor, calls him *thou* (Temp. 1.2.451). The clearest indication that *thou* could be insulting is Sir Toby's advice in *Twelfth Night*: if thou thou'st him some thrice, it shall not be amisse, (III.2.48). There is no contradiction between the friendly and hostile uses of *thou*, and similarly *you* can be used for two different reasons. The use of the plural pronoun implies aloofness, and this may result from either respect or dislike.

(e) *Thou* is used in invocations. Cassius, in speaking to Brutus, uses the respectful *you* (JC 1.2.57) but, when Brutus is absent, he uses the rhetorical *thou* (1.2.312). [Abbott 231–5, Franz 289]

77. In Old English the second person plural pronoun was *gē* in the nominative and *ēow* in the accusative and dative. Already by the middle of the sixteenth century *you* had become more common than *ye* in the subjective case, and in Shakespeare the most common use of *ye* is in rhetorical appeals and invocations: Therein, yee Gods, you make the weake most strong; (JC 1.3.91); O ye immortall Gods! (JC IV.3.156). *Ye* is sometimes used in the objective case, and here it may be an unaccented form of *you*: I never lov'd you much, but I ha' prais'd ye, (Ant. II.6.78); I thanke ye, (AYL II.7.135). [Abbott 236, Franz 288]

78. The third personal pronouns are used to mean 'man' or 'woman': Ile bring mine action on the proudest he That stops my way in *Padua*: (Shrew III.2.234); Lady, you are the cruell'st shee alive, (TN I.5.260). [Franz 290]

79. A pronoun in the objective case is sometimes used, without the preposition that would be necessary today, to refer to someone who is in some way the indirect object of the verb: See, how this River comes me cranking in, (1H4 III.1.98); but heare me this: (TN V.1.123). In the first example *me* means 'to my disadvantage', and in the second it means 'from me'. [Abbott 220, Franz 293]

80. One special category of the use of pronouns without prepositions is the ethic dative, which is used in narrative to indicate that the person to whom the pronoun refers has some special interest in the events described. It is a colloquial device used to make a narrative more lively: He pluckt me ope his Doublet (JC 1.2.267); And hee would manage you his Peece thus: and hee would about, and about, and come you in, and come you in: (2H4 III.2.332). The use of this device can lead to wilful misunderstanding. Petruchio uses the ethic dative: knocke me heere soundly (Shrew 1.2.8), but Grumio deliberately misinterprets it as a direct object. [Abbott 220, Franz 294]

81. The use of *it* as the object of a verb has a parallel in the colloquial speech of today, as in *to try it on*, *Mr. Britling Sees It Through*. The idiom is found in Shakespeare: Courage Father, fight it out (3H6 1.4.10); I cannot daub it further. (Lear IV.1.55). The pronoun *it* is often used with nouns to give them the force of

verbs: Ile Queene it no inch farther, (WT IV.4.458); I come to wive it wealthily in *Padua*: (Shrew I.2.75). [Abbott 226, Franz 295]

82. An apparently redundant personal pronoun is sometimes found:

(a) To achieve emphasis a personal pronoun, when the subject of a sentence, may be repeated at the end of the sentence: I will not trust you, I, (MND III.2.340); He cannot flatter, he, (Lear II.2.104). [Franz 298]

(b) When a clause introduced by *that* is the subject of a sentence, it is sometimes reinforced by the pronoun *it*: That I have tane away this old mans Daughter, It is most true: (Oth. I.3.78). Similarly, when the subject is an infinitive: To chide at your extreames, it not becomes me: (WT IV.4.6). [Franz 301]

(c) The subject of a sentence is sometimes reinforced by a personal pronoun immediately following it: The skipping King hee ambled up and downe, (IH4 III.2.60); The King he takes the Babe To his protection, (Cym. I.1.40). [Abbott 243, Franz 299]

(d) When the subject of a sentence is separated from its object by a long parenthesis, a pronoun may be inserted to reinforce either the subject or the object: But this same *Cassio*, though he speake of comfort, Touching the Turkish losse, yet he lookes sadly, (Oth. II.1.31). [Franz 300, 303]

83. Personal pronouns, especially *I*, are sometimes omitted in everyday colloquial expressions, as in present-day English *Thank you*. *Prithee* is the usual Elizabethan equivalent of present-day *Please*: Prethee peace. (Temp. II.1.9); Beseech you give me leave to retire my selfe. (Cor. I.3.30). The second personal pronoun is sometimes omitted: What hast heere? (WT IV.4.260), and the third person neuter pronoun is often omitted with impersonal verbs, as in *please you* and *methinks*. [Franz 306]

84. Personal pronouns are used as reflexives beside forms in *-self*. Examples are: Therefore prepare you, (Ham III.3.2); Ile go hide me. (MWW III.3.34). The personal pronoun is often used as a dative of advantage instead of a pronoun in *-self*: I can buy me twenty at any Market. (Macb. IV.2.40); Let every Souldier hew him downe a Bough, (Macb. V.4.4), [Abbott 223, Franz 307]

85. A pronoun in *-self* can be used as an emphatic substitute for the subjective case of a personal pronoun: My selfe have Letters of the selfe-same Tenure. (JC. IV.3.171); My selfe did heare it. (IH4 I.3.157). [Franz 308]

86. The usual royal plural form is *ourself*: We doe debase our selfe (R2 III.3.127); but we also find *ourselves*: our selves will heare Th' accuser, and the accused, freely speake; (R2 I.1.16). [Franz 309]

87. Personal pronouns, including those in *-self*, are sometimes used to express reciprocal relationships: Wee'l heare our selves againe. (Macb. III.4.31), i.e. 'We will hear each other'. There are other ways of expressing reciprocity. One easily intelligible way is illustrated in: A plague upon 't, when Theeves cannot be true one to another. (1H4 II.2.30). A more idiomatic way is: Sir, we have knowne togither in Orleance. (Cym. 1.4.35). [Franz 312]

Demonstrative

88. Before plural expressions of time the singular *this* is sometimes used because the speaker is thinking of the whole period of time, not the separate units: I have forsworne his company hourely any time this two and twenty yeare, (1H4 II.2.15); I have not seen him this two daies. (Lear 1.4.79). *Many a day* is interpreted as a singular expression meaning 'a long time' in: How does your Honor for this many a day? (Ham. III.1.91). Conversely *these* is sometimes used before *kind* or *sort* when followed by *of* and a plural noun, as in: These kind of Knaves I know, (Lear II.2.107). This construction is still common in colloquial speech today. [Franz 316]

89. *Same* is sometimes used to strengthen a demonstrative: take this same letter (Merch. III.4.46); yond same blacke cloud (Temp. II.2.19). *The same* is sometimes used instead of a personal pronoun, a construction today regarded as a feature of commercial English: Give me the paper, let me reade the same, (LLL I.1.116). [Franz 317]

90. *Self* is used in the same way as *same* to strengthen a demonstrative: if you please To shoote another arrow that selfe way Which you did shoot the first, (Merch. 1.1.147); I am made of that selfe-mettle as my *Sister*, (Lear 1.1.71). In the last quotation the Quarto reading ('The self-same metal') is a pointer to the later history of this construction.

91. *Yon, yond* and *yonder* are all used in Shakespeare as demonstrative adjectives. Today they have diverged: *yon* is Northern and Scots dialect, *yond* is archaic, and *yonder* is poetical: yon grey Lines (JC II.1.103), yond gull *Malvolio* (TN III.2.74), yonder City (Troil. IV.5.211). [Franz 319]

Possessive

92. The possessive pronouns like *his* and *her* have today become mere possessive adjectives, but in Shakespeare they have enough of their original pronominal function to allow a possessive pronoun to stand as the antecedent of a relative: And do you now strew Flowers in his way, That comes in Triumph over *Pompeyes* blood? (JC I.1.55), i.e. 'in the way of him who comes'. [Abbott 208–9]

93. Another survival of the days when possessive pronouns were not mere possessive adjectives is the use of *both* and *all* in agreement with the implied personal pronoun. Examples are: both our remedies Within thy helpe and holy phisicke lies: (RJ II.3.51), i.e. the remedy for us both; this will breake out To all our sorrowes, (John IV.2.101), i.e. 'to the sorrow of us all'. [Franz 324]

94. *His* is sometimes used in the sense 'of this one' in antithesis with 'of the other one': Desire his Jewels, and this others House, (Macb. IV.3.80). In Old English, *his* was the genitive of the neuter personal pronoun as well as of the masculine. *Its* came into use towards the end of the sixteenth century and is found occasionally in Shakespeare spelt *its* (as at Meas. 1.2.4), or *it's* (as at WT 1.2.151), but *his* is the usual neuter possessive. *It*, a provincial form of the possessive, still common in the North and North Midlands[1] is occasionally found in Shakespeare, especially with reference to children: (The innocent milke in it most innocent mouth) (WT III.2.101); It lifted up it head, (Ham. 1.2.216). In most of the passages where the First Folio shows *it* used in this way, the later Folios have *its* or *it's*.

95. *Mine* and *thine* are not normally used before consonants after the first half of the sixteenth century. Before vowels or *h* they are sometimes used attributively by Shakespeare, although *my* and *thy* are more common: How much I have disabled mine estate (Merch. 1.1.123); Thou shalt not know the sound of thine owne tongue. (Merch. 1.1.109). [Franz 326]

96. *Mine*, *hers* and *theirs* are used as possessive adjectives even when preceding their nouns, when linked with another possessive adjective by *and*: And his, and mine lov'd darling. (Temp. III.3.93); Mine and my Fathers death come not upon thee, (Ham. V.2.341);

1. See Joseph Wright, *The English Dialect Grammar* (OUP, 1905), § 411.

By hers, and mine Adultery: (Cym. v.5.186); Even in theirs, and in the Commons eares (Cor. v.6.4). [Abbott 238]

97. An effect similar to that gained by the ethic dative (see § 80) is obtained by the use of the possessive adjective *your*, which is used colloquially to indicate that the person addressed has a special interest in the subject under discussion: Your worm is your onely Emperor for diet, . . . Your fat King, and your leane Begger is but variable service to dishes, (Ham. iv.3.21); Your Serpent of Egypt, is bred now of your mud by the operation of your Sun: so is your Crocodile. (Ant. ii.7.29)

98. When a noun preceded by *my* or *thy* is qualified by an adjective, the adjective usually precedes the possessive: sweet my Coz (AYL 1.2.1); good my Lord (Ham. 1.2.169); deere my Liege (R2 1.1.184). [Franz 328]

99. The *-es* of the genitive ending of nouns is sometimes replaced by the possessive pronoun *his*, especially after proper names ending in *-s*: the Count his gallies, (TN III.3.26); *Charles* his glikes (1H6 III.2.123). [Abbott 217]

100. In present-day English the adjective *other* generally follows a possessive adjective, except in legal English. In Shakespeare it often precedes: With *Pointz*, and other his continuall followers. (2H4 IV.4.53); a thousand other her defences, (MWW II.2.258). [Franz 329]

101. Beside the possessive pronoun we find examples of the personal pronoun preceded by *of*, a construction which survives today in a few set phrases, such as *for the life of me*: Tell thou the lamentable fall of me, (R2 v.1.44). [Franz 323]

102. The relative pronoun is sometimes separated from its antecedent in sentences where today we should use a personal pronoun preceded by *and*:

Now presently Ile give her father notice
Of their disguising and pretended flight:
Who (all inrag'd) will banish *Valentine*:

(TGV II.6.36) [Abbott 263]

103. The modern rule, which keeps *who* for persons and *which* for things, is not always observed in Elizabethan English. Later editors, especially Pope, have sometimes emended the text to make it conform to later practice: Usurping Ivie, Brier, or idle Mosse,

Who all for want of pruning, with intrusion, Infect thy sap, (Err.
II.2.178; Hanmer reads *which*); The first of gold, who this inscrip-
tion beares, (Merch. II.7.4; Pope reads *which*).

Which is sometimes used of persons: he which hath your Noble
Father slaine, (Ham. IV.7.4); The Mistris which I serve, quickens
what's dead, (Temp. III.1.6) [Franz 335]

104. The use of *who* for *whom* is more common when it is interrogative than when it is a relative pronoun, since in English there
is always a tendency to assume that the first noun or pronoun in a
sentence is its subject. When the pronoun is preceded by a preposition, *whom* has a better chance of survival. During the seventeenth century the feeling for grammatical correctness became
stronger and we often find *who* in the Quarto and First Folio
replaced by *whom* in the later Folios: *Clarence*, who I indeede have
cast in darknesse, (R3 1.3.327; F2–4 read *whom*); you have oft
enquired After the Shepheard that complain'd of love, Who you
saw sitting by me on the Turph (AYL III.4.50; F2–4 read *whom*).
[Franz 333]

105. The use of *whom* for *who* is less common than that of *who*
for *whom*. When it does occur, the most frequent cause is probably
confusion with an accusative and infinitive construction (See § 67).
Whoever is used as an objective pronoun: Who ere I woe, my selfe
would be his wife. (TN 1.4.42). [Franz 334]

106. *Who* is used in the sense 'whoever' or 'he who': Is Proclamation made, That who finds *Edward*, shall have a high Reward,
and he his Life? (3H6 V.5.9). *Whoso* is used in the sense 'whoever':
who so empties them, (R2 II.2.130). [Franz 336]

107. *The which* occurs as a variant of *which*: that is one of the
points, in the which women stil give the lie to their consciences.
(AYL III.2.407); At the which, let no man wonder. (MND V.1.134).
[Franz 337]

108. *That . . . as* is often used where we should say *that . . .
which*, thus giving *as* nearly the function of a relative pronoun: I
have not from your eyes that gentlenesse And shew of Love, as I
was wont to have: (JC 1.2.33); your Highnesse is not entertain'd
with that Ceremonious affection as you were wont, (Lear 1.4.59).
[Abbott 280]

109. There are many sentences without the subjective relative
pronoun which would be used in present-day English. These
sentences show a paratactic construction, common in Early

English and found in modern English dialects:[1] There is a man haunts the Forrest, (AYL III.2.375); There be some Sports are painfull; (Temp. III.1.1). It is not quite correct to describe this construction as the omission of a relative pronoun, since the paratactic construction is very old, and it may be said that in constructions of this kind the relative was never there to be omitted.

110. In the sentence 'Marke but my Fall, and that that Ruin'd me' (H8 III.2.439) the first *that* is a demonstrative and the second a relative pronoun. Sometimes a single *that* has to satisfy both functions: Now followes, that you know (Ham. 1.2.17). The relative may be understood even when it is in an oblique case: Thy Honorable Mettle may be wrought From that it is dispos'd: (JC 1.2.313). [Abbott 244, Franz 348]

Interrogative

111. *What* is used as an interrogative pronoun meaning 'who': What are they that would speake with me? (Ham. IV.6.1); What's he That was not borne of woman? (Macb. V.7.2).

It is used in rhetorical questions with the meaning 'why': But what talke wee of Fathers, when there is such a man as *Orlando*? (AYL III.4.43); What shall I need to draw my sword? (Cym. II.4.30).

It is used as an exclamation of impatience to attract attention: What *Jessica*? (Merch. II.5.4).

Just as *who* is used for 'whoever' (see § 106), so *what* is used for 'whatever' or 'any': I love thee not a Jarre o' th' Clock, behind What Lady she her Lord. (WT 1.2.43). [Abbott 253–6, Franz 342]

112. The interrogative pronoun *whether* 'which of two' is no longer in general use, but it is common in Shakespeare: Whether doest thou professe thy selfe, a knave or a foole? (AW IV.5.26); whether had you rather lead mine eyes, or eye your masters heeles? (MWW III.2.2). [Franz 338]

113. When *any* is used as a pronoun today, it is plural; in Shakespeare it could also be singular: But is there any else longs to see this broken Musicke in his sides? (AYL 1.2.149). Similarly *some* as a pronoun is today plural, its singular function having been taken over by *somebody* and *someone*. In Shakespeare it is often uncertain whether *some* is singular or plural: How happy some,

1. See Joseph Wright, op. cit., § 423.

ore other some can be? (MND 1.1.226); Goe some of you, and fetch a Looking-Glasse (R2 IV.1.268). This request is followed by a stage direction: 'Enter one with a Glasse'. [Franz 350, 354]

114. *One* is used as an indefinite pronoun 'someone, somebody': there's one at the gate. (TN 1.5.132). [Franz 349]

115. *Every* is used as a pronoun 'everyone'; And after, every of this happie number . . . Shal share the good of our returned fortune, (AYL V.4.178). [Franz 352]

116. *A thing* is used in the sense 'something': I told you a thing yesterday, (Troil. 1.2.186); I shall discover a thing to you, (MWW II.2.186). [Franz 355]

117. The word 'something' is often understood in the sentence which accompanies a gift: Well Sir: here is for your paines: (TGV 1.1.143). [Franz 355]

118. *Aught* has now been replaced by *anything* except sometimes in poetry and often in dialect. It is frequent in Shakespeare, beside its negative *naught* (or *nought*) 'nothing': What's aught, but as 'tis valew'd? (Troil. II.2.53); wee'l Heare nought from Rome in private. (Cor. V.3.91). [Franz 356]

119. *Somewhat* is today usually an adverb. In Shakespeare it is sometimes used as a pronoun meaning 'something', a use which will cause no surprise to dialect speakers who use *summat* in this sense today: Well, somewhat we must do: (R2 II.2.116).

120. The *body* that we have today in *somebody* was used separately as an indefinite pronoun, as it is still frequently used in Scottish dialects: Ah, sirra, a body would thinke this was well counterfeited: (AYL IV.3.166).

ARTICLES

121. The definite article is used to indicate the most outstanding member of any group; when it is used in this way in present-day English it generally has the pronunciation [ði:]: I am alone the Villaine of the earth (Ant. IV.6.30). Before names of persons the definite article indicates a man of rank: The *Dowglas* and the *Hotspurre* both together (1H4 V.1.116). It is often used before titles: From the Count *Orsino*, is it? (TN 1.5.108). [Franz 257-9]

122. The definite article is sometimes used before a noun in the vocative: The last of all the Romans, far thee well: (JC V.3.99).

123. The definite article is often used before *death*, usually to

indicate that it is judicial: Either to dye the death, or to abjure For ever the society of men, (MND I.1.65). [Franz 262]

124. The nominative and accusative singular neuter of the definite article in Old English is *þæt*. There is a trace of this form in *tother*, from *that other*; tother day (Ham. II.1.56). Later the origin of the *t* was forgotten and the article *the* was added: O' th' tother side (Troil. v.4.8). [Franz 269]

125. The definite article is often omitted:

(a) before a noun which is already defined by another noun, especially in a prepositional phrase: for honor of our Land (H5 III.5.22); in number of our Friends (JC III.1.216);

(b) in similes: With teares as salt as Sea (2H6 III.2.96);

(c) before superlatives: Where is best place to make our Batt'ry next? (1H6 I.4.65);

(d) in many adverbial phrases, such as *at door, at end.*

126. In origin the indefinite article is an unaccented variant of the numeral *one* (OE *ān*). In Shakespeare it sometimes has the meaning 'the same': my selfe, and a sister, both borne in an houre (TN II.1.20); These Foyles have all a length, (Ham. v.2.277). [Abbott 81]

127. An indefinite article (or *one* or *this*) is sometimes inserted before a numeral in order to show that the objects mentioned can be considered collectively as a single group: like a-manie of these lisping-hauthorne buds (MWW III.3.74); but one seven yeeres (Cor. IV.1.55); Within this three Mile may you see it comming (Macb. v.5.37). [Abbott 87, Franz 271]

128. An indefinite article is sometimes inserted between an adjective and the noun it qualifies, as in the idiom *many a man*: but poore a thousand Crownes (AYL I.1.2); What poore an Instrument May do a Noble deede (Ant. v.2.236). [Abbott 85, Franz 275]

129. The indefinite article is used before the name of a military leader as a battle cry: A Clifford, a Clifford (2H6 IV.8.55); A *Talbot*, a *Talbot* (1H6 I.1.128). [Franz 278]

130. The indefinite article is often omitted:

(a) in comparisons: More tuneable then Larke to shepheards eare (MND I.1.184);

(b) in adverbial phrases, such as *at end, to purpose*; creeping like snaile (AYL II.7.146).

(c) in poetry: in glorious Christian field (R2 IV.1.93).

(d) after *never*: Never Master had A Page so kinde, (Cym.

v.5.85). The omission of the indefinite article before *little* is liable to cause a modern reader to misunderstand the line: Hold little faith, though thou hast too much feare (TN v.1.174).

(e) before nouns used predicatively in a semi-adjectival sense: A mellifluous voyce, as I am true knight. (TN II.3.54). [Abbott 84, 89, 90, Franz 267–8, 277]

ADJECTIVES

131. By functional shift several parts of speech are sometimes used as adjectives: as hush as death (i.e. 'silent', Ham. II.2.508). A noun in apposition is often used as an adjective: all the Region Kites (Ham. II.2.607), his Musicke Vowes (Ham. III.1.163); Draw them to Tyber bankes (JC I.1.63); loud and coward cries (Lear II.4.43). The use of adjectives as nouns is more widespread in Shakespeare than today, when such adjectives are generally plural or abstract. In Shakespeare adjectives were often used as nouns in the singular: 'Tis not enough to helpe the Feeble up, But to support him after. (Tim. I.1.110). An adjective often seems to be used as a noun because it agrees with a noun that is understood: Ile make division of my present with you: (TN III.4.380). 'Possessions' is understood.

Some adjectives, especially French loan-words describing persons, come to be regarded as nouns and so take plurals in -s: even as bad as those That Vulgars give bold'st Titles (WT II.1.93); Let but the Commons heare this Testament: (JC III.2.135); Landlesse Resolutes (Ham. I.1.98); mighty opposites (Ham. v.2.62). [Abbott 5, 433, Franz 358, 359, 362]

132. Adjectives, especially those ending in -*ful*, -*less*, -*ble*, or -*ive*, can be used with either an active or a passive meaning: a carelesse Trifle (Macb. 1.4.12); the sightlesse Curriors of the Ayre (Macb. 1.7.23). The couriers are invisible, not blind. [Abbott 3]

133. The use of the pronoun *one* in apposition to an adjective in the superlative is an old construction which has today been replaced by a partitive genitive. It survives occasionally in Shakespeare: And he is one The truest manner'd: (Cym. 1.6.166). [Franz 365]

134. A few adjectives call for separate comment:
Alone is used in the sense 'above all things, to an unrivalled extent': I am alone the Villaine of the earth, (Ant. IV.6.30); so full

of shapes is fancie That it alone, is high fantasticall (TN 1.1.14). [Abbott 18]

Many is sometimes preceded by the indefinite article: I doe know A many fooles (Merch. III.5.72). In this construction *many* may be derived from, or have been confused with, OE *menigo*, sb. It survives as a vulgarism in the speech of Sarah Gamp in Dickens's *Martin Chuzzlewit*.

Right is used to mean 'real, thorough', as it is in some modern English dialects: I am a right maide for my cowardice; (MND III.2.301). [Abbott 19]

135. The comparative ending is sometimes used to tone down an adjective, without any very explicit comparison being intended: it is common for the yonger sort To lacke discretion. (Ham. II.1.116).

The superlative is sometimes used when only two things are compared: To prove whose blood is reddest, his or mine. (Merch. II.1.7); of two usuries the merriest was put downe, and the worser allow'd (Meas. III.2.5).

The superlative is sometimes used absolutely in the sense 'very': A little ere the mightiest *Julius* fell (Ham. 1.1.114).

ADVERBS

136. Some adverbs are formed by adding the prefix *a-* to nouns. In the First Folio the *a-* is sometimes joined to the noun by a hyphen and sometimes treated as a separate word. The *a-* is the unaccented form of the preposition *on*: a bed (Cor. III.1.262), *a-worke* (Ham. II.2.510). The prefix *a-* is also added to adjectives used as nouns: I made her weep a good (i.e. 'in good earnest'; TGV IV.4.170), and then before other adjectives: For *Cassius* is a-weary of the World: (JC IV.3.95). [Abbott 24]

137. In Old English many adverbs were formed from adjectives by the addition of *-e*. With the loss of final unaccented *-e* in late Middle English these adverbs became indistinguishable from adjectives, and the use of adjectives as adverbs was extended to words, like *excellent*, which did not form adverbs by the addition of *-e*: Thou didst it excellent (Shrew Induction 1.1.89); 'Tis Noble spoken. (Ant. II.2.99); how Prodigall the Soule Gives the tongue vowes: (Ham. 1.3.116). [Franz 368]

138. Some adverbs end in *-s* from the genitive of nouns, as in:

Come thy wayes (TN II.5.1); 'Tis but early dayes (Troil. IV.5.12). But say, is *Warwicke* friends with *Margaret*? (3H6 IV.1.115) illustrates a confusion, frequent in substandard speech today, between 'Are Warwick and Margaret friends?' and 'Is Warwick a friend of Margaret?' [Abbott 25]

139. Some adverbs are used to moderate or tone down a following adjective, as the word *rather*, which became general in the eighteenth century, is used today. The most common adverbs of this kind in Shakespeare are *something* and *somewhat*: with a white head, & somthing a round belly. (2H4 I.2.207). *Pretty* is used once in the sense 'rather': a prettie wise fellow (AW II.3.215).

140. As an adverb of agreement we find *Ay* (often spelt *I*) beside *yes*. Today *ay* is dialectal or archaic or reserved for special uses, as at formal meetings, but in Shakespeare it is used more generally. Stephano, asked if he will kill Prospero, replies 'I on mine honour.' (Temp. III.2.123). *Yea* is often used by lower-class characters, such as Mouldy and Wart (2H4 III.2.115, 151). Falstaff calls a tailor who refuses him credit 'a Rascally-yea-forsooth-knave' (2H4 I.2.42).

Negative Adverbs

141. *Never* is used as an emphatic particle meaning 'not': I thinke His father never was so true begot, (John II.1.130). It is used with *so* to mean 'however': be he ne're so vile, This day shall gentle his Condition. (H5 IV.3.62). [Franz 407–8]

No is a direct negative; *nay* is used to correct or clarify a statement made by somebody else:

Ros. —Thou speak'st wiser then thou art ware of.
Touch. Nay, I shall nere be ware of mine own wit, till I breake my shins against it. (AYL II.4.56) [Franz 404]

Not is used as a negative particle before a verb without the auxiliary *do*: it not belongs to you (2H4 IV.1.98). [Franz 405]

Nothing is used as a negative particle 'not, by no means': That you do love me, I am nothing jealous: (JC I.2.162). [Abbott 55, Franz 407]

142. In spite of the assertion that 'your foure negatives make your two affirmatives' (TN V.1.26), the usual function of a double negative is to strengthen a negative statement:

I have one heart, one bosome, and one truth,
And that no woman has, nor never none
Shall mistris be of it, save I alone.   (TN III.1.170)

I cannot goe no further   (AYL II.4.8)

One of the negatives of a double negative construction may be
implicit: You may deny that you were not the meane (R3 1.3.89).
[Abbott 406, Franz 410]

Intensive Adverbs

143. Intensive adverbs are used to add emphasis and they therefore have a short life. Modern intensives like *awfully* and *tremen-
dously* are not found in Shakespeare, but he uses adverbs like *clean*,
that are still current: Your Lordship (though not clean past your
youth) hath yet some smack of age in you: (2H4 1.2.111), and
others that are no longer in general use. These include:

All in the sense 'altogether, exclusively': Why have my Sisters
Husbands, if they say They love you all? (Lear 1.1.102). *All* is
sometimes joined with a following adjective: this, your all-
lycenc'd Foole ('privileged to do anything'; Lear 1.4.218), her
all-disgraced Friend ('completely disgraced'; Ant. III.12.22). *All
thing* is used as an adverb: all-thing unbecomming (Macb. III.1.13).

Excellent 'extremely': Excellent, excellent well: y'are a Fish-
monger. (Ham. II.2.174).

Far 'very': But farre unfit to be a Soveraigne (3H6 III.2.92).
[Abbott 40]

Mainly 'very': I am mainely ignorant What place this is: (Lear
IV.7.65).

Monstrous in the sense 'very'. In the first of the following
examples it is used with deliberate absurdity: Ile speake in a
monstrous little voyce (MND 1.2.54); Skill infinite or monstrous
desperate (AW II.1.187).

Much is used adverbially to mean 'very' even before positive
adjectives: now I am much ill. (2H4 IV.4.111). [Abbott 51]

Passing 'very': For *Oberon* is passing fell and wrath, (MND II.1.20).

Right 'very' is preserved today in titles like *the Right Reverend* and
in dialects: Thou art right welcome, as thy master is: (AYL II.7.196).

Shrewdly 'severely, keenly': He's shrewdly vext at something.
(AW III.5.91).

Throughly has now been replaced by its variant *thoroughly*: My poynt and period will be throughly wrought, (Lear IV.7.97).

Vengeance is used once as an intensive: hee's vengeance prowd, and loves not the common people. (Cor. II.2.5).

Wondrous 'surprisingly, extraordinarily': That is, hot ice, and wondrous strange snow, (MND V.1.60). [Franz 370–96]

Adverbs of Time

144. Many Shakespearean adverbs of time are archaic and others have undergone changes of either form or meaning.

Afore 'formerly, previously' has today been replaced by *before*, but *afore* survives in dialects: if hee have never drunke wine afore, (Temp. II.2.77).

After 'afterwards' is still used adverbially in dialects: First, let her shew her face, and after, speake (Meas. V.1.168).

Alway 'always' is today archaic and poetical: O may such purple teares be alway shed (3H6 V.6.64).

Anon 'immediately', like all adverbs of similar meaning, came to mean 'presently, by and by': he wil be here anon (MWW IV.2.41). It occurs in the phrases *ever and anon*, *still and anon* 'every now and then': Still and anon cheer'd up the heavy time; (John IV.1.47).

Before-time 'formerly' is sometimes printed without a hyphen: I have Before time seene him thus. (Cor. 1.6.25).

Betime has been replaced by *betimes*, which is itself now archaic: Put up thy sword betime, (John IV.3.98).

Briefly means not only 'in a few words' but also 'in a short time' or 'very recently': 'Tis not a mile; briefely we heard their drummes. (Cor. 1.6.16).

Eftsoons 'by and by' was already archaic at the time of Shakespeare. The only occurrence in his works is: Eftsoones Ile tell thee why, (Per. V.1.256).

Erewhile 'a short time ago' was already archaic: Else your memorie is bad, going ore it erewhile. (LLL IV.1.89).

Erst 'once, formerly' is now archaic and poetical: Thy company, which erst was irksome to me I will endure; (AYL III.5.95).

Evermore 'always' is now found mainly in religious use, but more generally in Shakespeare: I evermore did love you (MND III.2.306).

Oft in everyday speech has now been replaced by *often*: some love that drew him oft from home (Err. V.1.56).

Often is sometimes used adjectivally in the sense 'frequent': my (F1 by) often rumination (AYL IV.1.19).

Otherwhiles 'at times' survives in dialects: Otherwhiles, the famisht English, like pale Ghosts, Faintly besiege us one houre in a moneth. (1H6 I.2.7).

Presently has both the older meaning 'at once' and the modern meaning 'by and by'. The old: Goe presently enquire, and so will I Where money is, (Merch. I.1.183). The new: Meete presently at the Palace, (MND IV.2.37).

Seld is a rare variant of *seldom*: As seld I have the chance; (Troil. IV.5.150).

Since 'ago' after expressions specifying a period of time: Who halfe an houre since came from the Dolphin, (John V.7.83).

Sometime is found besides *sometimes* without any rigid difference of meaning. It often means 'from time to time': I sometime lay here in *Corioles*, At a poore mans house: (Cor. I.9.80); The Love that followes us, sometime is our trouble, (Macb. I.6.12), and it can be used in the sense 'formerly': Respecting this our Marriage with the Dowager, Sometimes our Brothers Wife, (H8 II.4.180). It can also be used adjectivally: our sometimes Sister, (Ham. I.2.8).

Still is often used in the sense 'always': Thou still hast bin the Father of good Newes. (Ham. II.2.42). In the idiom *still an end, an end* is from ME *on ende* 'endlessly, always': A Slave, that still an end, turnes me to shame: (TGV IV.4.67).

Straight 'immediately': I will about it strait; (Meas. I.4.85).

Suddenly means 'quickly' without necessarily having the idea of unexpectedness that it has today: I will your very faithfull Feeder be, And buy it with your Gold right sodainly. (AYL II.4.100).

Tofore 'formerly' was already archaic in Shakespeare's time: O would thou wert as thou to fore hast beene, (Tit. III.1.294).

What and *when* are often used elliptically as exclamations of impatience: What *Lucius*, hoe? (JC II.1.1); When *Lucius*, when? (JC II.1.5).

Yesternight 'last night'; cf. MnE *yesterday*: For yester-night by *Catesby* was it sent me, (R3 III.6.6).

Yet is used in the sense 'now': How yet resolves the Governour of the Towne? (H5 III.3.1). [Franz 412–424]

Adverbs of Place

145. *Abroad* has a wider sense in Shakespeare than today, when it generally has associations with crossing the sea. A common meaning in Shakespeare is 'out of doors': Raine within doores, and none abroad? (2H4 IV.5.9); A troubled mind drave me to walke abroad, (RJ I.1.127).

Away is sometimes used in its etymological sense 'on one's way' without the implication that movement is from here to somewhere else: Come away, Servant, come: (Temp. 1.2.187).

By as an adverb is today generally coupled with another adverb or a verb (as in *close by*, *stand by*). It is used in Shakespeare in the sense 'nearby': I stole into a neighbour thicket by, (LLL V.2.94); Now go with me, and with this holy man Into the Chantry by: (TN IV.3.23).

Forth means 'forward' of either time or place: Lay forth the gowne. (Shrew IV.3.62); from this day forth, Ile use you for my Mirth, (JC IV.3.48).

Hence does not imply motion. It is used in the sense 'in another place, elsewhere': Freedome lives hence, and banishment is here; (Lear I.1.184).

Hitherto is used of place as well as time: England, from Trent, and Severne, hitherto, By South and East, is to my part assign'd: (1H4 III.1.74).

Other where means 'in another place': How if your husband start some other where? (Err. II.1.30).

Some whether means 'to some place or other': Some whether would she have thee goe with her. (Tit. IV.1.11). [Franz 425–32]

Adverbs of Manner

146. *Again* often involves opposition and means 'in return', 'on the other hand': The wall me-thinkes being sensible, should curse againe. (MND V.1.183); Th'one is my Soveraigne, . . . th'other againe Is my kinsman, (R2 II.2.112).

Almost is used with the meaning 'even': Would you imagine, or almost beleeve (R3 III.5.35).

Along 'at full length': my selfe, Did steale behinde him as he lay along Under an oake, (AYL II.1.29); There lay hee, stretch'd along like a Wounded knight. (AYL III.2.254).

Belike 'perhaps': Belike you meane to make a puppet of me, (Shrew IV.3.103).

But is often used in the sense 'only': Burne but his Bookes, (Temp. III.2.103). It is sometimes used pleonastically with *only*: discourse (will) grow commendable in none onely but Parrats: (Merch. III.5.50).

Case is used adverbially to mean 'by chance': If case some one of you would flye from us. (3H6 V.4.34).

Even is used as an intensive 'just, exactly': Villaine, thou liest, for even her verie words, Didst thou deliver to me on the Mart. (Err. II.2.164). The precision can refer to time, and then *even* means 'at this very moment': a certaine convocation of wormes are e'ne at him. (Ham. IV.3.21).

Happily is occasionally used as a variant of *haply* 'perhaps': That the soule of our grandam, might happily inhabite a bird. (TN IV.2.54). See also § 41.

How is occasionally used to mean 'however': I never yet saw man, How wise, how noble, yong, how rarely featur'd, But she would spell him backward: (Ado III.1.59).

Inly 'inwardly': I have inly wept, (Temp. V.1.202).

Jump 'exactly, just': Ile set her on my selfe, a while, to draw the Moor apart, And bring him jumpe, when he may *Cassio* finde Soliciting his wife: (Oth. II.3.391).

Like 'in the same way' is shortened from *alike*: My fellow ministers Are like-invulnerable (Temp. III.3.66).

Othergates 'in another manner': hee would have tickel'd you other gates then he did. (TN V.1.193).

Out 'fully, thoroughly': thou was't not Out three yeeres old. (Temp. I.2.39); Thou hast beate mee out Twelve severall times, (Cor. IV.5.127).

Peradventure 'by chance': if peradventure this bee true: (Ado I.2.19).

Round(ly) 'openly, straightforwardly': No, I went round to worke, And (my yong Mistris) thus I did bespeake (Ham. II.2.139).

Severally, 'separately', as in the frequent stage-direction *Exeunt severally*: I will heare *Cassius*, and compare their Reasons, When severally we heare them rendred (JC III.2.9).

So. The Idiom *or so* is used today to indicate that a preceding numeral is approximate. In Shakespeare it could be used more generally to indicate vagueness: Ile make one in a dance, or so:

(LLL v.1.160); Good sir, or so, or friend, or Gentleman. (Ham. II.1.46).

Something is used adverbially in the sense 'somewhat'; A good swift simile, but something currish. (Shrew v.2.54).

To. In the first half of the seventeenth century *to* and *too* begin to be distinguished in spelling. *To(o)* as an adverb is used after verbs: goe too, thou art made if thou desir'st to be so: (TN II.5.167); Can Honour set too a legge? (1H4 v.1.135).

It could be repeated for emphasis: O, but I love his Lady too-too much, (TGV II.4.205). In the sixteenth and seventeenth centuries *too blame* is often used. *Blame*, originally a verb, came to be misunderstood as an adjective, and the function of *too* was changed to give it the meaning of our *too*. This misunderstanding has clearly taken place when *blame* is compounded with another adjective: In faith, my Lord, you are too wilfull blame, (1H4 III.1.177). [Franz 433–56]

PREPOSITIONS

147. Prepositions originally indicated local relations but in course of time they have come to represent a large number of abstract relationships. There was great variety in the use of prepositions in Elizabethan times; some verbs which today take only a single preposition could then take any one out of a group of half a dozen. A few Elizabethan prepositions, such as *sans* 'without' and *mauger* 'in spite of', have passed out of use, but many prepositional phrases, such as *in comparison with*, have been introduced since the time of Shakespeare. When Elizabethan usage differs from that of today, it is often possible to find a modern parallel to a Shakespearean construction with a verb of similar meaning. Shakespeare can say *Or have we eaten on the insane Root?* (Macb. 1.3.84); we should use *of*, but we can say *He lives on bread*. Some prepositions, such as *for* and *after*, are now also used as conjunctions. On the whole, the number of prepositions has increased while the range of meanings of each preposition has decreased. For example, many of the meanings of *by* have been taken over by *near, in accordance with, by reason of, owing to*.

A preposition sometimes follows the noun which it governs. This construction is rare in prose but is sometimes found in verse to meet the demands of rhyme or metre: For feare least day should looke their shames upon, (MND III.2.385, rhyming with *gone*). The placing of a preposition after its noun is especially common in relative clauses: the thousand Naturall shockes That Flesh is heyre too (Ham. III.1.62); The labour we delight in, Physicks paine: (Macb. II.3.53).

Confusion between two constructions may lead to the repetition of a preposition, one before the verb, the other after: In what enormity is *Martius* poore in? (Cor. II.1.18); Of what kinde should this Cocke come of? (AYL II.7.90). [Abbott 407, Franz 689]

148. It is often said that prepositions were omitted in certain circumstances in Elizabethan English. Such a statement implies that constructions with prepositions are older than those without. This is not necessarily true, and it would be better to say that Elizabethan English expressed certain ideas without prepositions which are today expressed with prepositions. The following are the chief conditions where prepositions are often not used in Shakespeare:

(a) After verbs of motion: ere we could arrive the Point propos'd, (JC I.2.110). [Abbott 198]

(b) After verbs or adjectives indicating worth or value: he hath disgrac'd me, and hindred me halfe a million, (Merch. III.1.58).

(c) After some verbs which are today intransitive but which were transitive in Shakespeare's time: he hath bin all this day to looke you. (AYL II.5.34). [Abbott 200]

(d) In adverbial expressions of time or manner: Which time she chaunted snatches of old tunes. (Ham. IV.7.178).

(e) Before a relative pronoun, *that* being regarded as equivalent to 'to whom': A Bed-swarvar, even as bad as those That Vulgars give bold'st Titles; (WT II.1.93). Sometimes both preposition and relative pronoun are to be understood: Thy Honorable Mettle may be wrought From that it is dispos'd (JC I.2.303). [Abbott 201]

149. Details of the changes in usage of some prepositions follow:

A. In the Folios we sometimes find *a* where present-day English has *o*': What is't a Clocke? (R3 V.3.47), [Abbott 140]

150. *Afore* meaning 'before', either of time or place, is now dialectal: I shall be there afore you. (Lear I.5.4).

151. *After* in the sense 'according to' remains today in a few set phrases; it was used more widely in Shakespeare: After my seeming (2H4 V.2.129).

152. *Against* is used of time in the sense 'in expectation of': I must imploy you in some businesse Against our nuptiall, (MND I.I.124).

153. *Aloft* 'above' occurs once as a preposition: but now I breath againe Aloft the flood, (John IV.2.138).

154. *At* varies with *in* before the names of large cities and sometimes even countries: I told him that your father was at *Venice*, And that you look't for him this day in *Padua*. (Shrew IV.4.15); When at *Bohemia* You take my lord, (WT I.2.39).

155. *Athwart* 'across' is preserved in dialects and naval language: Nor never lay his wreathed armes athwart His loving bosome (LLL IV.3.135). [Franz 467]

156. *Besides* is used as a preposition interchangeably with *beside*: how fell you besides your five witts? (TN IV.2.90).

157. *Betwixt* is today poetical or dialectal and in Shakespeare it is less common than *between*: were there twenty brothers betwixt us (AYL I.I.52).

158. *But* is used as a preposition to mean 'except': my Honor is at pawne, And but my going, nothing can redeeme it. (2H4 II.3.7).

159. *By* originally meant 'near': a certaine aime he tooke At a faire Vestall, throned by the West, (MND II.1.157).

Hence it comes to mean 'concerning': How say you by the French Lord, Mounsier *Le Boune*? (Merch. I.2.57).

It often means 'by reason of': The Bishop of Yorke, Fell Warwickes Brother, and by that our Foe, (3H6 IV.4.12).

160. *Cross*, an apheitic form of *across*, has the same meaning: I charge thee waft me safely cross the Channell (2H6 IV.1.114).

161. *For* originally meant 'in front of'. A man who stands in front of another may be there as either his friend or his enemy, and we thus get two groups of meanings of the preposition. The larger group is that where *for* has the sense of support rather than opposition.

It means 'instead of': see what now thou art, For happy Wife, a most distressed Widdow: For joyfull Mother, one that wailes the name: (R3 IV.4.97);

'as regards': For your intent . . . It is most retrograde to our desire: (Ham. I.2.112);

'because of': yet I must not, For certaine friends that are both his, and mine, (Macb. III.1.119);

'in the capacity of': If thou be'st as poore for a subject, as hee's for a King, thou art poore enough. (Lear 1.4.21).

The use of *for to* with the infinitive is now a vulgarism but it is not uncommon in Shakespeare. It arose from the weakening of the prepositional function of *to*, which came to be regarded merely as a sign of the infinitive. Hence *for* was added to give the notion of purpose. Then *for to* in its turn was weakened and it came to be regarded as a mere sign of the infinitive: Forbid the Sea for to obey the Moone, (WT 1.2.427).

The meanings of *for* arising from the idea of opposition include 'in spite of': Faith the Priest was good enough, for all the olde gentlemans saying. (AYL V.1.3); and 'for fear of': Yet here they shall not lye, for catching cold. (TGV 1.2.136).

When *for* is used after a negative statement, it is often difficult to say whether it means 'because of' or 'in spite of': My Father is not dead for all your saying. (Macb. IV.2.36).

162. *Fore* is occasionally used with the meaning of the much more common *before*: What would you 'fore our Tent? (Troil. 1.3.215).

163. *From* can mean 'away from' and hence 'outside': But this is from my Commission (TN 1.5.201). It is sometimes strengthened by the addition of the adverb *off* or *out*: And you must cut this flesh from off his breast, (Merch. IV.1.302); From out the fierie Portall of the East, (R2 III.3.64).

164. *In* (sometimes weakened to *i'*) is often used where we should use *on*: would he were knockt ith' head. (Troil. IV.2.34).

It is often used in expressions of time to mean 'at' or 'during': How? The Duke in counsell? In this time of the night? (Oth. 1.2.93).

It often has a causal function: All the Conspirators save onely hee, Did that they did, in envy of great *Cæsar*: (JC V.5.69).

It sometimes means 'with regard to, concerning': Our feares in *Banquo* sticke deepe, (Macb. III.1.49).

165. *Intill* occurs once for 'into' in the Clown's song in *Hamlet*. In Middle English it is a Northern dialectal form: Age . . . hath shipped me intill the Land (Ham. V.1.81).

166. *Into* normally refers to motion while *in* refers to a state, but *into* can be used when a verb describing a state implies previous action: A Jewell lockt into the wofulst Caske, (2H6 III.2.409).

167. *Of* is used to mean 'from' more widely than it is today: For which I doe discharge you of your office, (Meas. V.1.465).

From this it is a natural development to 'as a consequence of':
And thus doe we of wisedome and of reach . . . By indirections
finde directions out: (Ham. II.1.64).

Verbs of entreating often take 'of': I shall desire you of more
acquaintance, (MND III.1.182).

Several verbs could be used with either a direct object or *of*
followed by a noun: I am your husband if you like of me. (Ado
v.4.59).

It sometimes means 'with regard to, concerning': is not this the
day That *Hermia* should give answer of her choice? (MND IV.1.138).

Of sometimes means 'by reason of': of his gentlenesse . . . he
furnishd me From mine owne Library, with volumes, (Temp.
I.2.165).

After past participles *of* often means 'by': Left and abandoned
of his velvet friend; (AYL II.1.50).

Of is used to mean 'by' before an agent, from whom an action
proceeds: receyv'd Of the most Pious *Edward* (Macb. III.6.26).

It is also used after verbs of supplying: I am provided of a
Torch-bearer. (Merch. II.4.24).

Of naturally follows a verbal noun, which is generally preceded
by the preposition *a* or *on*. When this preposition is omitted, the
verbal noun is liable to be regarded as a present participle: Heere
was he merry, hearing of a Song. (AYL II.7.4).

168. *On* and *of* are often interchanged, perhaps because they are
both sometimes weakened to *o'*. The use of *on* for *of* is especially
common at the end of a sentence and before pronouns, especially
when the pronoun is contracted; the use of *on* before pronouns is
common in colloquial speech: Yet he would be King on't, (Temp.
II.1.156); two on's Daughters, (Lear I.4.114); we are such stuffe
As dreames are made on; (Temp. IV.1.156).

On and *upon* represent juxtaposition of any kind, literal or
metaphorical: Reade on this booke, (Ham. III.1.44); And be not
jealous on me, (JC I.2.71).

On and *upon* are used with expressions of time, meaning 'at':
Even on the instant. (Oth. I.2.38), You come most carefully upon
your houre. (Ham. I.1.5).

They are used to express a causal relationship 'in consequence of':
When he shal heare she dyed upon his words, (Ado IV.1.225).

They are used in asseverations when the speaker mentions something that he values as evidence of the truth of an assertion: Upon

mine honour, Sir, I heard a humming, (Temp. II.1.317); Thou didst swear to me upon a parcel-gilt goblet (2H4 II.1.83).

They mean 'on the strength of, by virtue of': Upon my power I may dismisse this Court, (Merch. IV.1.104).

They mean 'according to': As I remember *Adam*, it was upon this fashion (AYL I.1.1).

They are used after verbs of thinking: I thinke not on my father, (AW I.1.89).

169. *Out* is sometimes used as a preposition to mean 'out of': you have pusht out your gates, the very Defender of them, (Cor. V.2.40); for then thou was't not Out three yeeres old. (Temp. I.2.40).

170. *Thorough* is a variant of *through*: thorough the streets (MWW IV.5.34).

171. *To* originally described motion towards, hence it described addition, a sense preserved in the stressed variant *too*. The sense 'in addition to' is preserved in: And to that dauntlesse temper of his Minde, He hath a Wisdome, that doth guide his Valour, (Macb. III.1.52).

With expressions of time *to* can mean 'at': For all the world, As thou art to this houre, was Richard then, (1H4 III.2.93).

It can mean 'as far as': Worthy *Othello*, I am hurt to danger, (Oth. II.3.197).

After a noun indicating liking *to* is often used where we should use 'for': Me-thinkes I have a great desire to a bottle of hay: (MND IV.1.35).

When *to* is used metaphorically it generally expresses the direction of an emotion which may be either hostile or friendly. If hostile, we should say 'against'; if friendly, 'for' or 'with': 'tis a fault to Heaven, A fault against the Dead, (Ham. I.2.101); I have businesse to my Lord, (Troil. III.1.55).

To can mean 'compared with': *Paris* is durt to him, (Troil. I.2.255).

A verb of motion is often understood before *to*: Ile to my booke, (Temp. III.1.94); So to your pleasures, (AYL V.4.198).

172. *Toward* and *towards*, both meaning 'to', are interchangeable, with no marked preference for either form: Let us toward the King: (Macb. I.3.152); we love him highly, And shall continue our Graces towards him. (Macb. I.6.29).

There are a few examples of the splitting of *toward* by the noun

which it governs, an archaism at the time of Shakespeare: Tapers
burnt to Bedward. (Cor. 1.6.32); Their powers are marching unto
Paris-ward. (1H6 III.3.30.)

173. *Unless* is occasionally used as a preposition, with the sense
'except': heere nothing breeds, Unlesse the nightly Owle, or fatall
Raven: (Tit. II.3.96).

174. *With,* like *by,* indicates proximity, including that of cause
and effect: I live with Bread like you, (R2 III.2.175).

It is used of an agent: he was torne to pieces with a Beare
(WT V.2.72).

It may indicate the basis of an accusation: I rather will suspect
the Sunne with gold Then thee with wantonnes: (MWW IV.4.5).

It is used after past participles to mean 'by': He is attended with
a desperate traine, (Lear II.4.308).

175. *Withal* is the emphatic form of *with* and is used when the
preposition follows its object: Ile tel you who Time ambles withall, who Time trots withal, who Time gallops withal, and who he
stands still withall (AYL III.2.327).

When used adverbially *withal* means 'moreover', 'nevertheless':
I must have liberty Withall (AYL II.7.48); I thinke withall, There
would be hands uplifted in my right: (Macb. IV.3.41).

176. *Without.* The original sense of this preposition was 'out-
side': Without the perill of the *Athenian* Law (MND IV.1.158).

177. There are prepositional phrases, some of which have survived without ever becoming completely anglicized. Such a phrase
is *in lieu of*: In lieu of all thy paines and husbandrie, (AYL II.3.65).
A phrase no longer in current use is *long of* 'caused by': all this is
long of you. (Cor. V.4.29).

CONJUNCTIONS

178. Since the time of Shakespeare certain conjunctions have
passed out of general use, although some of them, such as *afore,*
have remained in dialects. Others, such as *whiles* and *sith,* are now
archaic or poetical. [Franz 545]

179. In Early English *that* was often used to convert an adverb
or a preposition into a conjunction. Later *that* was sometimes added
after other conjunctions: If that this simple Sillogisme will serve,
so: (TN I.5.55); when that my father liv'd (John I.1.95). *As* is used
in the same way: Thereafter as they be (2H4 III.2.53); When as the

Enemie hath beene tenne to one: (3H6 1.2.75). [Franz 546–7]

180. Various phrases are used to express conditions. They include *upon condition, conditionally that, provided (that)* and *say (that)*: Upon condition *Publius* shall not live (JC IV.1.4); Conditionally, that heere thou take an Oath, To cease this Civill Warre: (3H6 1.1.196); say that she were gone, Given to the fire, a moity of my rest Might come to me againe (WT II.3.7). A conditional conjunction can be replaced by inversion of subject and verb: wert thou not my brother, I would not take this hand from thy throat, till this other had puld out thy tongue for saying so, (AYL 1.1.60). [Franz 565]

181. *Or . . . or* are used as correlatives where today we should use *either . . . or*: Why the Law *Salike*, that they have in France, Or should or should not barre us in our Clayme. (H5 1.2.12). *Nor . . . nor* are used where today we should use *neither . . . nor*: Ile then nor give nor hazard ought for lead. (Merch. II.7.22). [Abbott 136, Franz 586–7]

182. *Or whether . . . or whether* are used for *whether . . . or*:

Or whether doth my minde being crown'd with you
Drinke up the monarks plague this flattery?
Or whether shall I say mine eie saith true,

(Sonnet 114.1) [Abbott 136]

183. We sometimes find *neither . . . or*: thou shalt well perceive That neither in birth, or for authoritie, The Bishop will be overborne by thee: (1H6 V.1.58). [Franz 588]

184. *Neither* is sometimes omitted as a correlative where we should expect *neither . . . nor*:

But my five wits, nor my five sences can
Diswade one foolish heart from serving thee, (Sonnet 141.9).

185. When more than two things are mentioned, *nor* can be omitted before one or more of them:

For I have neyther wit, nor words, nor worth,
Action, nor Utterance, nor the power of Speech,
To stirre mens Blood, (JC III.2.225).

186. The negative particle *ne* for *nor* was already archaic at the time of Shakespeare. It occurs twice, one occurrence being in the

archaic prologue to *Pericles*: All perishen of man, of pelfe, Ne aught escapen but himselfe (Per. II. Prol. 35); my maidens name Seard otherwise, ne worse of worst extended With vildest torture, let my life be ended. (AW II.1.175). [Franz 587]

187. Some Shakespearean uses of particular conjunctions call for comment:

Against or *'gainst* is used to indicate the time when something may be expected to happen: Ile charme his eyes against she doth appeare. (MND III.2.99); Some sayes that ever 'gainst that Season comes (Ham. 1.1.158). [Franz 557]

188. *And* is used in the sense 'and therefore': Thou art inclinde to sleepe: 'tis a good dulnesse, And give it way: (Temp. 1.2.185). [Abbott 95, Franz 590]

It is used in the sense 'even' to fill out the line in a song: When that I was and a little tine boy, (TN V.1.398); He that has and a little-tyne wit, (Lear III.2.74).

And and its unaccented variant *an* are used in the sense 'if'. It is probable that the hypothesis was originally expressed by the subjunctive, as in: Goe not my Horse the better, I must become a borrower of the Night, (Macb. III.1.26). When the subjunctive fell into disuse, the hypothesis was expressed by *and*: Plague on't, and I thought he had beene valiant, and so cunning in Fence, I'de have seene him damn'd ere I'de have challeng'd him. (TN III.4.310) [Franz 564]

And is used in the sense 'as if', and is followed by the subjunctive: I will roar and 'twere any Nightingale. (MND 1.2.86); he will weepe you an 'twere a man borne in Aprill. (Troil. 1.2.188). [Abbott 104]

189. *As* is often used for 'as if': One cry'd God blesse us, and Amen the other, As they had seene me with these Hangmans hands: (Macb. II.2.28). [Abbott 107]

It is sometimes used parenthetically to mean 'for so': Who dares receive it other, As we shall make our Griefes and Clamor rore, Upon his Death? (Macb. 1.7.78). [Abbott 110]

It is used in the sense 'for indeed' or 'and indeed': if I die for it, (as no lesse is threatned me) (Lear III.3.19); When I was young (as yet I am not old) (1H6 III.4.17). [Abbott 110]

It can be used to mean 'in proportion as', with or without the addition of *so*: And, as with age, his body ouglier growes, So his minde cankers: (Temp. IV.1.191); As *Cæsar* lov'd mee, I weepe for him; as he was Fortunate, I rejoyce at it; as he was Valiant, I honour him: (JC III.2.24).

It can mean 'in as much as': as thou art a Prince, I feare thee, as I feare the roaring of the Lyons Whelpe. (1H4 III.3.166).

It is used in asseverations, with and without *so*: So come my Soule to blisse, as I speake true: (Oth. v.2.250); Do not laugh at me, For (as I am a man) I thinke this Lady To be my childe *Cordelia*. (Lear II.7.68). [Franz 578]

It is sometimes used as a relative 'which' or 'where', senses still common in dialects: that gentlenesse And shew of Love, as I was wont to have: (JC I.2.33); Heere, as I point my Sword, the sunne arises, (JC II.1.106).

It often has the meaning 'namely, for example': And that which should accompany Old-Age, As Honor, Love, Obedience, Troopes of Friends, (Macb. v.3.25). [Abbott 113, Franz 584]

It is used with expressions of time: one *Lucio* As then the Messenger, (Meas. v.1.76). [Abbott 114, Franz 556]

As can be used with another conjunction to give a relative meaning to words normally interrogative: one that was a wofull looker on, When as the Noble Duke of Yorke was slaine, (3H6 II.1.45). [Abbott 116]

190. *Being that*, like *seeing that*, is used as a conjunction: Being that I flow in greefe, The smallest twine may lead me. (Ado IV.1.252). The construction is preserved in modern dialects. [Franz 563]

191. *But* often means 'except' or 'except that': and, but hee's something stain'd With greefe (that's beauties canker) thou might'st call him A goodly person: (Temp. I.2.414). [Abbott 120]

It is used after negative statements and questions to indicate an exception: Can you not hate me, as I know you doe, But you must joyne in soules to mocke me to? (MND III.2.148). [Franz 567]

It is used with a negative verb of believing or thinking to express an emphatic affirmative: if thou follow me, doe not beleeve, But I shall doe thee mischiefe in the wood. (MND II.1.236). [Franz 569]

It is used in the sense 'if not': beshrew my soule, But I do love the favour, and the forme Of this most faire occasion, (John v.4.49). [Abbott 126]

It often follows negative comparisons where we should use 'than': I thinke it be no other, but enso (Ham. I.1.108). [Abbott 127]

When there is no negative, *but* passes naturally from 'except' to 'only': He who shall speake for her, is a farre-off guiltie, But that he speakes (wt ii.1.104); Where *Brutus* may but finde it: (jc 1.3.144). *Nobbut* is still used in dialects in the sense 'only'. [Abbott 128]

But does not necessarily immediately precede the word it qualifies, and its position in the sentence may be misleading: Where one but goes a breast (Troil. iii.3.155). *One but* means 'only one'.

The same love of emphasis which led to the double negative and the double comparative led also to the use of *but* as well as *only* in the same sentence: He onely liv'd but till he was a man, (Macb. v.8.40). [Abbott 130]

192. *Ere* 'before', today only poetical, is frequent in Shakespeare: Ere I learne love, Ile practise to obey. (Err. ii.1.29). [Franz 558]

193. *Except* is used in the sense 'unless': Mourne not, except thou sorrow for my good, (1h6 ii.5.111). [Franz 570]

194. *For* and *for that* often mean 'in order that': And for the time shall not seeme tedious, Ile tell thee what befell me (3h6 iii.1.9); For that our kingdomes earth should not be soyld . . . Therefore, we banish you our Territories. (r2 1.3.125). [Franz 573]

For and *for that* both mean 'because': And for the morning now is something worne, Our purpos'd hunting shall be set aside. (mnd iv.1.186); Yet in some sort they are better than the Tribunes, For that they will not intercept my tale; (Tit. iii.1.38).

For because shows confusion between *because* (from *bi cause* = *by cause*) and *for cause that*:

> I have bin studying, how to compare
> This Prison where I live, unto the World:
> And for because the world is populous,
> And heere is not a Creature, but my selfe,
> I cannot do it: (r2 v.5.1)

For why 'because' is substandard today but not so in Shakespeare: If she doe chide, 'tis not to have you gone, For why, the fooles are mad, if left alone. (tgv iii.1.98). [Franz 560]

195. *Howbeit that*, *however*, *howsoever*, and *howsome'er* are used as concessive conjunctions to mean 'though': how ere thou art a fiend, A womans shape doth shield thee. (Lear iv.2.66); how

somere their hearts are sever'd in Religion, their heads are both one, (AW 1.3.59); The Moore (howbeit that I endure him not) Is of a constant, loving, Noble Nature, (Oth. II.1.297). [Franz 574]

196. *Like as* is used in the sense 'as if': It lifted up it head, and did addresse It selfe to motion, like as it would speake: (Ham. 1.2.216). [Franz 582]

Like and *like as* are sometimes used instead of *as* to compare two sentences: And like as rigour of tempestuous gustes Provokes the mightiest Hulk against the tide, So am I driven by breath of her Renowne, (1H6 v.5.5). [Franz 583]

197. *Notwithstanding* is occasionally used in the sense 'although': notwithstanding thy capacitie, Receiveth as the Sea. Nought enters there, . . . But falles into abatement, and low price (TN I.1.10).

198. *Or* 'before' is used to strengthen the conjunction *ere*: dying, or ere they sicken, (Macb. IV.3.172). [Abbott 131]

199. *Seeing* (*that*) 'since' as a conjunction survives in dialects. It is found in Shakespeare both with and without *that*: seeing gentle words will not prevayle (2H6 IV.2.182); It seemes to me most strange that men should feare, Seeing that death, a necessary end Will come when it will come. (JC II.2.35).

200. *Since* is used for 'when' after verbs of knowing or remembering: thou remembrest Since once I sat upon a promontory, (MND II.1.148). [Abbott 132]

201. *So* and *so that* are used in the sense 'provided that, if': I prethee go, and get me some repast, I care not what, so it be holsome foode, (Shrew IV.3.15); So that you had her wrinkles, and I her money, I would she did as you say. (AW II.4.20). [Abbott 133, Franz 565]

So . . . as is used more freely in Shakespeare than today, when *so* is chiefly used in negative sentences: So well thy words become thee as thy wounds, (Macb. I.2.43); So long as I could see (TN 1.2.17). [Franz 580]

202. *That* is used in the sense 'with the result that': Have you not made an Universall shout, That Tyber trembled underneath her bankes (JC I.1.49). [Franz 571]

That can be used as a temporal conjunction meaning 'when': I was your Mother, much upon these yeares That you are now a Maide, (RJ 1.3.72).

To avoid the repetition of a conjunction the second one may be replaced by *that*: Though yet of *Hamlet* our deere Brothers death

The memory be greene: and that it us befitted To beare our hearts in greefe . . . (Ham. 1.2.1). [Franz 548]

That often means 'since, in as much as': O she is rich in beautie, onely poore, That when she dies, with beautie dies her store. (RJ 1.1.220).

203. *When.* A clause introduced by *when* is not necessarily temporal. It may be adversative, with *when* meaning 'whereas', or conditional, with *when* meaning 'if': How angerly I taught my brow to frowne, When inward joy enforc'd my heart to smile? (TGV 1.2.62); what a thing should I have beene, when I had beene swel'd? (MWW III.5.18).

204. *Where* does not always refer to place; it can mean 'when': Thou art not for the fashion of these times, Where none will sweate, but for promotion, (AYL II.3.59).

Where can mean 'whereas': And where thou now exact'st the penalty, . . . Thou wilt . . . Forgive a moytie of the principall, (Merch. IV.1.22).

205. *Where as* can be used for 'where': You do prepare to ride unto S. *Albons*, Where as the King and Queene do meane to Hawke (2H6 1.2.57). [Abbott 135]

206. *While* was originally a noun meaning 'time'. Today, as a conjunction, it means 'during the time when'. In Shakespeare, as in some modern dialects, it could mean 'until': We will keepe our selfe till Supper time alone: While then, God be with you. (Macb. III.1.43).

Whiles, derived from *while* with the addition of adverbial -*s*, was used with the same meaning: Then but forbeare your food a little while: Whiles (like a Doe) I go to finde my Fawne, (AYL II.7.128). [Abbott 737, Franz 555]

207. *Without* in the sense 'unless' is now dialectal. It is used in Shakespeare only by characters of low social standing: A very reverent body: I such a one, as a man may not speake of, without he say sir reverence, (Dromio, Err. III.2.91); He may staie him, marrie not without the prince be willing, (Dogberry, Ado III.3.82). [Franz 570]

VERBS

208. Many verbs which are today intransitive were in Shakespeare's day used transitively. It is often possible to find a verb of

similar meaning to that of the Shakespearean verb which is today used without a preposition: ere we could arrive the Point propos'd, (JC 1.2.110; cf. MnE *reach*); Smoile you my speeches, as I were a Foole? (Lear 11.2.77; cf. MnE *deride*). The transitive use may also be causative: She lingers my desires (MND 1.1.4); she hath recovered the King, (AW 111.2.20).

The verb *to fear* had the transitive meaning 'to frighten' already in Old English. This use survives in Shakespeare: Thou seest what's past, go feare thy King withall. (3H6 111.3.226). [Abbott 291, Franz 630]

209. Many verbs which are today intransitive were used reflexively by Shakespeare: endeavour thy selfe to sleepe, (TN IV.2.104); [Franz 628]

210. The use of transitive verbs intransitively is less common than the converse practice: There wanteth now our Brother Gloster heere, (R3 11.1.43); And what so poore a man as *Hamlet* is, May doe t'expresse his love and friending to you, God willing shall not lacke: (Ham. 1.5.185). [Abbott 293, Franz 629]

211. The number of impersonal verbs has diminished in the course of the history of English, partly because the decay of inflexional endings has sometimes left it uncertain whether an impersonal construction was intended. Some verbs are used both personally and impersonally:

Diomed   I doe not like this fooling.
Thersites Nor I by *Pluto*: but that that likes not me, pleases me best.   (Troil. V.2.101)

Other impersonal constructions are: it charges me in manners, the rather to expresse my selfe: (TN 11.1.16), i.e. it is incumbent on me; It doth import him much to speake with me (Troil. IV.2.51).

The verb *list* 'pleases' was originally impersonal, but in Shakespeare it is always personal: goe to bed when she list, rise when she list, all is as she will: (MWW 11.2.121). There is no final -*s* in *list* because the verb is from Old English 3 sg. *lysteþ*, with syncope of the unaccented vowel and assimilation of the final consonant.

212. Old English and Middle English had constructions of the type *me were better*. This became *I were better* through the influence of phrases like *you were better*, which could be either personal or impersonal. The transition from an impersonal construction has taken place in: thou wer't better be hang'd: (2H4 1.2.106). The

latest stage in the history of the construction shows the comparative giving way to the superlative: I were best not call; (Cym. III.6.19).

Shakespeare does not use the comparative *liefer*, although he often uses *as lief*: I had as liefe have beene my selfe alone. (AYL III.2.270). *I had rather* came into use during the fifteenth century and has now replaced *I had lever*. Beside *I had rather* we find *I would rather*, a development encouraged by the fact that *I had* and *I would* could both be reduced to *I'd*: I would rather hide me from my Greatnesse, . . . Then in my Greatnesse covet to be hid, (R3 III.7.161).

213. Shakespeare makes frequent use of the historic present to make the description of past events more vivid and interesting. He sometimes uses it in the same sentence as a straightforward preterite:

> He tooke me by the wrist, and held me hard;
> Then goes he to the length of all his arme;
> And with his other hand thus o're his brow,
> He fals to such perusall of my face,
> As he would draw it. Long staid he so,
>
> (Ham. II.1.87) [Franz 633]

214. The present perfect tense with the auxiliary *have* is today used to refer to a period of time beginning in the past but extending to the present or to past events which have given rise to current events; the preterite is used to describe completed events in the past. Sometimes Shakespeare uses the preterite where we should use the present perfect: You spoke not with her since. (Lear IV.3.37); I saw not better sport these seven yeeres day: (2H6 II.1.2).

Sometimes he uses the present tense where we should use the present perfect: How does your Honor for this many a day? (Ham. III.1.92); That's the worst Tidings that I heare of yet. (1H4 IV.1.127). [Abbott 346–7]

The Subjunctive

215. The subjunctive is used more freely in Shakespeare than today. The distinction between indicative and subjunctive is often blurred by the similarity in form between the two. Indications of

the subjunctive are forms of the 3 sg. present without final *-s* and the use of *were* with a singular subject. In the present tense *be* is not necessarily subjunctive. It is often used in questions: Be the Players ready? (Ham. III.2.109). After conjunctions like *though* and *if*, we sometimes find *be* as the subjunctive singular even when other verbs are in the indicative: Though *Page* be a secure foole, and stands so firmly on his wives frailty; (MWW II.1.239). [Franz 636]

216. In principal clauses the subjunctive is used, especially in the 3 sg. present, to express a wish: Good now sit downe, & tell me he that knowes (Ham. I.1.70); Long live she so; And long live you to thinke so. (Oth. III.3.228). The wish may be a curse: A burning divell take them. (Troil. V.2.193), or a threat: Deny me this, And an eternall Curse fall on you: (Macb. IV.1.104). The subjunctive is sometimes accompanied by inversion of the position of a pronoun and its verb: Goe we to our Tent: (Cor. 1.9.92); Joine we together for the publicke good, (2H6 1.1.199). In Shakespeare, as today, *let* is often used jussively: Let each man render me his bloody hand. (JC III.1.184). In the second person singular and plural the imperative is used, often accompanied by a pronoun: come you to me at night, (MWW II.2.280); Goe beare thou this Letter to Mistris *Page* (MWW 1.3.78). There are survivals of an unaccented pronoun in the archaic *lookee* and *harkee* and in *mind you*. [Franz 637, 649]

217. In subordinate clauses the subjunctive is used after verbs of commanding or wishing: Fortune forbid my out-side have not charm'd her: (TN II.2.19); We enjoyne thee, As thou art Liege-man to us, that thou carry This female Bastard hence, (WT II.3.173). [Abbott 369, Franz 647]

218. In subordinate clauses the subjunctive is often used after verbs of thinking: I thinke it be no other, but enso; (Ham. I.1.108).

219. In subordinate clauses the subjunctive is often used after impersonal constructions like *it is best*: 'Twere best he speake no harme of *Brutus* heere? (JC III.2.72). [Franz 641]

220. In final clauses the subjunctive is sometimes used, though the auxiliary *shall* is more common: Come thick Night, And pall thee in the dunnest smoake of Hell, That my keene Knife see not the Wound it makes, (Macb. 1.5.51); three of Mr Fords brothers watch the doore with Pistols, that none shall issue out: (MWW IV.2.51). [Franz 642]

221. In conditional clauses, introduced by *if*, we find both indicative and subjunctive: If money goe before, all waies doe lye open. (MWW II.2.175). When a comparison is introduced by *as if*, the subjunctive is generally used: I warrant it greeves my Husband, As if the cause were his, (Oth. III.3.3). Inversion in a conditional clause is more common in Shakespeare than today, when we generally prefer to use an auxiliary verb: And for that dowrie, Ile assure her of Her widdow-hood, be it that she survive me (Shrew II.1.124); Live *Roderigo*, He calles me to a restitution large (Oth. v.1.15), i.e. 'if Roderigo lives'. [Abbott 361, Franz 644]

222. In concessive clauses, introduced by such conjunctions as *though* or *albeit*, the indicative is generally used when the verb refers to something which the speaker regards as a fact; the subjunctive is used when it refers to something which the speaker regards as uncertain: they'll not shew their teeth in way of smile Though *Nestor* sweare the jest be laughable. (Merch. 1.1.55), beside: for all you are my man, goe wait upon my Cosen *Shallow*: (MWW 1.1.278). [Franz 645]

223. The subjunctive is sometimes used in relative clauses which express a wish: Therefore take with thee my most greevous curse, Which in the day of Battell tyre thee more Then all the compleat Armour that thou wear'st. (R3 IV.4.186). [Franz 648]

224. *Were* as a subjunctive is used more freely than the subjunctives of other verbs. It is used after *if* and *though* and in dependent sentences: if thy pocket were enrich'd with anie other injuries but these, I am a Villaine: (1H4 III.3.180); No marvaile then, though he were ill affected, (Lear II.1.100).

Were is used in subordinate clauses after verbs of knowing, not merely after verbs of thinking: I would I had thy inches, thou shoulds't know There were a heart in Egypt. (Ant. 1.3.40).

225. The preterite and past perfect subjunctives are used in principal sentences to imply a condition: She were an excellent wife for *Benedick* (Ado II.1.368); I had peopel'd else This isle with *Calibans*. (Temp. 1.2.350). *Could* and *might* are used as auxiliaries to replace the subjunctive: I could wish he would modestly examine himselfe, (Ado II.3.214); I might not this beleeve Without the sensible and true avouch Of mine owne eyes. (Ham. 1.1.56). [Franz 638]

Infinitives

226. Today we use the infinitive without the preposition *to* after certain verbs, such as *bid*, *shall* and *can*. In Shakespeare's day the number of verbs after which *to* could be omitted was much larger: I pray desire her call her wisedome to her. (Lear IV.5.35). After expressions like *it is best* and *he were better* we find infinitives both with and without *to*: she were better love a dreame: (TN II.2.27), beside: You were best to tell *Anthonio* what you heare (Merch. II.8.33). Conversely, verbs which do not take *to* today are sometimes found in Shakespeare with *to*, perhaps to meet the demands of metre: Heare me with patience, but to speake a word, (RJ III.5.160). [Franz 650–1]

227. When an auxiliary verb is followed by two infinitives, we sometimes find *to* used before the second infinitive but not before the first: Make thy two eyes like Starres, start from their Spheres, Thy knotty and combined locks to part, (Ham. 1.5.17). [Abbott 350, Franz 653]

228. The accusative and infinitive construction is common after verbs of thinking or desiring: I thinke this Lady to be my childe *Cordelia*. (Lear IV.7.69). The verb 'to be' has often to be understood: Meaning me a beast. (AYL IV.3.49). With the decay of inflexions, by the sixteenth century there was no distinction in form between the subjective and the objective case of nouns, and consequently we sometimes find that in pronouns, where there is a distinction, the subjective case is used with an infinitive where historically we should expect the objective: Heaven would that shee these gifts should have, and I to live and die her slave. (AYL III.2.161). One reason for the use of the subjective case of the pronoun is that there is sometimes a conflict between the grammatical and the psychological subject. The subjective case of a pronoun is sometimes used in exclamations when we have to understand an expression like 'It is monstrous to think' before it: All Sects, all Ages smack of this vice, and he To die for't? (Meas. II.2.5). [Franz 656]

229. The infinitive preceded by *to* is used in Shakespeare where today we should use a verbal noun preceded by another preposition: To fright you thus, Me thinkes I am too savage: (Macb. IV.2.70), i.e. 'in frightening you'. [Abbott 356]

230. An infinitive can be used instead of a causal subordinate

clause: If this be so, why blame you me to love you? (AYL V.2.117)
i.e. 'because I love you'; you your selfe Are much condemn'd to
have an itching Palme, (JC IV.3.9), i.e. 'for having an itching palm'.
[Franz 655]

231. An infinitive can be used instead of a conditional clause:
you might have saved mee my paines, to have taken it away your
selfe (TN II.2.5), i.e. 'if you had taken it'. [Franz 655]

232. Today we use the infinitive as a noun to form the subject
of a sentence, as when we say *To err is human*. In Shakespeare the
infinitive could also be used as the object of a verb: To doe this
deed, Promotion followes: (WT 1.2.354), i.e. 'Promotion will
follow the doing of this deed'. [Abbott 357]

233. To avoid repetition, the second of two infinitives may be
replaced by *it* or *'t*: But shall we dance, if they desire us too't?
(LLL V.2.145). [Franz 656]

234. One use of the infinitive is to describe something that is
fit or suitable: This disturbed Skie is not to walke in. (JC 1.3.40).

235. Shakespeare often uses the active infinitive where we
should use the passive: what's to do? (TN III.3.18); the best is yet
to doe (AYL 1.2.119). [Franz 654]

236. The perfect infinitive is used after a preterite to refer to a wish
that has not been fulfilled: I thought thy Bride-bed to have deckt
(sweet Maid) And not t'have strew'd thy Grave. (Ham. V.1.268).
[Franz 657]

Participles and Verbal Nouns

237. The present participle is normally active and the past participle is normally passive, but some exceptions occur: Tell him, from
his all-obeying breath, I heare The doome of Egypt (Ant. III.13.76),
i.e. 'obeyed by all'; Revenge the geering and disdain'd contempt
Of this proud King, (1H4 1.3.182); O grim lookt night, (MND
V.1.171). There is always the possibility of influence of the
adjectival ending (OE -ede) on the past participle. [Abbott 372, 374,
Franz 661]

238. The gerund, or verbal noun, in -ing may or may not be
preceded by a-, an unaccented variant of the preposition *on*.
Examples are: There is some ill a bruing (Merch. II.5.17), beside:
whil'st this Play is Playing, (Ham. III.2.94). A gerund with passive
meaning is sometimes used as an attributive adjective: Thy lips,
those kissing cherries, (MND III.2.139).

239. Today the -*ing* form of a transitive verb is normally
followed by a noun in the genitive when it is preceded by *the* but
by a noun in the objective when it is not preceded by an article:
for stealing sheep beside *for the stealing of sheep*. In this respect, however, Shakespeare's syntax was not as regular as ours: th' Bishop
of *Bayon*, then French Embassador, Who had beene hither sent on
the debating A marriage 'twixt the Duke of *Orleance* and Our
daughter *Mary*: (H8 II.4.173); Leave wringing of your hands,
(Ham. III.4.34). Constructions with and without *of* occur in a
single line: Here stood he in the dark, his sharpe Sword out,
Mumbling of wicked charmes, conjuring the Moone (Lear II.1.39).
[Franz 665, 667, 669]

240. There was a dative absolute construction in Old English,
but the fairly frequent absolute constructions in Elizabethan
English are probably in the main the result of imitation of the
Latin ablative absolute. Most absolute constructions are temporal,
but a few are conditional: This seene, *Orlando* did approach the
man, And found it was his brother, (AYL IV.3.119), beside: A
gracious King, that pardons all offences Malice ne're meant: (H8
II.2.68). The absolute construction is not confined to participles;
it is found also with adjectives: With this she fell distract, And (her
Attendants absent) swallow'd fire. (JC IV.3.154); I should not
seeke an absent argument Of my revenge, thou present: (AYL
III.1.3). An absolute participle is sometimes used with a preposition: after all this fearefull Homage done, (2H6 III.2.224). Since the
decay of inflexions has blurred the distinction between cases, the
subjective case of pronouns is sometimes found in an absolute
construction: First *Kildares* Attendure; Then Deputy of Ireland,
who remov'd Earle *Surrey*, was sent thither, (H8 II.1.42). [Abbott
377, Franz 660]

241. The suffix -*ed* is sometimes added to a phrase: For putting
on so new a fashion'd robe (John IV.2.27). There are other
examples which may be constructed in this way, although they
could also be interpreted in a more conventional manner. In: Ile
get me such a coulour'd Perrywig: (TGV IV.4.196), the last four
words may mean 'a periwig of such a colour' or 'a coloured periwig like that'. Similarly in: there's no man is so vaine, That would
refuse so faire an offer'd Chaine. (Err. III.2.185), *faire* may qualify
offer'd or *Chaine*. [Franz 662]

242. A hanging participle is sometimes used, with no noun

with which it can agree: Or in the night, imagining some feare, How easie is a bush suppos'd a Beare? (MND V.I.21). The present participle has come to assume the function of a causal conjunction. As a development of this construction, *being* comes to be used as a conjunction meaning 'in view of the fact that', very much as some speakers today use *seeing as*: you loyter heere too long, being you are to take Souldiers up, in Countries as you go. (2H4 II.I.197). Sometimes a pronoun on which a participle depends can be understood from a possessive adjective: Comming from *Sardis*, on our former Ensigne Two mighty Eagles fell, (JC V.I.80); *coming* means 'as we came', and it agrees with *we* that is implied in *our*. [Abbott 378–9, Franz 663]

Auxiliary Verbs

243. A verb of motion is often omitted after *shall, will, must, let* or *be* when followed by an adverb or a prepositional phrase: thou shalt not from this grove, (MND II.I.146); Lets away (MWW V.2.14); let us to the King: (WT IV.4.723). Verbs of motion are sometimes omitted after other verbs when the meaning is clear: He purposeth to Athens, (Ant. III.I.35); Bid them all home, (Cor. IV.2.1). [Franz 621]

244. *Be.* Many verbs which are constructed with the auxiliary *to have* at the present day are constructed with *to be* in Shakespeare, without the modern distinction of using *is* for state and *has* for action: he is retyred to Antium. (Cor. III.I.11); *Malcolme*, and *Donalbaine* . . . Are stolne away and fled, (Macb. II.4.26). [Franz 631]

245. *Can* is not merely an auxiliary verb. The original meaning was 'to have knowledge or skill', and this sense persists: I've seene my selfe, and serv'd against the French, And they can well on horseback (Ham. IV.7.84); What can mans wisedome In the restoring his bereaved Sense; (Lear IV.4.8).

246. *Do* is used today in questions and negative statements. In Shakespeare we often find both of these types of sentence constructed without an auxiliary: Revolt our Subjects? (R2 III.2.100); Gives not the Hawthorne bush a sweeter shade? (3H6 II.5.42); it not appeares to me, (2H4 IV.I.107). Today in positive statements *do* is used to express emphasis, but in Shakespeare it often seems to be used without emphasis, which is adequately expressed by the

following infinitive: I do intreat you, not a man depart, (JC
III.2.65); I do assure you, The King cry'de Ha, at this. (H8 III.2.59).
Franz (§ 595) suggests that *did* is used in the following passage to
indicate that the events described did in fact take place, however
improbable they might seem:

> Horsses do neigh, and dying men did grone,
> And Ghosts did shrieke and squeale about the streets.
>
> (JC II.2.23)

But there is nothing improbable about the first two of these events,
and Abbott (§ 304) is more likely to be right in suggesting that the
purpose of the auxiliary is to represent excited narrative. Sometimes the reason for the use of *do* seems to be metrical; it is a
device to introduce an extra syllable into a line. There is confirmation of this view in the greater frequency of occurrence of *do* in
verse as compared with prose. There seems to be no reason other
than metrical for the use of *did* in: When I did him at this advantage
take, (MND III.2.16). [Abbott 305–6, Franz 597]

247. *Have*. In subordinate clauses after a main verb in the
preterite, *had* followed by a past participle is used to describe something that has not in fact taken place: I thought your Honour had
already beene at Shrewsbury. (1H4 IV.2.56); I thought that all
things had bin savage heere, (AYL II.7.107). [Franz 657]

248. *May* and its preterite *might* are often used where we should
use *can* and *could*: You may away by Night: (1H4 III.1.141); But I
might see young *Cupids* fiery shaft (MND II.1.161). *May* is today
used optatively; in Shakespeare *might* could also be used in this
way: Lord worship might he be, (Merch. II.2.100). [Abbott 312–3,
Franz 604]

249. *Must* is from OE *mōste*, the past tense of *mōt* 'he is obliged'.
It is sometimes used to indicate something planned for the future
without any notion of compulsion: Hee must fight singly to
morrow with *Hector*, (Troil. III.3.247); Descend, for you must be
my Torch-bearer (Merch. II.6.41). [Abbott 314, Franz 607]

250. *Shall*. Many of the differences in use between *shall* and *will*
have arisen since the time of Shakespeare. In Shakespeare *shall* is
used in all three persons to indicate the normal future; *will*
generally involves some volition: And if I die, no soule shall
pittie me. (R3 V.3.201); If much you note him You shall offend
him, and extend his Passion, (Macb. III.4.56).

113

There is often an element of inevitability in the use of *shall* which gives it the meaning 'will have to': hee that escapes me without some broken limbe, shall acquit him well: (AYL I.I.130); Your Grace shall pardon me, I will not backe: (John v.2.78).

The inevitability associated with *shall* introduces an element of compulsion and this could arouse resentment: Marke you His absolute Shall? (Cor. III.I.89).

Shall is often used in temporal and conditional clauses where today we use the present tense: When she shall heare this of thee, with her nailes Shee'l flea thy Wolvish visage. (Lear I.4.329); If you shall send them word you will not come, Their mindes may change. (JC II.2.95). [Abbott 315, 317, Franz 608, 610]

251. *Should.* Corresponding to the use of *shall* for the future, we find *should* for the conditional in all three persons. In some of the occurrences we should today use the auxiliary *would*: If he should offer to choose, and choose the right Casket, you should refuse to performe your Fathers will, if you should refuse to accept him. (Merch. I.2.99).

Just as *shall* is used to mean 'is to', so *should* can mean 'was to' without any idea of moral obligation: I warrant you, hee's the man should fight with him. (MWW III.I.68).

Should is used to express an opinion about which the speaker is not quite certain: By Heaven, that should be my Handkerchiefe. (Oth. IV.I.163). [Franz 612, 613, 615, 620]

252. The preterite auxiliary *used to* is common today, but in Shakespeare it is found also in the present and the present perfect: they alwayes use to laugh at nothing. (Temp. II.I.175); Th'unstained Sword that you have us'd to beare: (2H4 V.2.114).

253. *Will* generally involves volition but it is occasionally used to express a simple future: Perchance I will be there as soone as you. (Err. IV.I.39).

Will is used to describe an habitual tendency: hee will be talking as they say, (Ado III.5.39); foule deeds will rise, Though all the earth orewhelm them to mens eies. (Ham. I.2.257). [Franz 616, 620]

254. *Would* is used to express an inclination or wish: that we would doe We should doe when we would: (Ham. IV.7.119).

Would sometimes means 'was (or were) accustomed to': But still the house Affaires would draw her hence: (Oth. I.3.147). [Abbott 330]

CHAPTER 4

Accidence

᠅᠅᠅᠅᠅

255. By the time of Shakespeare the process of simplification of the older inflexional endings had already been carried out almost to the stage reached in present-day English; differences between Shakespearean and present-day usage are mainly in points of detail. We sometimes find a mixture of forms, as in the formal *-eth* ending of the 3 sg. pres. ind. beside the more common *-es*. The reduction of unaccented words is a frequent colloquialism, and this produces a number of variants: *hem* is reduced to *'em*, *have* to *ha*, *he* to *a*, *it* to *'t*, *I will* and *I shall* to *Ile* and *thou wilt* to *thou'lt*. Prepositions are especially liable to lose their final consonants in colloquial speech. Such forms occur for *on*, *of*, *in*, *upon* and *with*.

256. Some of Shakespeare's contemporaries made free use of grammatical constructions which were already becoming archaic, but in contrast to Spenser and the Authorized Version of the Bible, Shakespeare looks forward rather than backward in matters of grammar. Archaisms are frequent in the lines in *Pericles* spoken by Gower as Prologue (see § 442). Elsewhere in Shakespeare the prefix *y-* (OE *ge-*) is found once in *yclad* and fairly often in *ycleped*.

NOUNS

257. Abstract nouns are often used for concrete nouns of related meaning. Prospero calls Ariel *my diligence* (Temp. v.1.241), and Iago addresses his wife as *Filth* (Oth. v.2.232). Other examples are *basenesse* 'base fellow' (MWW 11.2.19); *blasphemy* 'blasphemer' (Temp. v.1.218).

258. Nouns ending in *-s* are often unchanged in the genitive: since *Pythagoras* time (AYL 111.2.186). Proper names are often similarly unchanged: our Rome gates (Cor. 111.3.105); Draw them to Tyber bankes (JC 1.1.63). Nouns are sometimes unchanged in

the genitive when followed by a word beginning with *s*-: for sport sake (1H4 II.1.80); for Conscience sake (Cor. II.3.32).

The apostrophe is not generally used before *s* to indicate a genitive. The genitive is not a new formation from the subjective case, as it is in present-day English *wife's*; the spellings in Shakespeare show that the *f* has been voiced in the genitive singular of *wife* and *life*, as it has in the subjective plural: *your wives cloathes* (MWW IV.2.146); *his sweete lives losse* (John IV.3.106).

259. Some nouns could be regarded as either singular or plural. *Doors* and *gates* are often used with a singular meaning, perhaps because they were double: stand at her doores, (TN I.4.16). *Riches* (OF *richesse*) is used in both singular and plural: The Riches of the Ship is come on shore: (Oth. II.1.83), beside: Since Riches point to Misery and Contempt (Tim. IV.2.33). *Alms* (OE *ælmesse*) is singular: That hath receiv'd an Almes (Cor. III.2.120). *News* and *tidings* are both singular and plural: *these dead newes* (John V.7.65) beside: *the newes was told* (1H4 I.1.58); *this ill-tydings* (R2 III.4.80) beside: *these ill-tydings* (John IV.2.132). *Letters* may refer to a single letter: I have letters that my sonne will be heere to night (AW IV.5.91). *Corpes* is used as a plural with the meaning 'bodies' at 2H4 I.1.192.

Double plurals are sometimes found: *Galowses* (Cym. V.4.210); *your teethes* (JC V.1.40). *Beefs* and *muttons* may seem to belong to Shylock's idiolect in: As flesh of Muttons, Beefes, or Goates, (Merch. I.3.168), but *Beeves* occurs elsewhere in: now hath he Land, and Beeves (2H4 III.2.352). The plural *Sheepes* occurs in word-play with *Ships* at LLL II.1.219. There are a few survivals of the Old English plural in *-an* in the poetic plural *eyne* 'eyes' (OE *ēagan*, pl.), which occurs several times, usually in rhyme, as in MND I.1.242 and Ant. II.7.120. The plural *shooen* 'shoes' occurs at 2H6 IV.2.192 and the variant *shoone* at Ham. IV.5.24.

260. Nouns ending in a sibilant are sometimes unchanged in the plural: Are there ballance heere? (Merch. IV.1.255). Except after sibilants, the ending *-es* did not normally constitute an extra syllable, but the metre shows that there are occasional words in which the *e* is pronounced even when it does not follow a sibilant: To shew his teeth as white as Whales bone. (LLL V.2.332); You sent me for a ropes end as soone, (Err. IV.1.98). *Aches* 'pains' is disyllabic because the *ch* was pronounced [tʃ]: Their feares of Hostile strokes, their Aches losses, (Tim. V.1.202).

261. After numerals nouns indicating distance, weight or value are often unchanged in the plural. The plural without ending probably goes back to the OE gen. pl. in -*a* with some help from the nom. and acc. pl. of neuter nouns with long stems, which had no inflexional ending: I would not loose the dogge for twentie pound. (Shrew Ind. 1.21); since I was three yeare olde (AYL v.2.64).

262. Some abstract nouns such as *behaviour*, *glory*, *funeral* which are today normally used in the singular were sometimes used in the plural: His Funerals shall not be in our Campe, (JC v.3.105); my Behaviours (JC 1.2.42). On the other hand, some nouns, such as *nuptials* and *victuals*, which are now plural, were then often singular: You had musty victuall, and he hath holpe to eate it: (Ado 1.1.51); I must imploy you in some businesse Against our nuptiall, (MND 1.1.124).

263. The Old English gen. pl. ending -*ra* survives as -*der* in *alderliefest*: With you mine *Alder liefest* Soveraigne (2H6 1.1.28).

PRONOUNS

264. A few dialectal forms of personal pronouns are found in Shakespeare. In Southern dialects the first personal pronoun (OE *ic*) was often contracted with a following verb to give *chill* and *chud*, and these forms are used by Edgar in *King Lear*: Chill not let go, (IV.6.239), chill picke your teeth Zir (l.248), chud ha' bin zwagger'd out of my life, (l.242). There are many examples of the use of *a* or *a'* for *he* The pronoun *a* is used by both educated and uneducated speakers, but generally in contexts where colloquial language is appropriate: Here a comes me thinkes, (2H6 1.3.6); let his Father be what a will (Merch II.2.58); a pops me out (John 1.1.68); A shall not tread on me (Cor v.3.127). There are occasional examples of the accented neuter pronoun *hit* beside *it* (OE *hit*): nor keepe peace betweene Th'effect, and hit (Macb. 1.5.47; F1, 2, hit, F3, 4 it).

265. Today the third person plural pronoun '*em* for *them* is colloquial. It is fairly common in Shakespeare as an unaccented form but it is not restricted to colloquial use: God send 'em good shipping: (Shrew v.1.45); Let 'em enter: (JC II.1.76); Thy Asses are gone about 'em; (Lear 1.5.38).

266. In Old English, as we have seen (§ 94), *his* was the genitive of the neuter third personal pronoun as well as of the masculine,

and *his* is sometimes used as a neuter possessive in Shakespeare. To avoid confusion with the masculine, *it* is sometimes used as a neuter possessive. Most, but not all, of the occurrences are playful or familiar in tone, as when a child is addressed or spoken of. The Fool in *King Lear* says to Lear: For you know Nunckle, the Hedge-Sparrow fed the Cuckoo so long, that it had it head bit off by it young, (1.4.236). It is sometimes used in this way in the Authorized Version of the Bible: That which groweth of it owne accord, (Leviticus 25.5).

ADJECTIVES

267. Comparison with *-er* and *-est* is found in many adjectives which today use *more* and *most*: a properer man (AYL III.5.51), a perfecter gyber for the Table, (Cor. II.1.91), the Soveraign'st thing on earth (1H4 1.3.57). On the other hand we often find short and everyday adjectives compared by the use of *more* and *most*, perhaps to meet the demands of the metre: Hath not old custome made this life more sweete (AYL II.1.2), a Nuntio's of more grave aspect (TN 1.4.27). Participles used as adjectives are compared: the lyingst knave in Christendome (Shrew Ind. 2.24); *curster* (Shrew III.2.156).

268. When two adjectives become comparatives by the addition of *more*, a single *more* serves for both adjectives: *Dianas* lip Is not more smooth, and rubious: (TN 1.4.31); Our fancies are more giddie and unfirme, . . . Then womens are. (TN II.4.34).

269. Double comparatives and superlatives are common: for the more better assurance, (MND III.1.21); This was the most unkindest cut of all, (JC III.2.187), The worsser welcome: (Oth. 1.1.95). Words like *chief*, that express superlative ideas, can take the superlative ending: your chiefest thoughts (Merch. II.8.43). We also find the apparent contradiction: lesse happier Lands (R2 II.1.49).

270. *Enow* is descended from the OE pl. adj. *genōge*, while the more usual *enough* is from the OE sg. *genōh*: we were Christians enow before, (Merch. III.5.20).

Far. As a result of phonetic change, the OE adjective *feorr* 'far' and its comparative *fierra* fell together as *farre* in late Middle English. To avoid confusion the comparative was replaced by *further* (OE *furðra*) and *farther* (with *a* on the analogy of *far*). Occasional examples of the older use of *farre* as a comparative occur in Shakespeare: Not hold thee of our blood, no not our Kin, Farre then *Deucalion* off: (WT IV.4.440).

Little. The irregular comparison which in present-day English allows *little* to have a comparative *less* is for the most part preserved in Shakespeare, but the analogical superlative *litlest* occurs: Where love is great, the litlest doubts are feare, (Ham. III.2.181; Q2–5 reading).

Mickle. Beside *much* there are in Shakespeare six examples of the variant *mickle*, which seems not to have been regarded as an especially Northern form: in dutie bend thy knee to me, That bowes unto the grave with mickle age, (2H6 V.1.173; the King speaking); The one nere got me credit, the other mickle blame: (Err. III.1.45).

More originally meant 'larger'. This sense is preserved in: Why should their libertie then ours be more? (Err. II.1.10). The usual Middle English word to describe a greater number was *mo* (OE *mā*), originally an adverb though it was used as a substantive followed by a noun in the genitive plural. This survives in Shakespeare: many thousands moe (WT I.2.8). We sometimes find that the First Folio (1623) has *moe* while the later Folios (1632, 1663, 1685) have *more*, as in: Send out moe Horses (Macb. V.3.35; F1, 2 read *moe* while F3, 4 read *more*). This suggests that *moe* was passing out of use during the seventeenth century.

Nigh, near, next. Historically *near* is the comparative of *nigh*, and *next* is the superlative. Already in Shakespeare *near* has normally become a positive, though there are occasional examples of its use as a comparative: Better farre off, then neere, be ne're the neere. (R2 V.1.88). After verbs of motion it is often difficult to be sure whether *near* is positive or comparative: neere approches The subject of our Watch (Macb. III.3.7). In present-day English a distinction in meaning has developed between *nearest* and *next*, the former referring to proximity in space, the latter generally to proximity in time. This distinction is not always preserved in Shakespeare: Come (good boy) the next way home. (WT III.3.128).

NUMERALS

271. *Twain* derives from OE masculine *twēgen*, while *two* comes from OE feminine and neuter *twā*. *Twain* is today obsolete in the spoken language and archaic in the written. In Shakespeare it is

used as a substantive in the sense 'pair, couple': goe with me To blesse this twaine, (Temp. IV.1.103).

272. *Twenty* is used to indicate any fairly large number (§ 41), not necessarily exactly twenty: He would Kisse you Twenty with a breath. (H8 1.4.30); Good-even, and twenty (good Master *Page*) (MWW II.1.202).

273. Among the ordinal numerals *fift* and *sixt* (OE *fifta, sixta*) are the normal forms in place of the analogical forms *fifth* and *sixth* that are current today: the *fift houre* (Troil. II.1.132); *on the sixt* (Lear I.1.178). For our *eighth* Shakespeare has *eight* (OE *eahtoða* with syncope of *o*, assimilation of *tð* to *tt* and simplification of *tt*): *the eight hour* (JC II.1.213). *Tithe* (OE *tēoða*), now only a substantive, was originally an ordinal numeral meaning 'tenth': every tythe soul (Troil. II.2.19). For our *twelfth* Shakespeare has *twelfe* as a result of an attempt to simplify a heavy consonant group (OE *twelfta*). The title of a well-known play in the First Folio is *Twelfe Night*; cf. also: O the twelfe day of December. (TN II.3.90). *Prime* is occasionally used in the sense 'first': my prime request (Temp. I.2.423). The plural *dismes* occurs once in the sense 'tenth men': 'mongst many thousand dismes (Troil. II.2.19).

274. *Certain* is used as an adjective meaning 'some', not followed by *of*, and as a substantive meaning 'a certain number', followed by *of*: Bury it certaine fadomes in the earth, (Temp. V.1.55); I would send for certaine of my Creditors: (Meas. I.2.135).

As both adjective and substantive it may be qualified by *some*: Some certaine dregges of conscience are yet within mee (R3 I.4.123); I have mov'd already Some certaine of the Noblest minded Romans (JC I.3.121).

ADVERBS

275. When two or more adverbs are used in succession, we often find that only the last of them has a characteristic adverbial ending: Ile serve thee true and faithfully till then. (LLL V.2.840); And I, most jocund, apt, and willinglie, To do you rest, a thousand deaths would dye. (TN V.1.135).

276. The comparatives of adjectives can be used adverbially: you have spoken truer then you purpos'd (Temp. II.1.20); Thou speak'st wiser then thou art ware of. (AYL II.4.56).

Comparative adverbs in *-ier* are sometimes found: You have taken it wiselier then I meant you should. (Temp. II.1.21); I should freelier rejoyce in that absence (Cor. 1.3.3).

277. In compounds consisting of an adjective followed by a participial adjective in *-ed*, the adjective is sometimes compared by the addition of *-er*, *-est*, where today we should use *more*, *most*: The villaine is much lighter heel'd then I: (MND III.2.415); I thinke *Crab* my dog, be the sowrest natured dogge that lives: (TGV II.3.5).

Ratherest is used by Holofernes: untrained, or rather unlettered, or ratherest unconfirmed fashion, (LLL IV, 2.16).

278. Double comparison is found in adverbs as in adjectives: He beares himselfe more proudlier, (Cor. IV.7.8); I cannot hate thee worser then I do, (Ant. II.5.90).

VERBS

279. Some verbs which were originally strong occasionally have weak preterites and past participles: I shak'd you Sir. (Temp. II.1.319), when Degree is shak'd, (Troil. 1.3.101). The originally strong verb *help*, which has today become entirely weak, has the strong preterite *holp*, pp. *holpen; helped* is rare in Shakespeare. Verbs borrowed from other languages have often undergone the influence of analogy. *Strive* (OF *estriver*) has today become a strong verb on the analogy of *drive*, preterite *drove*; a weak preterite *strived* occurs in Shakespeare. *Catch* (ONF *cachier*) has the preterite *caught* on the analogy of archaic preterites like *laught* (pret. of *latch*) and *raught* (pret. of *reach*); Shakespeare has this form beside *catched*. The two preterites seem to have acquired different shades of meaning in: None are so surely caught, when they are catcht, As wit turn'd foole, (LLL V.2.69).

280. Strong forms of weak verbs are less common than weak forms of strong verbs. The usual past participle of *strew* (OE *streowian*) is *strew'd* or *strewed*, but a strong form *strewne* rhyming with *throwne* occurs in TN II.4.59. The usual pp. of *sweat* (OE *swǣtan*) is *sweat*, with syncope of *e* and assimilation and simplification of consonants from OE *-swǣted*, but a strong pp. occurs in *sweaten* (Macb. IV.1.63), rhyming with *eaten*.

281. As a result of the decay of inflexional endings in later Middle English, the old infinitive ending found in Middle English as *-en* has almost completely disappeared, but a trace of it is found

in one of the archaic prologues in *Pericles*: though he strive To killen bad, (II, Prologue 19).

282. The final -*t* of the 2 sing. pres. ind. often disappears when the next word begins with a consonant that would make pronunciation of the -*t* difficult. In speech a group of words pronounced without a pause between them is treated in the same way as a single word. Just as speakers today usually omit the *t* in the pronunciation of *Christmas* and *postman*, so in Shakespeare we find: thou mistakes me much (2H6 V.1.130). When the next word begins with *th*-, the final -*t* is particularly likely to disappear: What may this meane? That thou dead Coarse againe in compleat steele, Revisits thus the glimpses of the Moone, (Ham. 1.4.51). When forms like *are* and *shall* are used for the 2 sg. they are probably due to analogy, but phonetic change may have helped in the creation of such forms as *shall* in: an angel shall thou see (LLL V.2.103, F2 reading), and: Thou an Egyptian Puppet shall be shewne In Rome as well as I: (Ant. V.2.207).

283. The usual ending of the 3 sg. present indicative is -(*e*)*s*. The metre shows that the *e* of this ending is usually syncopated, even when it is kept in spelling. The ending -*th* is frequent in *hath*, *doth* and *saith*, but in other verbs it is not common. Examples are: shee enlargeth her mirth (MWW II.2.229): He hath wrong'd me (MWW I.1.102). We often find -*s* in prose dialogue but -*eth* in proclamations and stage directions. It may well be that one reason for the use of the ending -*eth* is that it makes an extra syllable, which is often useful in verse, whereas the ending -*es* does not, except when the stem of the verb ends in a sibilant.

284. There are a few survivals of the Middle English dialectal endings of the plural of the present indicatives, -*en* in the Midlands and -*es* in the North. It is natural that the deliberately archaic language of Gower as Prologue in *Pericles* should include examples of the -*en* ending: All perishen of man, of pelfe, (II, Prol. 35); Where when men been, there's seldome ease, (II, Prol. 28). Another example is assigned to Puck: And waxen in their mirth, (MND II.1.56).

The 3rd plural pres. ind. in -*es* is fairly common in the First Folio, though less common in modern editions, where editors have often emended such forms. Forms in -*es* are sometimes fixed by rhyme, as in: Whiles I threat, he lives: Words to the heat of deedes too cold breath gives. (Macb. II.1.60); The great man downe, you marke his favourites flies, The poore advanc'd, makes Friends of Enemies: (Ham. III.2.214). Examples not in rhyme are: My old bones akes: (Temp. III.3.2); His teares runs downe his beard like winters drops (Temp. v.1.13). Editors are too ready to emend such forms but, in their defence, it has to be admitted that there are some examples that are clearly misprints: Comes shall we in, (Tim. I.1.284); Sir *Protheus*, your Fathers call's for you, (TGV 1.3.88). There are a few examples of the survival of the Middle English Southern dialectal ending -(e)th, especially in *hath* and *doth*. They include: All his successors (gone before him) hath don't (MWW 1.1.15); Looke how thy wounds doth bleede (Troil. v.3.82).

285. Some strong verbs of Classes IV and V, such as *bear*, *break*, and *speak*, today normally have *o* in the preterite with *a* as an occasional archaism. Forms with *a* are more common in Shakespeare than today, though even there they are less common than forms with *o*. An example is *I bare* (Err. II.1.73). Such forms go back to OE preterite singulars with stem-vowel *æ* lengthened on the analogy of the long vowel in the preterite plural. In the seventeenth century they seem to have been regarded as archaic and suited to a dignified style. Preterites with *a* are occasionally found on the analogy of verbs of Classes IV and V in verbs of other conjugations, such as *drive*, pret. *drave* (Troil. III.3.190).

In strong verbs of Class III there is at the present day some variation between *a* and *u* as the stem-vowel of the preterite; *a* goes back to the OE preterite singular, *u* to the preterite plural. In Shakespeare preterites with *u* are more common than they are today. The verbs *ring*, *shrink*, *spin*, *sting* and *wring* have only forms with *u* in the preterite. An example of a form with *u* where present-day English has *a* is: I am sure thy father drunke wine (AW II.3.105).

286. Strong past participles often occur without their final -*en* or -*n*: That Jade hath eate bread from my Royall hand (R2 v.5.85); H'as broke my head a-crosse, (TN v.1.178). On the other hand, we find a few past participles in Shakespeare with the -*en*, which has been lost in those verbs in present-day English. Examples are: a Deere, stroken by many Princes (JC III.1.209); this glorious and well-foughten field (H5 IV.6.17). *Lyen* shows the analogy of forms of the present: Many a poore mans sonne would have lyen still, (John IV.1.50). *Loden* (OE *hladen*, pp. of *hladan*) shows the analogy of the noun *load*: Loden with Honor (Cor. v.3.164) beside: Laden with Gold (Ant. III.11.5).

287. There are several examples of the use of the preterite of a strong verb as a past participle, a practice which may have been helped by the falling together of the preterite and past participle of weak verbs after the loss of final -*e*: These errors are arose (Err. v.1.388); Be shooke to ayrie ayre (Troil. III.3.225); He might have tooke his answer long ago. (TN 1.5.281). Beside *drove* (2H6 III.2.84) we find *droven* once, with the vowel of the preterite but the ending of the past participle: we had droven them home (Ant. IV.7.5). In some verbs the use of preterites as past participles has survived to the present day. Examples are: *held, stood.*

288. In the 2 sg. pret. ind. of weak verbs, syncope of unaccented vowels often led to the creation of heavy groups of consonants which were difficult to pronounce. This difficulty was sometimes overcome by the omission of one consonant. Hence *likd'st* became *lik'st* and *lookd'st* became *look'st*. An example is: Thou refts me of my Lands. (Cym. III.3.103). The analogy of the plural may have combined with phonetic changes to produce forms like *would* in: I doe relent: what would thou more of man? (MWW II.2.26).

289. With the exception of verbs ending in -*t* or -*d*, the *e* of the weak preterite ending -*ed* is usually silent, and is often omitted in spelling, with or without an apostrophe. The unvoicing of final *d*, which comes to stand next to a voiceless consonant as a result of the syncope of *e*, is sometimes recorded in spelling, and we find *lackt* and *lack't* beside *lack'd*.

Weak verbs ending in -*t* are often unchanged in the preterite: I fast, and pray'd for their Intelligence (Cym. IV.2.347); There they hoyst us (Temp. 1.2.148). The preterite *spet* (Merch. 1.3.113) has *e* by shortening of the *ǣ* of OE *spǣtte*. The ME variant *spatte* gave *spat* after the loss of final -*e*, and from this the infinitive *spit* was formed on the analogy of *sit*, preterite *sat*.

290. The French loan-word *catch*, as we have seen (§279), has two preterites in English. *Catched* is formed on the pattern of native weak verbs; *caught* is formed on the analogy of *laught*, preterite of the obsolete verb *latch*. In Shakespeare *catched* is more common than *caught*.

291. Weak verbs ending in -*t* or -*d* are often unchanged in the past participle: Well hast thou acquit thee: (R3 V.5.5); I of Ladies most deject and wretched, (Ham. III.1.162); For tis the sport to have the enginer Hoist with his owne petar, (Ham. III.4.206). Beside these past participles we sometimes find new formations in -*ed*. We thus get

double forms, such as *blended* (Troil. IV.5.87) beside *blent* (TN 1.5.258), *builded* (Ant. III.2.30) beside *built* (R2 II.1.43), *girded* (Sonn. 12.7) beside *gyrt* (3H6 IV.8.20). The past participle *fet* is from OE *-fett*, pp. of *fetian*. It occurs in Shakespeare both alone and in the compounds *deep-fet* and *far-fet*: Whose blood is fet (H5 III.1.19); my deep-fet groans (2H6 II.4.33); Yorke, with all his farre-fet pollicie, (2H6 III.1.293). MnE *fetched* is a new formation from the infinitive. Some past participles in *-ate* are borrowed from Latin participles (§19) and occur in Shakespeare without the analogical *-ed* that they have in present-day English: when Degree is suffocate, (Troil. 1.3.125).

292. The participial prefix *y-* (OE *ge-*), as we have seen (§256), was already archaic at the time of Shakespeare and is occasionally found in the plays: it is ycliped, Thy Parke, (LLL 1.1.240); *Judas I am, ycliped Machabeus* (LLL V.2.601); Her words yclad with wise-domes Majesty, (2H6 1.1.33).

293. A few verbs call for separate comment.

Be. The usual forms of the present indicative are: *am, art, is, are,* beside the much less common *be, be'st, be, be.* Be'st or *beest* is often used after *if*: if thou beest *Stephano*, touch me, and speake to me: (Temp. II.2.105). *Be* is more common in the plural than in the singular: Be my Horsses ready? (Lear 1.5.37); There be some Sports are painfull; (Temp. III.1.1). The plural form *been* occurs only in one of the archaic prologues in *Pericles*: Where when men been, there's seldome ease, (II. Prol. 28).

The usual forms of the preterite indicative are *was, wert, was, were.* *Wert* is first recorded in the sixteenth century, replacing earlier *were* (OE *wǣre*). A less common Shakespearean form is *wast*, formed on the analogy of the 1 and 3 sg. pret. ind. Examples are: she was dead, ere thou wast borne. (R3 II.4.33; the Quartos have *wert* for *wast*); Thou wast ever an obstinate heretique (Ado 1.1.236).

294. *Dare* has 3 sg. pres. ind. *dare* beside *dares*: the little hang-man dare not shoot at him, (Ado III.2.9) beside: the folly of my soule dares not present it selfe (MWW II.2.253). In the sense 'issue a challenge' the 3 sg. is always *dares*: he dares us too't. (Ant. III.7.31). The preterite form *durst* is sometimes used with present meaning: My Lord, I love you; And durst commend a secret to your eare. (H8 V.1.16).

295. *Have.* In unaccented positions *have* is sometimes reduced to *ha'* or *a*, especially in colloquial prose: Come you shall ha't (AW

v.2.39); she might a bin a Grandam ere she died (LLL v.2.17).

296. *Hight* 'was called' was already archaic at the time of Shakespeare. It is used in the present tense in contexts which call for archaism, such as the Prologues in *Pericles* and the play within the play in *A Midsummer Night's Dream*. Examples are: this Maid Hight *Philoten*: (Per IV. Prol. 17); This grizy beast (which Lyon hight by name) (MND v.1.139); This childe of fancie that *Armado* hight, (LLL.I.1.171).

297. *Methought*. The second element of *methought* is from OE *þūhte*, preterite of *þyncan*, 'to seem', whereas *thought* in *I thought* is from OE *þōhte*, preterite of *þencan* 'to think'. *Methought* in Shakespeare sometimes has a final -*s*: Me thought that I had broken from the Tower (R3 1.4.9); me thoughts I did requoyle Twentie three yeeres, (WT 1.2.154).

298. *Ought* is historically the preterite of *owe* (OE *āgan*, pret. *āhte*). It is used once by Shakespeare in this sense: You ought him a thousand pound (1H4 III.3.156, Mistress Quickly). *Ought* in Shakespeare usually means 'should' and, like *should* but unlike present-day *ought*, it is used with an infinitive without the preposition *to*: you ought not walke (JC 1.1.3). *Owe* is often used in Shakespeare in the sense 'possess'; in this sense it is later replaced by *own* from OE *āgnian*.

299. *Quoth* (OE *cwæð* pret. of *cweðan*) is used in the 3 sg. as both present and preterite, and it is not always easy to say which tense is intended. The use in the present was probably due to a misunderstanding of the function of the final -*th*. The rounding of the vowel by the preceding *w* may have been encouraged by lack of stress. The verb is generally used mockingly or ironically. *Quoth* is probably in the present tense in: Did they, quoth you? (LLL IV.3.221).

Quotha 'said he' is used sarcastically in repeating something said by another character: The humour of it (quoth'a?) heere's a fellow frights English out of his wits. (MWW II.1.140). It is reduced to *ke-tha* in Per. II.1.83.

300. *Shall* is sometimes reduced colloquially to [s], probably as a regional feature: thou'se heare our counsell. (RJ 1.3.9); ice try whether your Costard, or my Ballow be the harder; (Lear IV.6.246).

301. *Will*. For the verb *will* Shakespeare has several forms with *o* or *oo*, representing a vowel rounded by the influence of the preceding *w*: Woo't weepe? Woo't fight? Woo't teare thy selfe? Woo't drinke up *Esile*, eate a Crocodile? (Ham. v.1.298).

302. *Wont* is in origin a past participle, from OE *gewunod*, ME *iwuned*. It was usually followed by the preposition *to*, and the final *t* of *wont* is probably due to assimilation. In much the same way, the *d* of *used* in *used to* [ju:stu] is generally unvoiced today. An example of the normal use of *wont* as a past participle is: Your worship was wont to tell me (Merch. ii.5.8). *Wont* is also used as a preterite and a present: *Talbot* is taken, whom we wont to feare: (1H6 i.2.14); I beare it on my shoulders, as a begger woont her brat: (Err. iv.4.37). A new participial adjective *wonted* was formed with a double participial ending: his wonted way (Ham. iii.1.41).

303. *Wot.* Several forms descended from OE *witan* 'to know' survive. They are not generally in colloquial use but seem to be used as rhetorical archaisms. *Wot* 1, 3 sg. has formed the basis of a new present participle *wotting*: the Gods themselves (Wotting no more then I) are ignorant. (WT iii.2.76). From the infinitive stem (OE *witan*) we have *to wit* 'that is to say' (AYL v.1.59) and *wittingly* 'knowingly' (Ham. v.1.13). The ME adjective *iwis* 'certain' (OE *gewiss*) was sometimes misunderstood to be a pronoun followed by a verb, as is suggested by the word-division: I wis your Grandam had a worser match. (R3 i.3.102).

CHAPTER 5

Word-Formation

𒀭𒀭𒀭𒀭𒀭𒀭

304. A study of the elements used in the formation of words is often the best way of arriving at the meaning of those words. There are in Shakespeare many unfamiliar words made up of familiar elements whose meaning is clear even though the reader may never have met the words before. Examples are nouns like *lewdsters*, adjectives like *cuckoldly* and *wittolly*, and adverbs like *invectively*. A study of word-formation can help in the interpretation even of familiar words if they are used with an unfamiliar meaning. Hamlet says: Ile have grounds More Relative than this: (II.2.632). Hilda Hulme[1] suggests that *relative* may have the meaning 'able to be related, having some chance of being believed'. To justify this interpretation she is able to quote the meaning of such words as *uncomprehensive* and *unexpressive*, containing the same suffix *-ive*.

305. *Backformation.* Compounds consisting of a noun followed by a verb are often backformations from compounds in which the noun was the object of the verb. Examples are: Ile fortune-tell you. (MWW IV.2.192); I must conicatch, (MWW I.3.33).

306. *Blends.* Examples of blend-words in Shakespeare are *Triumpherate* from *triumph* and *triumvirate* (Ant. III.6.29); *rebus'd* from *rebuke* and *abused* (Shrew I.2.7). *Me thoughts* (Merch. I.3.70) may be due to confusion of *methinks* and *methought*. *Extraught* (3H6 II.2.142) is a blend of *extract* and *raught*.

307. *Malapropisms.* There are innumerable examples of confusion between words that resemble each other in form. Such solecisms have since the time of Sheridan been called malapropisms; Shakespeare's chief offenders are Mistress Quickly and Dogberry, but almost any low-life or foolish character is liable to provide a few examples. Malapropisms are often devised as appurtenances to characterization, but their chief purpose is to provide humour. Like puns, they keep the spectator or reader alert in the attempt to

1. Op. cit., pp. 29–33.

recognize what is the word intended. The malapropisms in *The Merchant of Venice* are shared between Old Gobbo and his son. The latter has fairly straightforward examples, like *impertinent* for *pertinent* (II.2.145), *reproach* for *approach* (II.5.22), *exhibit* for *inhibit* (II.3.10) with *frutifie* for *certify* (II.2.142), which seems to be an imperfect attempt at *fructify*. Gobbo's examples need an intermediate stage since both form and meaning have undergone some change. He uses *infection* in the sense 'desire' (II.2.135) as the result of confusion with *affection*, and *defect* for 'gist' (II.2.150) by confusion with *effect*. Another play where malapropisms come thick and fast is *The Merry Wives of Windsor*. Examples are: *decrease* for *increase* (I.1.258, Slender), *dissolved* for *resolved* (I.1.162, Slender), *dissolutely* for *resolutely* (I.1.262, Slender), *detest* for *protest* (I.4.156, Mistress Quickly), *Allicholy* for *melancholy* (I.4.159, Mistress Quickly).

Malapropisms sometimes gain extra point because the word used by mistake is more appropriate than the word intended, as when Gobbo says: O heavens, this is my true begotten Father . . . I will trie confusions with him. (Merch. II.2.36).

One form of confusion takes a word not merely in the wrong sense but in one directly opposite to the correct meaning: I thanke God, I have as little patience as another man, and therefore I can be quiet. (LLL I.2.170).

308. *Refashioning.* In the course of the history of English some words have been refashioned to make them conform to the ultimate Latin etymology. Hence we find *Accompt* (R2 I.1.130). *Bankerout* (Err. IV.2.58) represents Fr. *banqueroute* (from It. *banca rotta*), which was later Latinized, in both spelling and pronunciation, to *bankrupt*. *Cry havoc* is the form which OF *crier havot* assumes in English. It was originally the signal to plunder, and it is used more generally in Shakespeare as an incentive to battle and slaughter. The best-known occurrence is its use by Antony: Cry havocke, and let slip the Dogges of Warre, (JC III.1.273).

PREFIXES

309. There was a need for new prefixes in Elizabethan times, since many of the prefixes handed down from Old English or Old French had disappeared or been reduced beyond recognition from lack of stress, as in *sport* from OF *disport*. Other prefixes had fallen

together: OE *a-*, *an-* and *of-* had all fallen together as *a-*. The very common OE prefix *ge-* had generally disappeared, though traces of it are to be found in unexpected places even today, as in *handywork* (OE *handgeweorc*), and *enough* (OE *genōh*). Some Old English prefixes have been replaced by adverbs, in accordance with the tendency for English to become a more analytical language. For example, OE *tōteran* has been replaced by *tear up*. One reason for the disappearance of the prefix *to-* may be the growing use of the preposition *to* as a mark of the infinitive.

310. The following prefixes call for comment:

a- is an unaccented variant of the preposition *on* or *an*. Many adverbs are formed from nouns by the addition of this prefix. Examples from Shakespeare now archaic or obsolete include *a-height*, 'on high', *a-high*, 'aloft', *a-row* 'one after the other'. These words are today generally replaced by adverbial phrases introduced by *on*, such as *on high*. Editors have sometimes replaced the prefix *a-* by *o'* as in the First Folio's: when I am a-horsebacke, (1H4 II.3.101). The prefix *a-* is sometimes the reduced form of *of*, as in *akin*, *adown*, *anew*. On the analogy of forms like *anew*, we sometimes find *a-* compounded with adjectives as in *a good* 'in good earnest' (TGV IV.4.170), *a cold* 'cold' (Lear III.4.61), *a-hungry* (MWW 1.1.277).

be- is an unaccented variant of the preposition *by*. It is used in verbs instead of a preposition to make an intransitive verb transitive, as in *behowl* 'howl at', *bespeak* 'speak to', *bemock* 'mock at', *bemoan* 'moan about'. It can be used to describe deprivation, as in *behead*, *bereave*, or to form verbs from nouns or adjectives, as in *bemonster*, *besot*, *befortune*. It is used with nouns to mean 'to give the name of', as in *bewhore* 'to call somebody a whore', *bemadam*. There are several pairs of verbs, one with and the other without the prefix *be-* that have similar meanings: *(be)friend* 'to favour', *(be)get* 'to procreate', *(be)dim* 'to darken'. Many words with the prefix *be-* are now obsolete, such as the verbs *belock* 'enclose', *bemoil* 'bedraggle', and the participial adjective *betumbled* 'disordered by tossing'.

de-. Intensive prefixes are sometimes liable to be misinterpreted as negatives; it is to avoid ambiguity of this kind that today *inflammable* is tending to be replaced by *flammable*. The prefix *de-* has undergone a similar fate, and *demerit* is used in Shakespeare in two opposite senses. In *Othello* 1.2.22 it has its older meaning 'merits, deserts', but in *Macbeth* IV.3.226 it means 'offences, sins' when Macduff blames himself for the death of his children: Not for their owne demerits, but for mine Fell slaughter on their soules.

dis- is used as a negative prefix, as in *discandy* 'to dissolve, melt', *disquantity* 'reduce the size of'. *Discovery* is often used in the sense 'uncovering, disclosure', as in: so shall my anticipation prevent your discovery (Ham. II.2.304). Although the prefix is found chiefly in Latin and French loan-words, it is occasionally found joined to native stems, as in *disbench, disburthen*.

en- is often confused with Latin *in-* and occasionally with English *in-*, giving pairs of forms like *enquire* and *inquire*, *engaged* and *ingag'd*. *En-* is used with nouns and adjectives to mean 'to put a person or thing in a specified situation', either literally or metaphorically, as in *endanger, enthrall, enskied, engaol, entomb, entame*. *En-* is sometimes used to change a noun into a verb as in *enwheel* 'to encircle'. Sometimes it modifies the meaning of a verb, as in *entwist* 'to twist around'. Sometimes it seems to have no other function than the metrical one of providing an extra unstressed syllable, as in: He may enguard his dotage with their powres, (Lear I.4.349).

enter- is sometimes confused with the Latin prefix *inter-*, from which it is derived, as in *enterview, enterchange*.

for- is often spelt *fore-*. Examples are *foredo* 'destroy', *foreslow* 'delay', *forespeak* 'gainsay', *forewearied* 'wearied out'.

mis- was a pejorative prefix in Old English, as in *misdēd*, and it has kept this sense, as in *misgovern*. It is often used with French loan-words, as in *misreport* 'to slander', and it sometimes replaces the OF prefix *mes-*, as in *mischief* (OF *meschief*).

out- is used in the sense 'exceed, surpass', with verbs resulting from the functional conversion of nouns. Such conversion is often found only in the compound, not in the simple word. Examples are *out-paramour, out-tongue, out-Herod*. This prefix is used to convert nouns into verbs, meaning to perform to excess an action implicit in the noun, as when Jessica (Merch. V.1.23) uses *out-night* 'to outdo in mentioning nights'.

to-. There is often some uncertainty about the function of *to*. When Mrs Page describes her plan to punish Falstaff, she says: Then let them all encircle him about, And Fairy-like to pinch the uncleane Knight; (MWW IV.4.56). It is uncertain whether the verb is *to-pinch* 'pinch thoroughly' or whether *to* is merely the sign of the infinitive. In the line 'Now the Gods to blesse your Honour'

(Per. IV.6.22), *to* is an intensive prefix and *to-blesse* means 'to bless entirely'.

un-. The native prefix *un-* often varies with Latin and French *in-* as a negative prefix, as in *uncapable, uncivil, uncertain* beside *incertain, incivil. In-* is generally used only with words of Romance origin, *un-* with words of any origin. Only *un-* is used with participles (as in *unwound*) or nouns (as in *unrest*). In dialects *un-* is often found where Standard English has *in-* or *im-*, as in *unpossible*. Sometimes the variation of the prefix provides a useful way of modifying the meaning of a word. *Infirm* has come to be used of physical disability, but the use of a different prefix allows the creation of *unfirme* in the sense 'fickle' (TN II.4.36) and 'weak with few supporters' (2H4 I.3.73). Shakespeare has more than six hundred words beginning with *un-*, half of them occurring only once. They often express concisely ideas that need a dozen words or so if they are paraphrased. For example, *unfoole* means 'to take from someone the reproach of being a fool' (MWW IV.2.113). When *un-* is prefixed to a noun, it converts it into a verb, adding the sense 'remove', as in *unhair, unsex, unchild*. When it is prefixed to a verb, it reverses an action, as in *unshout* 'not to shout', *unbuild* 'to pull down', *uncharge* 'to acquit of guilt'.

up- is used as a verbal prefix to express ideas which today are expressed by an adverb following a verb, as in *uprous'd, up-fill*.

SUFFIXES

311. When we compare Elizabethan words with those of the present day, we find three categories: those in which there has been a change of suffix, those in which a suffix has apparently been lost, and those in which one has been added. The first category needs special care because often the word is still in use today with its Elizabethan suffix but with a different meaning. Examples are *intelligent* 'intelligible', *credent* 'credible' but also 'credulous', *affecting* 'affected', *respective* 'regardful', *expediently* 'expeditiously'. Examples of words which have either lost their suffix or never had one, although they would have one today, are *cess* 'cessation', *attent* 'attentive', *illume* 'illuminate', *unthrift* 'good-for-nothing', *like* 'likely'. When Shakespeare speaks of 'the haught Northumberland' (3H6 II.1.169), it is not true to say that he has dropped the suffix of *haughty*, since *haught* existed beside *haughty* in Middle English.

Today we often use suffixes to convert one part of speech into another where Shakespeare would have used the same word by functional shift without any suffix. He uses *solicit*, *consult* and *expect* as nouns. Other examples are: *make prepare for Warre* (3H6 IV.1.131); *deepe exclaimes* (R3 1.2.53).

Some words have two suffixes today, but Elizabethan freedom in word-formation made it possible for them to be used with a single suffix. We thus have *child-nesse* (WT 1.2.170), since -*ness* could then be used to form abstract nouns from nouns as well as from adjectives. Examples of words which have a suffix in Elizabethan English where none is felt to be necessary today are *recordation* 'remembrance', *importance* 'import', *neglection* 'neglect'.

Many of the words containing prefixes and suffixes are very rare or even nonce-words, since, once the prefixes and suffixes were known and the patterns for their use established, any speaker or writer could create new words at will.

312. New suffixes can arise by misdivision. From *front* we have *frontelet*, with two suffixes. Then -*let* is regarded as a suffix and is used to form new words like *droplet* and *martlet*. We find blends, like *fishify*, in which the second element of *justify* has been transferred to another word. Suffixes are sometimes confused, as in *magnanimious*, *dexteriously*, *jealious* on the analogy of such words as *envious*. *Ingenuous* is often used where we should use *ingenious*.

313. The following suffixes call for comment:

-*able* is used to form adjectives from nouns, as in *peaceable* 'peaceful'. It is sometimes pejorative, as in *serviceable* 'officious'. The use of the suffix in a passive sense may have been aided by the influence of the adjective *able*, as in *bearable*. *Comfortable* is used in an active sense. It means 'affording help' as in: be comfortable to my mother (AW 1.1.86).

-*al* is used to form adjectives from nouns or adjectives. The adjectives so formed are sometimes used as nouns, as *rival*.

-*ance* varies with -*ence*. Double suffixes are formed by the addition of OF -*ie*. We thus get four suffixes, -*ance*, -*ence*, -*ancy* and -*ency*, all interchangeable, though one suffix tends to become established in a particular word. We find *persistence* beside *persistency* and *incidencie* 'happening, occurrence'.

-*ant*, the French present participial suffix, is used in *aydant* 'helpful' (Lear IV.4.17) and *conspirant* 'conspiring' (Lear V.3.135).

-*ate* is derived from the Latin participial ending. Words containing this suffix could be used as both infinitives and participles. Examples are *evitate* 'to avoid', *ruinate* 'to ruin'; *captivate* 'imprisoned', *emulate* 'envious', *gratulate* 'satisfactory'. See also §§ 19, 291.

-*ed* is used to form adjectives from adjectives and nouns. When the base is a noun, the meaning of the adjective so formed is 'provided with (the noun)' as in: grav'd in the hollow ground (R2 III.2.140). Other examples are: *Lorded* 'exalted' (Temp. I.2.97), *stranger'd* 'made a stranger' (Lear I.1.207), *leane-look'd* 'lean-looking' (R2 II.4.11). Adjectives formed by the addition of -*ed* to an adjective mean 'made (the adjective)': *feebled* 'enfeebled' (John V.2.146). Often the addition of -*ed* has little effect on the meaning of an adjective: *azur'd* 'azure' (Temp. V.1.43). The suffix -*ed* could be equivalent to that of -*able*: Inestimable Stones, unvalewed Jewels, (R3 I.4.27). Here *unvalewed* means 'invaluable'.

-*en* is used to form adjectives from nouns. It usually means 'made of', as in *brazen, earthen, golden, leaden, leathern, silken, threaden*, but sometimes it means 'covered with', as in *woollen* (applied to bagpipes, Merch. IV.1.56) and *Twiggen-Bottle* (Oth. II.3.152). Many of these adjectives are used metaphorically, as *hempen homespuns* 'coarse people', *brazen gates*, 'impregnable gates', *leaden slumber* 'heavy sleep', and *silken tearmes* 'delicate language'. Today adjectives in -*en* tend to be replaced by nouns in apposition, as when we speak of *gold coins*.

-*er* had three main sources: (1) OE -*ere*, (2) AN -*er* corresponding to OF -*ier*, (3) AN -*ur* corresponding to OF -*our*, Fr. -*eur*. There are several hundred nouns with this suffix in Shakespeare. They indicate dwellings (*villager*), occupations (*pulpiter, sworder*), or activities (*flatterer*). The suffix is doubled in *fruiterer* (Fr. *fruitier*), *caterer* (AN *acatour*). Shakespeare has *poulter* beside the present-day *poulterer*, with double suffix.

-*ess* is less common than today. Shakespeare uses *heir, Jew, priest* and *tiger* as feminine nouns, and he does not use the suffix -*ess* with any of them.

-*et* is found in *goblet, billet*, which lost their original diminutive force.

-*ful* 'full of' is very common. There is often a difference from modern usage in that -*ful* could have either an active or a passive meaning. *Fearful* could mean either 'full of fear' or 'causing fear'. *Dreadfull secrecie* means 'secrecy full of dread' (Ham. I.2.206).

-hood is used to form abstract nouns from nouns and, less often, from adjectives. It describes a state, as in *likely-hoode*, *child-hoode* or a group, as in *brotherhood*. The variant suffix *-head* goes back to OE *-hǣdu*.

-ic varies with *-ics*, and additional variants are provided by the use of the spelling *ck* for *c*. We find *Rhetoricke* and *Musicke* beside *Mathematickes* and *Metaphysickes* (all in Shrew I.1.35–7).

-ie and *-y* are used to form adjectives from nouns: *unheedy haste* (MND I.1.237), *Battie-wings* (MND III.2.365).

-ify is used chiefly with stems of foreign origin, to make verbs from adjectives or nouns, as in *amplify*, *beautify*, *stupify*, but it is used with a native stem in *fishified*.

Latin *-ile* had lost its *i* in French to give the *-le* which appears in *humble* and *subtle*. The suffix *-ile*, found in *facile* and *civil*, is a learned borrowing from Latin. It is often spelt *-ill* in Shakespeare, as in *civill* and *subtill*.

-ing. The OE suffix *-ung* died out in Middle English, but the less common variant *-ing* survived in a large number of verbal nouns, such as *building*, which became identical in form with the present participle. Plurals of verbal nouns in *-ing* are not uncommon in Shakespeare: *weepings*, *lamentings*, *prattlings*, *visitings*. The suffix *-ing* is also used to form verbal adjectives, where it varied with *-ive*, as in *persisting*, beside *persistive*.

-ise is used to form verbs from nouns and adjectives, as in *sluggardised* 'made lazy'.

-ish is used to form adjectives from nouns, as in *sottish*, or to tone down adjectives, as in *bluish*. It is often used pejoratively as in *womanish* beside *womanly*, *childish* beside *childlike*.

-ist is used of a person who follows a particular occupation or who holds certain ideas, as in *Brownist*, *votarist*, *statist*.

-ite describes a person from a particular place or belonging to a particular party. It is generally used disparagingly: *Nazarite*, *Ottamittes*.

-ive, added to participial endings, means 'tending to, inclined to', as in *speculative*, *submissive*. In Shakespeare the suffix sometimes has a passive meaning: th' insuppressive Mettle of our Spirits (JC II.1.133). The faire, the chaste, and unexpressive shee (AYL III.2.10).

-kin is a diminutive suffix, probably of Dutch origin, first found in the thirteenth century in proper names like *Wilekin*. It occurs in Shakespeare in *canakin* 'drinking-vessel', *jerkin* 'short coat', *malkin*

'kitchen maid' and in the corruption *by'r lakin* 'by our Lady'.

-less. Many adjectives in *-less* had a passive meaning, which they have since lost: *a carelesse Trifle* 'a trifle not worth bothering about' (Macb. 1.4.12), *sightlesse Curriors of the Ayre* 'invisible couriers' (Macb. 1.7.23).

-ling[1] is a diminutive suffix, as in *eanling* 'newly-born lamb', *fondling* 'darling', *firstling*.

-ling[2] is a suffix used to form adverbs from adjectives found in *darkling* 'in the dark'. In *headlong* and *flat-long* 'with the side of the blade', the *-ling* has been replaced by *-long*.

-ly is both an adjectival and an adverbial suffix (OE *-lic* adj., *-lice* adv.), and many words in *-ly* can be either adjectives or adverbs: *cleanly, cowardly*. When *-ly* came to be regarded as an adverbial ending, adjectives in *-ly* tended to be replaced by adjectives with other suffixes: *loathly* has been replaced by *loathsome*, *traitorly* by *treacherous*; *minutely* 'continual' has passed out of use in this sense. New formations in *-like* are found beside older formations in *-ly*: *life-like* beside *lively*. The voiceless *f* in *life-like* shows it to be a new formation. The suffix *-ly* is sometimes used to form adverbs from nouns: *angerly, hungerly*.

-meal, an adverbial suffix, goes back to an Old English dative plural in *-mǣlum*. It is found in *Limb-meale* 'limb from limb' (Cym. II.4.148), *by ynch-meale* 'little by little' (Temp. II.2.3).

-ment (from Fr. *-ment*) is used to form abstract nouns from verbs, as in *enticement, engrossment*, 'accumulation'. Some of Shakespeare's nouns in *-ment* are now obsolete: *allayment* 'mitigation', *cloyment* 'surfeit', *insultment* 'contemptuous triumph'. The suffix is often combined with a native first element, *bodement, bewitchment, blastment, fleshment* 'excitement', *fitment, strewment*.

Latin *-or* varies with OF *-our*, as in *labor* beside *labour*. Similarly *audito(u)r, creato(u)r*. It replaces earlier *-er* in *bachelor* and *sailor*.

-ous. There is some confusion of the suffixes *-ous*, *-ious* and *-uous*: My ingenuous Instrument (Cym. IV.2.187); What? that an Eele is ingenuous. (LLL I.2.28); Dexteriously, good Madona (TN I.5.68).

-ry is a double suffix formed from ONF *-er* followed by *ie*, as in *archerie*. It was then extended as an independent suffix to other words, such as *outlawry*.

-s, an adverbial suffix, is found in *otherwhiles* (1H6 I.2.7); *Come thy wayes* (TN II.5.1); *other gates* 'in another way' (TN V.1.193): *'Tis but early dayes* (Troil. IV.5.12). There are many pairs of adverbs, one

with and the other without the -s ending: *alway(s), backward(s), homeward(s). Eftsoons* 'by and by' has -s by analogy with such adverbs as *whiles*.

-ship, from OE *-scipe*, describes a state or a quality, as in *foxship* 'qualities of a fox', *mistership, moorship*, used in derision as a title when Iago describes himself as 'his Mooreships Auntient' (Oth. I.1.33).

-ster, from OE *-estre*, may have been originally feminine, but it seems more likely that it had become a depreciatory suffix. Most nouns formed with it in Shakespeare are used pejoratively: *gamester* 'gambler', *lewdster* 'libertine', *whitster* 'bleacher', *whipster* 'contemptible fellow', *tapster, youngster*.

-ure is used to derive nouns from verbs; the nouns then describe an action, a particular instance of an action, or its result, as in *departure, creature*. Many of these nouns are now obsolete: *expressure* 'expression', *insisture* 'persistency', *tainture* 'defilement'. The suffix is sometimes weakened to *-er* in Elizabethan English: *wafter, climater*.

COMPOUND WORDS

314. Shakespeare made great use of compound epithets, which express ideas picturesquely and concisely. Examples are *oak-cleaving thunderbolts, pity-pleading eyes, half-witted lord*. Some compound words have more than two elements, although the elements are not always linked by hyphens, as in: the alwaies winde-obeying deepe (Err. 1.1.63); The too and fro conflicting wind and raine, (Lear III.1.11). An apparent giant compound, 'A needy-hollow-ey'd-sharpe-looking-wretch' (Err. v.1.240) is not a genuine compound, since it can easily be split up into shorter words. R. A. Foakes, the editor of the New Arden edition of the play, suggests that the hyphens in the First Folio may represent Shakespeare's deliberate compression of the line into one breathless word.

315. *Substantival Compounds.* We often find two nouns joined together in such a way that one defines the other; usually the first defines the second. They may be either written as two separate words, or hyphened: Region Kites (Ham. II.2.607); *Caines* Jaw-bone (Ham. v.1.87). These compounds have to be distinguished from another type where the two elements are of equal status: but my Unckle Father, and Aunt Mother are deceiv'd. (Ham. II.2.394); This signior *Junior* gyant dwarfe, don *Cupid*, (LLL III.1.182).

One category of compounds, which tend to be used colloquially and disparagingly, consists of an adjective followed by a noun: *thick-lips*, *brazen-face*, *smooth-pates*. Capulet abuses Juliet as a *tallow-face*, and Falstaff is a *fatguts*. Such compounds are also used attributively, as a *false-heart traitor*, *curl'd pate ruffians*.

Compound nouns made up of a verb followed by its object are very common. These too tend to be derogatory: Some carry-tale, some please-man, some slight Zanie, Some mumble-newes, (LLL v.2.463). Other examples are *lack-love*, *pick-thanks*, *tell-tale*, *kill-courtesy*, *lack-brain*. Compounds of this kind are sometimes used attributively: *the hold-door trade*, *lack-lustre eye*. Many compounds of this kind are used as proper names like *Martext* or *Tearsheet*, or as nicknames like *my lord Lackbeard*.

The use of prepositions with compounds may sometimes seem strange today, but there are present-day parallels. *At over-night* (AW III.4.23) is similar in construction to Modern English *in the afternoon*. The first element of a compound noun may be an adverb: so that here men are punisht for before breach of the Kings Lawes, in now the Kings Quarrell: (H5 IV.1.177); *Harryes backe returne* (H5 v.Prol.41).

316. *Adjectival Compounds*. In the relationship between the two elements of a compound a preposition is often to be understood: *love-sick* means 'sick with love' and *threadbare* means 'bare to the thread'. The second element of an adjectival compound often has the suffix *-ed*, as in *ditch-delivered* 'born in a ditch', *time-honoured* 'honoured over a long period of time', *grim-looked*, *great-sized*, *long-legged*, *two-legged*, *slow-gaited*, *nimble-footed*, *big-boned*. These compounds sometimes exist side by side with similar compounds made up of an adjective and a noun: *a mad-braine rudesby* (Shrew III.2.10) beside *this mad-brain'd bridegroome* (Shrew III.2.165), *a false-heart Traitor* (2H6 v.1.143) beside *a false-hearted Rogue* (Troil. v.1.94). When the second element is a present participle, the first is often its direct object, as in *cloud-kissing*, *ear-piercing*, *love-lacking*. One type of compound consists of two adjectives of similar meaning which strengthen each other: *heady-rash* 'impetuous', *wilful-opposite* 'stubborn'. In such compounds the first element sometimes expresses a comparison: *rocky-hard*, *childish-foolish*. The two adjectives which make up a compound may be opposites: *odd-even*, *fortunate-unhappy*, *dumb-discursive*. It is sometimes uncertain whether we should regard a pair of words as a compound or as two adjectives, the first of

which is used adverbially: old Northumberland, Lyes crafty sicke. (2H4 Induction 36); Horrible steepe. (Lear IV.6.3).

Short phrases, especially those containing participles, are often compounded into epithets: my too much changed Sonne (Ham. II.2.36). A Jewell in a ten times barr'd up Chest, (R2 I.1.180), a world-without-end bargaine (LLL V.2.799).

CHAPTER 6

Pronunciation, Spelling and Punctuation

𝕾𝕾𝕾𝕾𝕾𝕾

PRONUNCIATION

317. Two questions are frequently asked about Shakespearean pronunciation. The first is how can we possibly know how the English language was pronounced at a time several centuries before mechanical recording of sound became possible? The second is what use is such knowledge? The answer to the second question must be primarily that if we are to talk of the melody of Shakespeare's verse, it is at least interesting to know how it sounded to him. When we are considering the validity of an emendation, it is useful to know which words were pronounced alike or nearly alike. Some knowledge of Shakespearean pronunciation is essential if we are to understand his versification. Finally, such knowledge is necessary if we are to understand Shakespeare's frequent examples of word-play. The question how we are to obtain the knowledge does not admit of a simple answer. We can establish probabilities by piecing together several different kinds of evidence. The chief evidence is that of spelling, considered in relation to the earlier and later history of English sounds in the light of general phonetic probability. We also have the evidence of rhymes and puns in Shakespeare's plays and the testimony of grammarians who, during Shakespeare's lifetime, described English pronunciation for the benefit of either Englishmen or foreigners. Metre does not give us information on many points, but the information that it does give in such matters as stress and silent letters is relatively reliable.

318. *Evidence of Spelling.* The instability of Elizabethan spelling is both an advantage and a disadvantage to a modern reader who wants to use it as evidence. It is an advantage because occasional spellings provide useful evidence of pronunciation which cannot be provided once spelling has become traditional. It is a disadvantage because we cannot assume that the spelling of the early printed

texts was that actually used by Shakespeare. An Elizabethan printer thought it no part of his duty to record the author's own spelling or pronunciation.

Occasional spellings are usually phonetic. Though the spelling is occasional, it betrays the usual pronunciation of the man who indulges in it. It is important to distinguish between phonetic spellings and phonetic doublets, where a difference of spelling reflects a difference of pronunciation. We have no direct evidence of the extent to which compositors interfered with Shakespeare's spelling, but we have some evidence about the practice of the time. Printers did not as a rule introduce their own eccentricities of spelling into the author's text. They made many mistakes, some of which were corrected by the proof-reader, but their deliberate interference was generally to preserve traditional spellings. The printer was more conservative than the author. Hence when we find eccentric spellings, they are more likely to be due to the author than to the printer.

319. *Metrical Evidence*. Many examples quoted of metrical irregularity are really examples of varieties of Elizabethan pronunciation. There are two main types of metrical irregularity: a tendency to treat two unaccented words as a single word and the shift of stress from one syllable to another. The elision of a vowel is sometimes proved by a rhyme, such as *foot*: *too't* or *note*: *know't*.

The evidence of rhymes is not very useful because of the frequency of assonance and inexact rhymes. By the sixteenth century a rhyming tradition had developed that was to some extent independent of contemporary pronunciation. Thus we find eye-rhymes, like *love* and *prove*, which may reveal the pronunciation of a former age. Rhymes in Shakespeare may be genuine, but they may also be regional or social variants, or eye-rhymes that would have been genuine rhymes only in the pronunciation of conservative speakers. The rhyme *coold*: *should* (VA 385) is genuine, because in Shakespeare's time an old-fashioned pronunciation [ʃuːld], existed beside [ʃʌd].

320. *Internal Evidence*. Apart from the evidence provided by spelling and metre, there are occasional pieces of internal evidence about pronunciation from the plays. One often-quoted example is Holofernes's criticism of Armado's pronunciation in *Love's Labour's Lost* (v.1.15). Although this criticism is included in a literary work, it is of a piece with the evidence of the early grammarians.

Holofernes is as precise as any of the sixteenth-century grammarians. He complains that Armado does not pronounce the *b* in *doubt* and *debt*, that the *l* in *calf* and *half* has been vocalized to *u*, and that he does not pronounce the *gh* in *neighbour*. He regards such pronunciations as 'abhominable'. These comments show that both the pronunciations that he dislikes and those that he recommends were current in the late sixteenth century, and they show that Holofernes, like most sixteenth-century grammarians, was fond of spelling pronunciations and hostile to sound changes that have since come to be generally accepted.

321. *Evidence of Early Grammarians.* The early grammars which provide evidence of Elizabethan pronunciation are of two kinds. One group is the work of foreigners who are interested in teaching their own language to Englishmen or English to their fellow-countrymen. They point out the nearest foreign equivalents of English sounds. The other kind of grammar is the work of Englishmen. They rely too much on ancient authority and they are too much influenced by spelling, but they often provide pointers to changes that were taking place even though they are liable to describe these changes as errors which they advise their readers to avoid. Some of them are spelling reformers.

The early grammar of most use to a student of Shakespeare's language is Alexander Gil's *Logonomia Anglica* (1619). Gil was headmaster of St Paul's School, London, and a classical scholar. He does not mention Shakespeare among his literary authorities, and this is not surprising; an academic like Gil would attach little importance to popular drama. As an academic, Gil was conservative, influenced by Latin and written English. For example, he reports the pronunciation of a fricative in *night* and *light*, though it had probably disappeared in pronunciation.

UNACCENTED SYLLABLES

322. Our knowledge of Elizabethan accentuation is mainly derived from the practice of the poets, and this was not necessarily the same as the colloquial usage of the time. In French and Latin loan-words the chief stress was generally on or near the final syllable, whereas in native words it was generally on the first syllable. Variation arises from a conflict between these two stress systems. In order to fit in with the metre, loan-words originally stressed on

their final syllable may be assumed to shift their stress to the first syllable when immediately followed by a stressed syllable, as in *lick absurd pompe* (Ham. III.2.65, Q2 reading), though probably there were many compromises involving level stress and inter-mediate stages between accented and unaccented syllables.

There is some variation of stress in native words. Compound words are stressed on the first or second syllable according to the stress on the following word, Cf. *day-light* (MND III.2.427 and III.2.433), *mid-night* (Temp. I.2.128) and *midnight* (Temp. I.2.228). Nouns, adjectives and verbs with the prefix *un-* show variation of stress, as in '*unkind* (RJ V.3.145) and *un'kinde* (Err. IV.2.21). *Antique*, spelt *anticke*, always has the stress on the first syllable; the modern pronunciation is due to the influence of the stress of other French loan-words, or the word may be a later re-borrowing from French. *July* (from Latin *Julii*) preserved its original Latin stress on the first syllable up to the time of Dr Johnson.

In native words verbal prefixes were generally unaccented, as in *forgive, arise*. This tendency was reinforced by the borrowing of many French words with chief stress on the ending and with no cognate noun. Hence we get the tendency, which survives today, to have disyllabic words stressed on the first syllable when they are nouns and on the second when they are verbs, as in *accent, rebel, increase*. Analogy has sometimes interfered with the operation of this tendency: *delay, escape, reproach* have stress on the final syllable even when used as nouns, by analogy with the verbs, while *forfeit* and *promise* have stress on the first syllable, even when verbs. Adjectives in *-ic* have the accent on the penultimate syllable on the analogy of adjectives ending in *-ical*, as in *rheu'matic*, earlier '*rheumatic*.

There are many passages in Shakespeare where the metre shows that the recessive tendency in accent has not gone so far as it has today. An example is: Why thy Canoniz'd bones Hearsed in death, (Ham. I.4.47), where *Canoniz'd* has its chief stress on the second syllables.

The practice of obscuring the vowels of unaccented syllables, so frequent in present-day English, was already fully established in the sixteenth century. The play on *dollor-dolour* (Temp. II.1.18) would have been impossible two hundred years earlier.

323. There was, indeed, much variation in the treatment of vowels of unaccented syllables. Thus a word like *temperate* might be either disyllabic or trisyllabic. Very often a syncopated vowel

is omitted in spelling, as in *boystrous* (Ham. III.3.22). The omission is sometimes indicated by an apostrophe, as in *sland'rous* (R3 I.2.96), *desp'rate* (AW V.3.178). Evidence of this kind is ignored by most modern editors, who silently insert apostrophes or expand contracted forms. We cannot be sure that loss of a vowel is always recorded in spelling, and modern readers, because of their reliance on spelling, are generally reluctant to admit syncope. The contraction of *I am* to *I'm* is very rare in Shakespearean spelling, though metre suggests that it was fairly common in pronunciation. Attempts have been made to use the variation between *them* and *'em* as evidence of authorship, but we have to remember that a printer would often normalize *'em* to *them*. Scansion is the best guide to the loss of unaccented vowels. The vowel of the second syllable of a compound word is often weakened and there may also be a loss of consonants, and the etymology of the word is consequently disguised. Examples are *a Cot-sal-man* 'a Cotswold man' (2H4 III.2.20), *Berard* 'bearward' (2H6 V.1.149).

Unaccented vowels were generally reduced to [ə] or [i]. Shakespeare sometimes has [i] where we have [ə], as in *taffety* (AW II.2.24). The interchange of *o* and *a* in *Ryalta* (Merch. I.3.20), *Gondilo* (Merch. II.8.8) and *stanzo* (AYL II.5.16) suggests that both *o* and *a* were reduced to [ə].

In pretonic syllables *i* alternates with *e*, as in *indure* (Ado II.1.362), *dispise* (Macb. IV.3.201), *enterview* (H5 V.2.27).

In unaccented positions *have* is often reduced to *a* or *ha*: Durst thou a lookt upon him, being awake? (MND III.2.69).

Pronunciation of the ending -*ture* as -*ter* is now a vulgarism but it was not so regarded in the seventeenth century. *Construe* was pronounced *conster* as late as the nineteenth century (see OED s.v. *construe*). Examples are *venter* (1H4 V.1.101), *conster* (Shrew III.1.31).

324. The Elizabethan fluctuation between a colloquial and a conservative pronunciation is to be seen in the treatment of endings like -*ion* and -*iage*. In everyday speech these endings were usually monosyllabic but the older pronunciation with syllabic *i* lingered on sometimes, as in *carriage* (RJ I.4.93), *Souldier* (JC IV.1.28), *patience* (AYL I.3.80).

There is some evidence from the metre of a tendency to insert a parasitic [ə] between two consonants one of which is *r* or *l*, as in the present-day substandard *umberella*. Examples are *Countrey* (TN

1.2.21), *Dowglas* (1H4 v.2.33). Sometimes the apparently parasitic [ə] is etymologically justified, as in *wondrous* (MND v.1.59), *Marshall* (1H4 IV.4.2).

325. Various forms of the verbs *be, have* and *will* are contracted with a preceding pronoun as in *I'd, thou'st*. An unusual contraction is Lady Capulet's *thou'se* 'thou shalt' (RJ 1.3.10), and a dialectal contraction is Edgar's *ice* 'I shall' (Lear IV.6.246). The pronouns *it* and *his* often lose their vowels when unaccented, as in *speak't againe* (Lear II.4.258), *in's garden house* (Meas. v.1.229). *It is* is often contracted to *'tis* in Shakespeare, whereas today it is usually contracted to *it's*.

326. *Aphesis.* The loss of an initial vowel or syllable has been common in English since long before the time of Shakespeare. The apostrophe is only occasionally used in the First Folio to indicate the loss. Examples are: *'gainst* 'against', *haviour* 'behaviour', *noyance* 'annoyance', *pear* 'appear', *quest* 'inquest', *rouse* 'carouse', *stonish* 'astonish'. Sometimes aphesis creates doublets with different meanings like *squire* and *esquire*, *fence* and *defence*.

327. *Syncope.* The loss of an unaccented syllable from the middle of a word is one of the most strongly marked features of colloquial English in the sixteenth and seventeenth centuries. There were often variants, one with and the other without syncope, and either form could be used to suit the demands of metre. Some of these variants have survived as doublets like *fancy* and *fantasy*. Syncope is sometimes indicated by spelling but not always. It is especially likely to take place when the vowel in question is followed by a liquid or a nasal, because these consonants form easily pronounceable groups when preceded by another consonant. Examples are: *parlous* 'perilous', *count'nance* 'countenance', and *ignomy* from *ignominy* with syncope of *i* and assimilation of *mn* followed by simplification of the resultant double consonant. The loss of a vowel may be accompanied by the loss of a consonant: *shall* is contracted to *s* or *se* in Lear IV.6.246, where it is a provincialism, and in RJ 1.3.9, where it is a colloquialism.

328. *Apocope* is the loss of an unaccented syllable at the end of a word. Examples are *the Capels Monument* (for *Capulet*, RJ v.3.127), *Couze* 'cousin' (1H4 III.1.88). A common type of apocope is the elision of the final vowel of unaccented particles like *by, to* and *the*, when followed by a word beginning with a vowel, as in *t'unsettle* (Lear III.4.167).

VOWELS

329. ME *a*. The fronting of [ɑ] to [æ], which began in the fifteenth century, was completed by the end of the sixteenth. There are a few *e*-spellings, like Mistress Quickly's *exion* (2H4 II.1.30).

The lengthening of *a* before [f, s, θ] began in the sixteenth century; the vowel was usually front at the time of Shakespeare.

Before a nasal followed by a voiced consonant many ME dialects had *o* instead of *a*. This *o* occasionally survives, as in *Stronds* (1H4 I.1.4).

The rounding influence of *w* on a following *a*, seen today in such words as *swan* and *was*, is not generally found in Shakespeare. *Swan* rhymes with *can* (*Phoenix and Turtle* 15) and *was* with *glasse* (Luc. 1764).

In some French loan-words *a* varies with *au* before *n* followed by a consonant, as in *auncient, daunger*, beside *ancient, danger*. By analogy the *au* spread to the native word *aunswer* beside *answer*. Forms with *u* are beginning to be less common by the time of Shakespeare.

In the sixteenth century *u* developed between *a* and a following *l*, and the *l* then disappeared. In present-day English the [au] has normally become [ɔ:], as in *walk*, but when the *l* is followed by a labial consonant, the vowel has become [ɑ:], as in *half* and *calm*.

330. ME [e] remained, sometimes spelt *ea* on the analogy of shortenings like *head*, as in *seaventie* (AYL II.3.71) and *creadit* (Meas. II.4.92). Several words have *a* where we should expect *e*. Most of these are from variants with *a*, such as *Wrastler* (AYL I.1.94). Kökeritz (p. 185) suggests that Mrs Quickly's *alligant* (MWW II.2.69) may be due to the influence of the following *l*, and Costard's *vara* 'very' (LLL V.2.487) may be a northernism. OED explains *Sacke* (1H4 I.2.7) as a hypercorrect pronunciation of *sec*, made possible by a tendency to pronounce [a] as [e].

There are many forms with *i* for ME *e*, and rhymes and puns show that the spelling reflects a sound change. The very frequent *Divell* (as at 1H4 I.2.126) shows raising of [e] after shortening of the long vowel (OE *dēofol*). Other forms with *i* are *Libbards* 'leopard's' (LLL V.2.551) and *togither* (Cym. I.4.34).

In ME *er* became *ar*, and *er* varies with *ar* today in such words as *person* beside *parson*. In Shakespeare forms with *a* are more common than they are today, and they occur especially in the speech of uneducated characters. Doll Tearsheet has *Marchants* (2H4 II.4.66), and Dogberry *desartlesse* 'deserving' (Ado, III.3.8). Other examples are *Parmacity* (1H4 1.3.58) and *parlous* 'perilous' (AYL III.2.46), and we find rhymes like *art*: *convert* (Sonn. 14.10).

331. ME [i] remained in Shakespeare and it still remains today. It was probably a rather open variety of the vowel, as is shown by frequent spellings with *e*, such as *Cesterne* (Ant. II.5.95). The rhyme *spirit*: *merit* (Sonn. 108.2) suggests that the first *i* of *spirit* was nearly like an *e*, but the rhyme *quite*: *spirit* (MND II.1.32) suggests that *spirit* could be written for its monosyllabic variant *sprite*. *Spirituall* is disyllabic in 1H6 III.1.50.

The rounding influence of *w* is seen in *woo't* (Ham. V.1.298 and elsewhere).

332. ME [o], as in *god*, has remained unchanged until the present day, though there is some evidence of unrounding to [ɑ] in the seventeenth and eighteenth centuries. Hamlet puns on *Mouse-trap* and *tropically* (III.2.247). Dr Caius's *by gar* (MWW 1.4.114) is probably from *by Gad*.

333. ME short *u* [u] had by the end of the sixteenth century become an unrounded centralized vowel not far removed from [ʌ].

334. ME *ā*. During the fifteenth century ME [ɑ:] fell in with [ai] and by the end of the century both sounds became [æ:]. In Shakespeare this has become [ɛ:]. Shakespeare rhymes *baite* with *state* (Err. II.1.94) and *tale* is a frequent pun with *tail* (as at Oth. III.1.8).

There are two pronunciations of *are*. The stressed form had [ɑ:] in Middle English and this gave [ɛ:] in Shakespeare, with the result that we find *are* rhyming with *compare* and *care* (Macb. IV.1.90). Side by side with this form, Middle English had an unstressed form with a short vowel and this form rhymes in Shakespeare with *star* and *war* (Troil. Prol.31).

335. ME close *ē* [e:], as in *see*, was raised to [i:] at the beginning of the fifteenth century and this pronunciation has remained ever since. In Shakespeare shortening of this [i:] is common. It rhymes with the ending *-y* in words like *story* (H8 Prol. 21). The spelling *bin* for *been* occurs frequently, and *beene* rhymes with *sinne* (Luc. 209). The pun *ship – sheep* (Err. IV.1.93) shows that the pronunciation [ʃip] for *sheep*, now dialectal, was then colloquial. *Friend* (OE *frēond*) and *fiend* (OE *fēond*), both had [e:] in Middle English, but

they have developed differently today as the result of the selection of different variants. In Elizabethan English both *friend* and *fiend* occur with both a long and a short vowel, but rhymes suggest that Shakespeare preferred a short vowel in both words.

336. ME open *ē* [ɛ:], as in *sea*, had two developments in Elizabethan English. One was the conservative [ɛ:], later [e:]; the other was the newer pronunciation [i:]. The latter sound has survived in present-day English; the former died out during the eighteenth century, with the exception of five words (*break*, *great*, *steak*, *yea* and *drain*) in which it has remained until the present day. The long vowel has often been shortened in present-day English, as in *head*, *deaf* beside *read*, *eat*. There are several rhymes which suggest that Shakespeare had a short vowel in words in which today the vowel is long: *intreats*: *frets* (VA 73) and *greater*: *better* (Sonn. 119.10).

337. ME [i:] had been diphthongized to [əi], by the time of Shakespeare, and ME [ɔi] had become a similar diphthong. We therefore find puns like *bile-boil* (TN II.5.3) and the inverted spelling *smoile* (Lear II.2.88).

In the adverbial ending *-ly* and the substantival ending *-y* we find double pronunciations: [əi] beside [i:]. Thus rhymes like *eie*: *chastitie*: *silently* (MND III.1.203) occur beside *be*: *jollity* (MND IV.1.95).

338. ME long close *o* [o:] had become [u:] in the fifteenth century, and this change is reflected in occasional spellings with *ou* beside the usual *oo*: *bloud* (John II.1.42), *floud* (1H4 V.1.48).

Well before the Elizabethan period, ME long open *o* [ɔ:], as in *go*, had fallen in with the [ou] of *know* to give [o:], and Shakespeare has rhymes like *blowe*: *so* (LLL IV.3.109) and *flow*: *go* (Cym. III.5.164). The normal pronunciation of *one* seems to have been [o:n], rhyming with *bone* (LLL V.2.331), but there are signs of the dialectal pronunciation that has given the modern pronunciation [wʌn] in Dr Caius's *van* (MWW III.1.81 Q).

339. ME long *u* [u:] was diphthongized during the fifteenth century and by the time of Shakespeare the diphthong was [əu]. This change was often hindered by a preceding labial consonant. We therefore find *swoonds* 'swoons' (Ant. IV.9.26); loss of *w* before the back rounded vowel gives the common variant *sound* (AYL V.2.29). ME [u:] has been shortened in *Huswife* (Ant. IV.15.44). Before [r], [u:] often became [o:] or [ɔ:], as in *houre*: *Siccamore* (LLL V.2.89). The development of [u:] before [r] could be monosyllabic (as in *power* Temp. 1.2.99) or disyllabic (as in *Power* Cor. 1.2.9).

DIPHTHONGS

340. There were fewer diphthongs in Elizabethan English than there are today. Words like *gate* and *go*, which have diphthongs today, still had long vowels. Diphthongs which today have [ə] as their second element as the result of developments before [r] had begun to develop in the fifteenth century. In Shakespeare the second element [ə] of the diphthong does not as a rule add to the number of syllables in a word, but there are occasional examples where it does. In the line 'As fire drives out fire, so pitty pitty' (JC III.1.171), the first *fire* seems to be disyllabic, the second monosyllabic.

341. ME [ou] as in *law*, had probably become [ɔ:] in Shakespeare, as is shown by the spelling *Kickshawes* (2H4 V.1.29) from French *quelquechose*.

342. ME [ei] fell in with [ɑi]. Hence in Shakespeare we find spellings like *obay* (Shrew. V.2.164), *waighty* (Shrew IV.4.26).

343. ME [eu], as in *new*, and [ɛu], as in *few*, fell together and were pronounced [ju:], as they are today.

344. ME *oi* [ɔi], as in *joy*, sometimes remains in Shakespeare, as indicated by the rhyme *destroy*: *Pardonne moy* (R2 V.3.145) but there is some evidence of a variant pronunciation [əi], rhyming with the regular [əi] from ME [i:] (see § 336).

CONSONANTS

345. Assimilation of *pb* to *bb* is found in *Courtcubbord* (RJ 1.5.5) and *cubbording* (Cor. 1.1.94). Intervocalic *p* is occasionally voiced, as in *debuty* (2H4 II.4.92, Q reading), *Libbards* (LLL V.2.551). *Sampire* (Lear IV.6.16) is the older form, later altered to *samphire*. As a result of faulty timing in the movement of the organs of speech, *p* sometimes appears between *m* and a following *t* or *s*. In *empty* (OE *ǣmetig*), the *p* has become a normal part of the present-day spelling, and it is found in occasional spellings in Shakespeare, such as *dreampt* (JC II.2.76) beside *dreamt* (1H4 IV.1.75). Rhymes such as *empty*: *plentie* (Temp. IV.1.110) suggest that the *p* was not always pronounced.

346. As today, *b* is usually silent after *m*, but Elizabethan spelling, more responsive to pronunciation than ours, sometimes reveals a change that is concealed by the conservative spelling

conventions of today. We thus find *dum* (JC III.2.229). There is further evidence of the change in the spelling of 'climb' and the rhyme *crime*: *time*: *clime* (Luc. 772). No *b* was normally heard in *doubt* and *debt*, but pedants like Holofernes tried to enforce its pronunciation without etymological justification (LLL V.1.25). Shakespeare rhymes *debt* with *Plantagenet* (R3 IV.4.20) and *doubt* with *out* (John IV.2.101).

347. In Early English, [f] was generally voiced to [v] between voiced sounds, a change which explains the difference in pronunciation between *wife* and *wives*. The [f] has often been restored by analogy, but we find several forms in Shakespeare in which the voiced form remains: *Wolvish* (Merch. IV.1.138), *leavy* (Ado II.3.75), *wives* gen. sg. (AYL IV.1.170). The southern voicing of initial *f* gives *vade* 'fade' (Sonn. 54.14) and leads to hypercorrect forms like *firago* (TN III.4.303).

348. Medial *v* often disappears in words like *ever*, *over* and *devil*. The loss of *v* is indicated by spellings like *who ere* (RJ V.3.173) and rhymes like *ore*: *before* (Sonn. 30.10). When the *v* remains in spelling, its loss is often suggested by the metre. *Eale* occurs for *evil* in a famous crux (Ham. 1.4.36). Loss of *v*, perhaps preceded by syncope and assimilation, has taken place in *Senights* (Oth. II.1.77. The loss of *v* in *Ease-dropper* (R3 V.3.221) may be due to its occurrence in a heavy consonant group. A *v* has been lost in the greeting *Godgigoden* (RJ 1.2.60), and loss of *v* is normal in *has*, sometimes spelt *ha's*. There is a similar loss of *v* in *so God sa'me* (H5 III.2.120, Macmorris). Confusion between *v* and *w*, frequent in Cockney but not confined to that dialect, is to be seen in *showe* for *shove* (Ham. III.3.58, Q2) and the dialectal *che vor'ye* 'I warrant you' (Lear IV.6.247).

349. *t* often disappears from groups of consonants: *insulment* (Cym. III.5.142), *Currence* 'currants' (WT IV.3.40), *russle* 'rustle' (Meas. IV.3.39). In the verbal ending *-st* of the 2 sg. present indicative, final *t* often disappears, especially when followed by a word beginning with a consonant: *revisits thus* (Ham. 1.4.53). In the 2 sg. pret. ind. of weak verbs we find *refts* (Cym. III.3.103), but it is more common for the tense ending *t* or *d* to drop out, leaving the ending *-st*: *lik'st* (Oth. III.3.109), *stroakst* (Temp. 1.2.333). Occasionally *t* disappears after *s*, as in *hoys'd* (R3 IV.4.529) beside *hoisted* (Err. V.1.21).

An excrescent *t* has sometimes been added at the end of a word after *n*: *Talent* 'talon' (1H4 II.4.362), *Orphants* gen. pl. (H8 III.2.399), *margent* (LLL V.2.8). A similar *t* has been added to a few words in present-day English, such as *peasant* and *parchment*.

350. Final *d* is sometimes unvoiced to *t* after *n*: *arrant* (Cor. V.2.66) beside the usual form *errand*, *reverent* for *reverend* (Err. III.2.91), *ballet* 'ballad' (WT IV.4.261).

d often disappears after *n* and occasionally after other consonants: *hansomely* (Tit. II.3.268), *canstick* (1H4 III.1.131, Qq reading), *wensday* (WT IV.4.281), *pun* v. (Troil. II.1.44). We sometimes find weak past participles without -*d*, such as *designe* (Ham. I.1.94 F1, *design'd* F2–4).

An excrescent *d* often appears at the end of a word after *l* or *n*: *vilde* (Ham. II.2.110), *sound* 'swoon' (AYL V.2.29), *swound* (AYL III.5.17), *Turbonds* (Cym. III.3.6). A similar excrescent *d* appears between *n* or *l* and *r* in *chiualdry* (H5 IV.6.19, Q reading), *Standlie* (R3 V.3.290, Q reading).

351. There are traces of the Middle English fluctuation between [d] and [ð] next to [r], whether the original consonant was [d] or [ð]: *murther* (Oth. V.1.28), *Fardingales* (Shrew IV.3.56) beside *Farthingale* (TGV II.7.51), *burthen* (Ham. III.1.54), *Fadome* (RJ I.4.85).

A dialectal change of final [θ] in *moth* to [t], reported by Kökeritz especially from the West Midlands (op. cit. p. 320) led to the falling together of *moth* and *mote* and to the use of *moth* as an inverted spelling for *mote* (Ham. I.1.112). Preservation of older forms (OE *fífta, sixta*) explains *fift* (Merch. I.2.138), *sixt* (Ado V.1.222). Loss of *t* or *th* before *d* or *n* explains *Twelfe Night, twelfe day* (TN II.3.90). The cardinal numeral *hundreth* (Tit. I.1.350) is from ON *hundrað*. Mistress Quickly's *wo't ta* (2H4 II.1.63, Q reading) shows assimilation of [θ] to [t]. Confusion between [f] and [θ], generally thought of as Cockney,[1] is found in *philhorse* 'thill-horse, shaft-horse' (Merch. II.2.102). Intervocalic [ð] has disappeared in *wher* (Lear II.1.81) and *where* (JC I.1.66) for *whether*. In other words containing the group *ther* the metre shows that it sometimes did and sometimes did not constitute an extra syllable.

Th is occasionally used as a spelling for *t*, as in present-day English *Anthony*. Shakespearean examples are: *anathomize* (AYL I.1.162), *gamouth* 'gamut' (Shrew III.1.71), *Anthony* (Ant. I.1.20).

Nosthrill (H5 III.1.16) keeps the earlier spelling (OE *nospyrl*), though the consonant had probably become *t* by the time of

1. William Matthews, *Cockney Past and Present* (Routledge, 1938), pp. 162f.

Shakespeare. *Drouth* (:*mouth*, Per III. Prol.8) and *heighth* (Ant. III.10.21) have the older form of the suffix used to form abstract nouns (OE - *ðo*); the *th* is still found in many regional dialects.

352. From the fifteenth century [l] began to disappear before consonants in colloquial speech, as in *should, would* and *shalt*. The protests of Holofernes (LLL V.1.25) against the loss of [l] suggest that Shakespeare favoured the colloquial pronunciation, and we find occasional spellings like *bauk* (Luc. 696). Some forms without *l*, such as *Fauconbridge* (LLL II.1.42) and *Raphe* (2H4 III.2.109), go back to Old French variants without *l*, and *Salvages* (Temp. II.2.63) is from OF *salvage*, a variant of *sauvage* (OED). *Alablaster* (Merch. I.1.84), a common spelling in the sixteenth and seventeenth centuries, may be due to confusion with *alablaster* from *arblaster* (see OED). *Bristow* (2H6 III.1.328) is the old form of the name (OE *Brycgstōw*) before the distinctive western development of [w] to [l].

353. An excrescent *n* sometimes appears before consonants in unaccented syllables, as in *Palentine* 'Palatine' (Merch. 1.2.49). There are parallels to the loss of *n* in *mallicholie* (LLL IV.3.13) and *Allicholy* (MWW 1.4.160) (see OED s.v. Melancholy sb.). Misdivision has led to *Nunckle* (Lear 1.4.117) and *an ayword* (TN II.3.152). It is likely that [ŋ] often became [n] in colloquial speech finally or before consonants, as is suggested by puns on *mountain-mounting* (LLL IV.1.4) and spellings like *Bullinbrooke* (R2 II.2.62) and *javelings* (VA 616).

354. Before consonants *r* disappeared in early Modern English. Before *s* the loss of *r* began in the fourteenth century. In Shakespeare we find *accust* 'accursed' (Macb. IV.3.107), *woosted-stocking* (Lear II.2.17). *Tortoyrs* (RJ IV.1.42) is an inverted spelling. Metathesis of *r* is found in *Aporne* (2H6 II.3.75). *Pomgarnet* (1H4 II.4.37) is from a doublet which had metathesis already in Old French. In Costard's *pursents* 'presents' (LLL V.2.489) there is a change of prefix.

355. The development of [sj] to [ʃ] or [ʒ] had begun as early as the fifteenth century, though it is not recognized by the orthoepists until the middle of the seventeenth century. At the time of Shakespeare colloquial speech probably had [ʃ] in *condition* and [ʒ] in *occasion*, though conservative speakers would still use [sj] and [zj]. We find spellings like *Marshall* 'martial' (H5 IV.8.46) and *martiall*, v. 'marshal' (Per. II.3.19). The metre shows that endings like *-cious* and *-tion* often had two syllables, but this evidence does not tell us how the consonant was pronounced. Medial *s* is voiced

in *Gozemore* 'gossamer' (Lear IV.6.49). Dogberry's *suffigance* (Ado III.5.54) and Nell Quickly's *Pulsidge* 'pulse' (2H4 II.4.26) anticipate Dickens's Sarah Gamp. In a suffix [tʃ] has been voiced to [dʒ] in *Estridges* (1H4 IV.1.98) by a change similar to that which has given our *knowledge*. Several words ending in -*s* have plurals in -*es* which are shown by the metre to be silent: *Carkasses* (Cor. III.3.122), *Conveyances* (Cor. V.1.54), *services* (WT II.1.17). *Zounds* (John II.1.466) preserves the voiced *s* of *God's*. The loss of initial *s* in *Parmacity* (1H4 I.3.58), a common variant of *spermaceti*, may have originated in contexts where the word was preceded by a word ending in *s*.

356. Initially *k* had disappeared before *n*, as is suggested by puns like *knight – night* (1H4 I.2.27) and *known – none* (Ado IV.2.23). Intervocalic *k* has disappeared in the past participle of *take*, which is usually spelt *tane* (as at RJ III.5.17).

357. The palatal fricative [ç] was disappearing before *t* during Shakespeare's lifetime. When Holofernes attacked those 'insociable, and poynt devise companions' who said *nebour* instead of *neighbour* and *ne* instead of *neigh* (LLL V.1.26), he was defending a conservative pronunciation used at the end of the sixteenth century by a dwindling number of speakers. We find in Shakespeare spellings like *hie* 'high' (Troil. II.2.113) and *lyte* 'light' (Troil. I.2.10) and inverted spellings like *bight* 'bite' (AYL II.7.184) and *spight* (RJ I.1.85). Loss of the fricative is suggested by rhymes like *despight : night* (VA 731). Between vowels [ç] often disappeared, as in the rhyme *hie : dry* (VA 551).

358. The velar fricative [x], spelt *gh*, when final, either disappeared or became [f]. The two developments are illustrated by the rhymes *bough : now* (VA 37) and *Macduffe : enough* (Macb. V.8.33). The fricative [x] has apparently become [f] before *t* in *daughter : after* (WT IV.1.27).

359. Initial [h] was not very strongly pronounced, since we find the article *an* before *h* even when the initial syllable is stressed, as in *an hundred* (JC II.2.77), and there are puns like *art – heart* (Shrew IV.2.10), and *eare – heere* (Shrew IV.1.60). In unaccented positions initial [h] is normally lost, as suggested by the rhyme *win her : dinner* (Shrew I.2.217). *Abhominable* (Meas. III.2.25) and *abhominations* (Ant. III.6.94) have *h* by mistaken association with *homo*, and Holofernes (LLL V.1.27) is anxious that the *h* in such words should be pronounced. The *h* in *preheminence* (Lear I.1.133) is probably to avoid hiatus.

360. Initial [j] sometimes disappears, as in *God 'ild you* (AYL v.4.56). A prosthetic [j] is found in *Yedward* (1H4 1.2.143), *yerewhile* (AYL III.5.105). *Popingay* (1H4 1.3.50) is the older form of the word which has become *popinjay* by association with *jay* (OED).

361. Close resemblance between *w* and *wh* is suggested by possible puns like *wight – white* (Oth. II.1.133) and *whether – [wether]* *– Sheepe* (TGV 1.1.80). Initial *w* was often still pronounced in the group *wr*, but spellings like *unrung* (Ham. III.2.252) and puns like *ring – wring* (Shrew 1.2.17) suggest that variants with silent *w* may also have been current. Loss of [w] before [u:] is found in the common *sound* for *swoon* (as at AYL v.2.29) and *w* has disappeared in the common oath *Zounds* (John II.1.466) and *greene-sord* (WT IV.4.155). The loss of initial *w* in *old* 'wold' (Lear III.4.126) is dialectal: EDD records it from Northamptonshire.

362. In the suffixes *-ward* and *-worth w* tends to disappear, though the influence of the spelling has led to the preservation or restoration of [w] in standard English. *Peniworths* is disyllabic at RJ IV.5.4 and so is *penyworths* at 2H6 I.1.222.

In French loan-words *qu* was pronounced [k], though we now have [kw] by the influence of the spelling: *banket* (AYL II.5.65). Hence Nell Quickly's *Canaries* for *quandary* (MWW II.2.63). The name *Jaques* could be monosyllabic, and Touchstone may be punning on its resemblance to *jakes* when he calls Jaques 'good Mr what ye cal't' (AYL III.3.77), but the metre shows that it could be disyllabic, as at AYL II.1.26 and LLL II.1.42. Slender's use of *Coram* for *Quorum* (MWW 1.1.6) suggests that in this Latin loan-word initial *qu* was perhaps pronounced [k].

SPELLING

363. Our knowledge of Elizabethan spelling has suffered because of the popularity of Shakespeare's plays, since this popularity has led to the widespread practice of publishing editions in modernized spelling. Hence many readers assume that Shakespeare's spelling was very much like ours. It would be unreasonable to require the schoolboy or the general reader to have his attention distracted by what seem to us to be eccentricities of spelling, but serious study of the plays must be based on editions which preserve the spelling and punctuation of the earliest texts. We cannot be sure that these are Shakespeare's own, but they are part of the evidence on which

our knowledge of the plays rests, and they can help in their interpretation. Pairs of words which today seem quite distinct often
resembled each other much more closely in Elizabethan spelling
and were therefore liable to be confused. The original spelling may
be necessary for the correct identification of a word. In *Hamlet*
III.2.65 there occur the words usually printed 'Where thrift may
follow fawning'. Q2–5 have *fawning* or *fauning*, while F1 has *faining*.
Hilda Hulme[1] takes the Folio reading to mean 'feigning', but
fawning and *faining* are variants, going back to Old English forms
with *a* and *æ* respectively. An editor who printed the modern form
feigning would be concealing the evidence for this explanation.
Banquo speaks of: great prediction Of Noble having and of
Royall hope, That he seems wrapt withall: (Macb. 1.3.55). Modern
editors read *rapt*, but Hilda Hulme points out[1] that the spelling
with *w* suggests that the imagery may be that of a garment and
quotes 'borrowed Robes' (l. 109) and 'strange Garments' (l. 145)
in support. In the early scenes of *Macbeth* (1.3.32, 1.5.7, II.1.21) the
Weird Sisters are in the First Folio called 'weyward Sisters'. It may
be that this repeated spelling is due to association with *wayward*
(OED s.v. Weird, *a*,). Stage directions are particularly liable to be
modernized or inserted by an editor. It is worth while to know
whether the admirably concise direction 'Enter Mariners wet'
(Temp. I.1.53) is the work of a contemporary of Shakespeare or of
a modern editor. The original stage directions often give a clue to
characterization. In Act V, scene 1 of *Love's Labour's Lost* Armado,
Holofernes and Nathaniel are in the First Folio described as
'Bragart', 'Pedant' and 'Curate' respectively. These descriptions
show that the three characters were recognized as stock-types.

364. It is mainly in the absence of uniformity that the spelling
of the sixteenth century differs from that of later times. There were
very few words that were never written as they are now, but side
by side with the spellings familiar to us there were many variants
that have now passed out of use. At the time of Shakespeare the
modern notion of correctness in spelling was only beginning to be
developed. The chief characteristic of Elizabethan spelling was the
large number of variants which it allowed. Any spelling that
represented the sound of a word according to current analogues
was accepted, and homophones were not distinguished in spelling

1. op. cit. p. 160   2. op. cit. p. 237.

as they often are today. Doublets have sometimes diverged in both spelling and pronunciation since Elizabethan times, but they were not then regarded as different words. We thus find *loose* used interchangeably with *lose*, *die* with *dye*, *metal* with *mettle*, *curtsy* with *courtsey*, *flour* with *flower*, *cloths* with *clothes*, and *draft* with *draught*. Some non-phonetic spellings are etymological, like *conceipt* for *conceit* and *sainct* for *saint*, and some of these etymological intrusions have remained to the present day, as in *scissors*, *scythe*, *debt* and *fault*. Sometimes they result from the adoption of the spelling conventions of foreign languages, giving *phang* and *curphew*, or native conventions may be applied to words of foreign origin, as in *ducket* beside *ducat*. This freedom in spelling is very useful to a modern investigator, since it enables him to tell which words were pronounced alike and which sounds had fallen together. Changes in spelling have lagged behind changes in pronunciation, and Elizabethan spelling, like that of today, represents a series of compromises between historical and phonetic spellings.

365. The following are the chief differences in detail between Elizabethan and present-day spelling. Sometimes the difference is one of degree, characteristics that are present today being found to a greater or less extent in Elizabethan times.

(a) Final -*e* is often used without etymological justification. As the result of a Middle English sound-change, in nearly all words ending in -*e* after a single consonant the stem-vowel was long, and the addition of final -*e* had thus become one of the ways of indicating vowel-length; this is probably the explanation of final -*e* in such words as *bone* (OE *bān*). With the loss of final -*e* in pronunciation at about the end of the fourteenth century, the use of -*e* in spelling became more and more arbitrary.

(b) The modern practice of using *u* for a vowel and *v* for a consonant became general during the first half of the seventeenth century. The First Folio (1623) generally follows the Middle English practice of using *v* initially and *u* medially to represent both vowel and consonant, as in *vnder*, *reuiue*.

(c) In the First Folio *i* is used to represent both the vowel and the consonant represented today by *i* and *j* respectively. The modern distinction between *i* and *j* developed soon after 1630 (See OED s.v. J).

(d) In Middle English, long vowels were shortened before double consonants or consonant-groups. Hence, doubling a consonant became a way of indicating that the preceding vowel was short, as in *coppy*, *pollicy*.

(e) A horizontal stroke is occasionally placed over a vowel to indicate the omission in spelling of a following *m* or *n*.

(f) *ee*, *oo* are often used to indicate the development of ME close *ē* [e:] and *ō* [o:], and *ea* and *oa* are used for the development of ME open *ē* [ɛ:] and *ō* [ɔ:].

(g) French loan-words ending in *-ic* often add a *k* to show that the consonant was pronounced [k], not [s], as in *magick*, *rusticke*.

(h) The spelling *vv* is occasionally used for *w*.

PUNCTUATION

366. There are two important differences between Shakespeare's punctuation and that of the present day. The first is that modern punctuation is logical, whereas Elizabethan was rhetorical. The second is that modern punctuation aims at uniformity, whereas an Elizabethan author could vary the punctuation to indicate his interpretation of a passage.[1] On the whole there were fewer stops then than now. For example, we often find a vocative or an appositional phrase used without commas: I prethee foolish greeke depart from me, there's money for thee, (TN IV.1.21); if my Uncle thy banished father had banished thy Uncle the Duke my Father, (AYL I.2.9).

367. A *comma* may be used to mark emphasis even if it separates a subject from its verb: I have heard that *Julius Cæsar*, grew fat with feasting there. (Ant. II.6.64).

Contrary to modern usage, a comma may be used in a comparison before *than*: Better a witty foole, then a foolish wit. (TN I.5.36).

A comma is often used where we should have a colon or a semicolon to indicate a longer pause: A Calender, a Calender, looke in the Almanack, finde out Moone-shine, finde out Moone-shine. (MND III.1.54).

368. A *semicolon* is used to emphasize the preceding word. In the following quotation the semicolon shows that *war* has stronger emphasis than the other nouns: Thus, what with the war; what with the sweat, what with the gallowes, and what with poverty, I am Custom-shrunke. (Meas. 1.2.84).

It is used to mark off a dependent clause at the beginning of a

1. See Percy Simpson, *Shakespearian Punctuation* (OUP, 1911), p. 8.

sentence: Say what you can; my false, ore-weighs your true. (Meas. II.4.170).

369. A *colon* is used to mark an emphatic pause: O pardon me, thou bleeding peece of Earth: That I am meeke and gentle with these Butchers. (JC III.1.254).

It is often used after a noun in the vocative: Gentlemen all: Alas, what shall I say. (JC III.1.190).

370. *Full stop.* In order to indicate a stronger pause than that required by a colon or semicolon, a full stop may be used even in an unfinished sentence:

> Such an Act
> That blurres the grace and blush of Modestie,
> Cals Vertue Hypocrite, takes off the Rose
> From the faire forehead of an innocent love,
> And makes a blister there. Makes marriage vowes
> As false as Dicers Oathes. Oh such a deed,
> As from the body of Contraction pluckes
> The very soule,   (Ham. III.4.40)

A full stop is often used to end an interrupted speech:

Gon. Had I plantation of this Isle my Lord.
Ant. Hee'd sow't with Nettle-seed.   (Temp. II.1.144)

371. A *question-mark* is often used where we should use an exclamation-mark: O what a deale of scorne, lookes beautifull? (TN III.1.157).

372. *Quotation marks* are often used at the beginning, but not the end, of each line of a quotation or a sententious passage. Quotations are sometimes introduced without any punctuation marks and without even a capital letter, as when Jessica says: His words were farewell mistris, nothing else. (Merch. II.5.46).

373. *Brackets* were used more freely than today, but, as today, they usually indicate a parenthesis: You doe looke (my son) in a mov'd sort, (Temp. IV.1.146). They are often used to enclose adjectival phrases which follow a noun: Then can I drowne an eye (un-us'd to flow) For precious friends hid in deaths dateles night, (Sonn. 30.5).

374. An *apostrophe* is used, more freely than today, to indicate the loss of an unaccented *e* in past participles, but the apostrophe is not used, as it is today, to distinguish the possessive from the subjective or objective plural of nouns.

375. *Initial capitals* are used not only for proper names but also for words which have a special significance in their context: But *Brutus* sayes, he was Ambitious: And *Brutus* is an Honourable man. (JC III.2.98).

376. *Italics,* which are today used to indicate emphasis, are very rarely used for this purpose in Elizabethan texts. There they are used, as Roman type had been used in black-letter texts, to distinguish proper names and quotations. Allied to the latter function is the use of italics to call attention to a sententia: *Some rise by sinne, and some by vertue fall:* (Meas. II.1.38).

CHAPTER 7

Metre

🔯🔯🔯🔯🔯

377. Apart from a few plays, such as *Much Ado About Nothing*, where prose is dominant, the usual Shakespearean practice is to make blank verse the normal medium of expression but to use prose for a number of special purposes. These are:

(a) In formal documents, letters and proclamations. Prose is used for anything that is to be read aloud.

(b) For reasoned argument. Iago, seeking to convince Roderigo, uses prose (Oth. 1.3.314).

(c) By characters of low social class, like the gravediggers in *Hamlet*, the shepherds in *The Winter's Tale* and Jack Cade in *2 King Henry VI*, though Hamlet uses prose sometimes and Falstaff nearly always. *The Merry Wives of Windsor* is nearly all in prose to accord with its bourgeois setting.

(d) In comic scenes, as in the Falstaff scenes of *King Henry IV*, the drinking scene in *Twelfth Night* and the porter's scene in *Macbeth*, and in wit-encounters, as in the Beatrice and Benedick scenes in *Much Ado About Nothing*.

(e) Whenever it is necessary to lower the dramatic pitch, as in *Coriolanus* 1.3, which consists in the main of a colloquial household scene between Volumnia and Virgilia.

(f) To express madness (as in Lear IV.6.122) or frenzy (as in Oth. IV.1.35).

(g) Prose is better suited than verse to the use of broken English, in which the speaker stumbles. Hence in *King Henry V* the scenes with Fluellen, Macmorris and Jamy and Henry's lovemaking (V.2.103) are in prose.

378. There are different kinds of Shakespearean prose. His normal prose style draws its strength from the spoken language of everyday life, but the prose of *Love's Labour's Lost* shows the influence of Euphuism. Another variety is that of light-hearted badinage, as used by Portia and Nerissa, Beatrice and Benedick,

Rosalind and Orlando. There is the affected speech of Osric and his like, frequently parodied. 'Fine writing' of prose is a subject of satire. Viola says: I would be loath to cast away my speech; for besides that it is excellently well penn'd, I have taken great pains to con it (TN 1.5.183).

A good example of the prose of reasoned argument is Brutus's address to the Roman people. By using prose he provides a more striking contrast to Antony's speech: Brutus is concerned with logic, Antony with emotion. The prose of Brutus is rhetorical, with balanced sentences and repetition. His refrain 'for him have I offended' (JC III.2.29) may be compared with Antony's 'For *Brutus* is an Honourable man', (III.2.86).

379. There is a special interest in scenes in which prose and verse are both used. The use of prose is a help in characterization, and to notice when it is used is a help in appreciating the action of the play. In *Troilus and Cressida* Thersites and the other satirical commentators use prose to distinguish them from the characters whom they criticize. In *2 King Henry VI* (IV.7) Lord Say, defending himself against Jack Cade's men, uses verse in contrast with the prose of his accusers. In *Love's Labour's Lost* Armado, the Euphuist, uses prose. It is chiefly in the early plays that we find dialogues, like that between Bottom and Titania, where one character speaks in verse while the other uses prose. In *1 King Henry IV* there is a clear distinction between the prose of the comic scenes and the blank verse of the noble characters, but Hotspur's dialogue with his wife in a domestic scene (III.1.229ff.) mixes verse with prose. In *Romeo and Juliet* (II.5) Juliet speaks verse, whereas the Nurse mixes prose and verse in speaking to her. In *Troilus and Cressida* Troilus consistently speaks verse in reply to the prose of Pandarus. In *The Tempest* most of the prose comes from Stephano and Trinculo. Caliban nearly always speaks in verse, even to them, and this fact throws light on Shakespeare's conception of Caliban: he is no clown, though he is a savage, and he is contemptuous of Stephano and Trinculo when they stop to pick up finery.

380. Some characters use both prose and verse, and it is sometimes possible to suggest reasons for the choice of one medium or the other. Hamlet uses verse in soliloquy and in talking to Horatio, but in his communication with a hostile court he uses prose, which is felt to be the natural medium for satirical utterances. He uses prose in talking to low-life characters like the gravediggers. In *As You*

Like It after Orlando's victory, the Duke asks his name (1.2.242). On hearing it, he reveals his heightened emotional tension by changing from prose to blank verse. There is an implication that prose is the natural medium in Jaques's sarcastic outburst: Nay then God buy you, and you talke in blanke verse. (IV.1.30). In *Twelfth Night* Olivia first addresses Viola in bantering prose, but when she begins to fall in love with her, she slips into blank verse.

Prose and verse are used to distinguish between different registers. In *1 King Henry IV* II.4 most of the scene is in prose, but Hal uses verse in his conversation with the Sheriff and Carrier, keeping them in their place (l.561). When they have left, the scene reverts to prose.

381. In the course of his career Shakespeare made less and less use of rhyme. There is a lot in *Love's Labour's Lost* but very little in *The Tempest*.[1] In the early plays rhymed couplets are sometimes introduced into the middle of a blank verse speech, especially when the lines are end-stopped. A rhymed couplet is often used at the end, or nearly at the end, of a scene or act, as at the end of Act I of *Hamlet* or after Hamlet's reproaches to his mother (III.4.214). A speech often ends with a rhymed proverb or maxim, and rhyme is sometimes used to indicate an aside, as in *Richard III* IV.4.15 and 20.

382. In dialogue it is common for a five-stress line to be divided between two speakers, but we also find short lines interpolated by a different speaker with no attempt to complete a five-stress line. An example is: What, lookt he frowningly? (Ham. 1.2.231). Ejaculations, like *fie*! and forms of address, like *my lord*, sometimes seem to be outside the metrical pattern of the line.

383. Four-stress lines, which were very common in Middle English poetry, are not at all common in Shakespeare. They are used especially by supernatural beings like the Weird Sisters in *Macbeth* and the fairies in *A Midsummer Night's Dream*. Occasional examples occur elsewhere:

Let's each one send unto his wife   (Shrew v.2.66)

The match is made, and all is done,   (Shrew IV.4.46)

Four-stress lines are sometimes found where a number of short clauses or nouns are linked together in one line. The frequent pauses mean that the line has to be pronounced slowly:

1. For metrical tables see E. K. Chambers, *William Shakespeare: A Study of Facts and Problems* (OUP, 1930), II, 398ff.

Earth gapes, Hell burnes, Fiends roare, Saints pray   (R3 IV.4.75)

Is Goades, Thornes, Nettles, Tayles of Waspes   (WT 1.2.328)

384. Long lines can usually be explained by allowing for the possibility of extra unaccented syllables, but occasionally a six-stress line or alexandrine seems to be substituted for the usual five-stress line, especially in the later plays:

A hundred thousand more: in surety of the which,

(LLL II.1.135)

Our Bosome interest: Goe pronounce his present death,

(Macb. 1.2.64)

Some apparent alexandrines should be regarded as couplets of three-stress lines, as in the dialogue between Anne and Gloucester in *King Richard III* (1.2.194). This metre is used especially in comic or burlesque scenes for rapid dialogue and retort. It is used, for example, together with four-stress lines, by Thisbe in *A Midsummer Night's Dream* (v.1.334).

385. There is often reason to believe that words written in full are shortened in ordinary speech, but we sometimes find the converse. In the following line *Ile* must be pronounced as though it were two syllables, and some editors emend *Ile* to *I will*:

Glendower   Ile not have it alter'd.
Hotspur   Will not you? (1H4 III.1.116)

The superlative suffix *-est* does not always count as a separate syllable. In the line: Which art my neer'st and dearest Enemie? (1H4 III.2.123), *neer'st* is apparently one syllable but *dearest* is two.

If a verb ends in a dental consonant, the *-ed* of its past participle counts as a separate syllable, but in past participles of other verbs the *-ed* may or may not do so. The retention of *-ed* as a separate syllable is most common in the early plays but is not confined to them. We sometimes find syncopated and unsyncopated forms in a single line: Some shall be pardon'd and some punished. (RJ v.3.308); Despis'd, distressed, hated, martir'd, kil'd, (RJ IV.5.59).

The plural and genitive singular of nouns ending in a sibilant are often pronounced, and sometimes written, without the inflexion counting as an extra syllable: I but their sense are shut, (Macb. v.1.29); And *Duncans* Horses, (A thing most strange, and certaine) (Macb. II.4.14).

The loss of an unaccented syllable is especially common at the beginning of a line, immediately after the caesura and in emotional passages. Failure to admit this practice has led to many unnecessary emendations. For example, in the line: Under my Battlements. Com you Spirits, (Macb. 1.5.41), Pope inserts *all* before *you*. The loss of unaccented vowels is especially common before and after *r*, as in *spirits, confederates*.

386. A single foot may contain more than one unaccented syllable. Pronouns, conjunctions and articles are especially common among these unemphatic extra syllables.

Anapaests are more common in Shakespeare's later plays than in the early plays. We cannot always be sure that an apparent anapaest is to be so regarded because of the possibility of syncope or elision: No man beares sorrow better. *Portia* is dead. (JC IV.3.147); What a haste lookes through his eyes? (Macb. 1.2.46).

387. Feminine endings are most common in the later plays, and are especially common in certain parts of *King Henry VIII*, a fact that has been adduced to show that in that play Shakespeare collaborated with other dramatists.

388. As a result of sound-changes taking place at the time of Shakespeare, we often find double forms that can be used interchangeably to suit the demands of metre. The ending *-tion* can have the older pronunciation with two syllables or the newer pronunciation with one. Compare: Which smoak'd with bloody execution (Macb. 1.2.18), with: You greet with present Grace and great prediction (Macb. 1.3.55).

389. The 3 sg. present indicative ending in *-eth* constitutes a separate syllable, whereas the ending *-es* does not, except when the stem of the verb ends in a sibilant. It sometimes seems that the choice of ending in verse is influenced by metrical convenience in the addition of an extra syllable: When Love begins to sicken and decay It useth an enforced Ceremony. (JC IV.2.20). The genitive singular ending in *-s* does not as a rule constitute a separate syllable, except after sibilants. When it does, it is an archaism: swifter then the Moons sphere; (MND II.1.7).

390. The author of a verse play tries to make his verse approach to conversational prose rhythm. He achieves this aim by varying the position of the syntactic pauses in relation to the lines of blank verse. End-stopped lines are most common in the early plays. In the later plays we find relative pronouns and auxiliary verbs separated from their verbs by the end of a line:

This ancient morsell: this Sir Prudence, who
Should not upbraid our course: (Temp. II.1.286)

In the later plays, too, we find an increasing number of speeches
which end in the middle of a line, the line being completed by
another speaker.

391. The king's opening speech in *Love's Labour's Lost* is in the
language of sonneteers, and two sonnets are incorporated in later
acts of the play: Nathaniel reads a sonnet written by Armado
(IV.2.105), and Longueville reads one of his own composition
(IV.3.60). In *Romeo and Juliet* (1.5.94) a complete sonnet is split up
into short speeches for Romeo and Juliet.

392. A trochaic foot is sometimes substituted for the more
usual iamb, especially at the beginning of a line or after the caesura:
Sleepe that knits up the ravel'd Sleeve of Care, (Macb. II.2.37);
Took pains to make thee speak, taught thee each houre (Temp.
I.2.354). Departure from the normal alternation of accented and
unaccented syllables is often the result of strong emotion, as in:
O, Trecherie! Flye good *Fleans*, flye, flye, flye, (Macb. III.3.17).
Disturbance of the normal iambic rhythm can have the effect of
calling special attention to a word occurring in an unexpected
position. In this way *flat* receives special emphasis in the line: How
weary, stale, flat, and unprofitable (Ham. 1.2.133).

393. Many disyllabic words could be pronounced with the chief
stress on either syllable. Compare the pronunciation of *upon* in the
two following lines: Why doe you put these sayings upon me?
(Meas. II.2.133), and: Upon my secure hower thy Uncle stole
(Ham. 1.5.59). Similarly in loan-words of more than two syllables:
My Manors, Rents, Revenues, I forgoe; (R2 IV.1.212) beside: The
Revennew whereof shall furnish us (R2 1.4.46).

394. When disyllabic adjectives are used attributively, the stress
sometimes shifts from the second syllable to the first to preserve
the alternation of accented and unaccented syllables that is found
in iambic verse and, to a lesser extent, in everyday speech: To do
no contriv'd Murder: (Oth. 1.2.3); to set the exact wealth of all our
states (1H4 IV.1.46). In polysyllabic words, Elizabethan English,
like American English today, often has one syllable with secondary stress: Why he a harmlesse necessarie Cat? (Merch. IV.1.55).

CHAPTER 8

Rhetoric

🐚🐚🐚🐚🐚

395. When a reader of today opens an Elizabethan textbook of rhetoric, he is struck by the wealth of technical terms. Opinions differ about the value a knowledge of these terms has for a modern reader. Many of them provide very learned-sounding words of Greek origin to describe very simple features of style, and there is little to be gained by memorizing such names when they are no longer currently used. Nevertheless, if a figure of speech had a name, the name itself may be unimportant, but its existence shows that the figure was felt to be common and important enough to be recognized. From the wealth of technical terms current in Elizabethan times, a few are chosen here to describe figures of speech which are distinctive and which are the result of deliberate effort and imitation on the part of the author, as distinct from those figures which might arise independently in any literature at any time. It is certain that Shakespeare knew more about the figures of rhetoric than the average reader of today, but it seems likely that he did not take them very seriously.

We find them illustrated most often in the early plays, and the real experts are the clowns. Touchstone seems to be parodying them when convincing William of his unworthiness:

> To have, is to have. For it is a figure in Rhetoricke, that drink being powr'd out of a cup into a glasse, by filling the one, doth empty the other. (AYL V.1.43)

Holofernes and Nathaniel in *Love's Labour's Lost* have studied rhetoric and they know all the stock devices of antithesis, repetition and variation, with a free use of inkhorn terms. Most of the characters in the play show Mr Polly's delight in new long words. Costard's repetition and praise of *remuneration* is ironical: 'Why? It is a fairer name then a French-Crowne' (III.1.140), but Nathaniel's admiration for *peregrinate* has no reservations: A most singular and choise Epithat (v.1.15). In much the same way Justice Shallow and Bardolph are enthusiastic about *accommodated* (2H4 III.2.74). Holofernes and Nathaniel illustrate a vice of their time: the excessive use of synonyms. Holofernes is concerned with the teaching of Latin as well as English, and therefore many Latin words are included among the synonyms:

> The Deare was (as you know) sanguis in blood, ripe as a Pomwater, who now hangeth like a Jewell in the eare of *Celo* the skie, the welken the heaven, and anon falleth like a Crab on the face of *Terra*, the soyle, the land, the earth. (LLL.IV.2.3)

396. *Alliteration*. In medieval times alliteration was an important structural feature of verse, but by the time of Shakespeare it had become an ornament. We may so regard the double alliteration when Duke Senior speaks of the 'churlish chiding of the winters winde' (AYL II.1.7). Then, as now, slight alliteration could be used without the hearer being conscious of it, but excessive alliteration was introduced either for burlesque, as in the play within a play in *A Midsummer Night's Dream*:

> Whereat, with blade, with bloody blamefull blade,
> He bravely broacht his boiling bloudy breast, (v.1.147)

or as an exercise in literary ingenuity, as when Holofernes, in *Love's Labour's Lost*, writes an epitaph on a deer and announces his intention of using heavy alliteration: I will something affect the letter, for it argues facilitie. The poem begins:

> The prayfull Princesse pearst and prickt a prettie pleasing Pricket, (LLL IV.2.57)

397. *Ambiguity* is frequent in the equivocation of clowns, who feel that they are not doing their job properly if they fail to call attention to the possibility of a double meaning. Prophecies and oracles are notoriously ambiguous. The spirits invoked by the conjurors in *2 King Henry VI* utter an ambiguous prophecy of a familiar kind made possible by the identity in English of the subjective and objective cases of nouns: The Duke yet lives, that *Henry* shall depose; (1.4.32). In *Macbeth* the prophecy that 'none of woman borne shall harme *Macbeth*' (IV.1.79) derives its ambiguity from the interpretation of the words 'of woman borne' as a literal description or as a rhetorical flourish.

398. *Anaphora* is the repetition of a group of words at the beginning of a number of successive sentences or clauses. Orlando, appealing to Duke Senior and anxious to show that he is a gentleman after his rude interruption of the meal has met with a courteous rebuke, makes use of this figure:

> If ever you have look'd on better dayes:
> If ever beene where bels have knoll'd to Church:
> If ever sate at any good mans feast:
> If ever from your eye-lids wip'd a teare, . . .   (AYL II.7.113)

It emphasizes the stylized nature of this appeal that the Duke replies to each of these clauses in turn.

399. *Cacozelia* is the affectation of using high-sounding words, which may be either new coinages from Latin or Greek or familiar words used in unfamiliar senses. Osric is a great practitioner:

> sir here is newly com to Court *Laertes*, believe me an absolute gentleman, ful of most excellent differences, of very soft society, and great showing: indeede to speake feelingly of him, hee is the card or kalender of gentry; for you shall find in him the continent of what part a Gentleman would see.
>
> (Ham. v.2.110)

Pistol combines cacozelia with the bombastic speech of a braggart and unusual word order, which together give his speech a characteristic rhythm.

400. *Diaeresis* is the logical division of a genus into its species. Each species is briefly described and this description provides a definition:

> I have neither the Schollers melancholy, which is emulation: nor the Musitians, which is fantasticall; nor the Courtiers, which is proud: nor the Souldiers, which is ambitious; nor the Lawiers, which is politick: nor the Ladies, which is nice: nor the Lovers, which is all these: but it is a melancholy of mine owne . . .   (AYL IV.I.10)

401. *Hendiadys* is the use of two nouns linked by 'and' for a noun and its modifier, as in 'Well ratified by Law, and Heraldrie' (Ham. I.1.87), where the last three words mean 'the laws of heraldry'. The letter which Edmund pretends that he has received from Edgar begins: This policie, and reverence of Age, makes the

world bitter to the best of our times: (Lear 1.2.49). It is probable that 'policie, and reverence' means 'policy of reverence'.

402. *Hypallage* is the figure which divorces appropriate partners when several related ideas are listed. Bottom is fond of it:

> The eye of man hath not heard, the eare of man hath not seen, mans hand is not able to taste, his tongue to conceive, nor his heart to report, what my dreame was. (MND IV.1.214)

This habit affects his imagery:

> I will aggravate my voyce so, that I will roare you as gently as any sucking Dove; I will roare and 'twere any Nightingale
> (1.2.82)

Another offender is Slender in *The Merry Wives of Windsor*:

> All his successors (gone before him) hath don't: and all his Ancestors (that come after him) may: (1.1.11).

403. *Hyperbole*, or exaggeration, is especially used by women characters. When Orlando protests that he has come within an hour of his promise, Rosalind replies:

> Breake an houres promise in love? hee that will divide a minute into a thousand parts, and breake but a part of the thousand part of a minute in the affairs of love, it may be said of him that *Cupid* hath clapt him oth' shoulder, but Ile warrant him heart hole. (AYL IV.1.45)

Portia indulges in hyperbole to express her love for Bassanio:

> though for my selfe alone
> I would not be ambitious in my wish,
> To wish my selfe much better, yet for you,
> I would be trebled twenty times my selfe,
> A thousand times more faire, ten thousand times
> More rich, (Merch III.2.152)

Falstaff seems to bring out hyperbole in others. Prince Hal describes him as 'this huge Hill of Flesh' (1H4 II.4.268); Doll Tearsheet says: Thou art as valorous as *Hector* of Troy, worth five of *Agamemnon*, and tenne times better then the nine Worthies (2H4 II.4.239).

Paulina uses hyperbole for vituperation in reproaching Leontes:

A thousand knees,
Ten thousand yeares together, naked, fasting,
Upon a barren Mountaine, and still Winter
In storme perpetuall, could not move the Gods
To looke that way thou wer't.   (WT III.2.211)

404. *Metonymy* replaces a subject by an adjunct or an adjunct by a subject. In *Love's Labour's Lost* Katharine describes Cupid as 'a shrewd unhappy gallowes' (V.2.12). *Gallowes* is used by metonymy for *gallows-bird* 'one deserving to be hanged', as when Gonzalo says of the Boatswain, 'his complexion is perfect Gallowes' (Temp. I.1.28). Rosalind says: I must comfort the weaker vessell, as doublet and hose ought to show it selfe coragious to pettycoate; (AYL II.4.5).

405. *Oxymoron* has been defined as a witty absurdity. Orlando says to Adam: besides this nothing that he so plentifully gives me, (AYL I.1.16).

406. *Parison* is the figure in which several successive phrases or clauses are of corresponding structure. Nathaniel says to Holofernes:

I praise God for you sir, your reasons at dinner have been sharpe & sententious; pleasant without scurrillity, witty without affection, audacious without impudency, learned without opinion, and strange without heresie.   (LLL.V.1.2)

407. *Repetition* is a common rhetorical device. Antony's repetition of *ambitious* and *honourable* in his funeral oration on Caesar is a famous example, and it allows the audience to trace the crowd's growing realization that the latter word is used ironically. Another example is in a speech by Isabella in *Measure for Measure*:

Angelo   And she will speake most bitterly, and strange.
Isabella   Most strange: but yet most truely will I speake,

That *Angelo's* forsworne, is it not strange?
That *Angelo's* a murtherer, is't not strange?
That *Angelo* is an adulterous thiefe,
An hypocrite, a virgin violator,
Is it not strange? and strange?

Duke   Nay it is ten times strange?   (V.1.37)

Edmund's soliloquy on his illegitimacy (Lear I.2.1) provides a

good example of the use of repetition. He first repeats the word
'base' as though incredulous that it should be applied to him: Why
brand they us With Base? with basenes Barstadie? Base, Base?
and he then goes on to repeat the word 'legitimate', applying it, in
derision, to Edgar:

> Well then,
> Legitimate Edgar, I must have your land,
> Our Fathers love, is to the Bastard *Edmond*,
> As to th'legitimate: fine word: Legitimate.

408. Several characters have the mannerism of piling up synonyms or near-synonyms. The favourite number is three, and we
often find that of the three words one is of native origin, one from
French and one from Latin. This practice was common in Middle
English, when it served a practical purpose in a multilingual
community, and it has since survived as a feature of legal English,
where the use of several near-synonyms is a precaution against
accidental exclusions. In Shakespeare the practice is the result
partly of exuberance and partly of a desire to make provision for
the audience's failure to understand one of the words; the remain-
ing words serve as a gloss.

Sir Nathaniel speaks of 'a companion of the Kings, who is
intituled, nominated, or called, *Don Adriano de Armatho*' (LLL
V.I.7). Armado himself is fond of the practice: I meane, setting
thee at libertie. Enfreedoming thy person: thou wert emured,
restrained, captivated, bound. (III.I.124). It is used especially when
a character with some pretensions to culture is trying to impress
someone who has none, as when Touchstone says to William:

> Therefore you Clowne, abandon: which is in the vulgar, leave
> the societie: which in the boorish, is companie, of this female:
> which in the common, is woman: which together, is, abandon
> the society of this Female, or Clowne, thou perishest: or, to thy
> better understanding, dyest; or (to wit) I kill thee, make thee
> away, translate thy life into death, thy libertie into bondage:
> (AYL V.I.49)

Quince, as the intellectual among the Athenian rude mechanicals,
uses the same device: I am to intreat you, request you, and desire
you, to con them by toomorrow night: (MND I.2.101).

409. In their different ways Holofernes and Osric, Nell Quickly and Ancient Pistol are all fascinated by words. When a speaker's fascination with words outruns his knowledge, the result is likely to be a malapropism; when he has control of the situation, the result may well be a pun. Two main categories of puns may be distinguished: the homonymic and the semantic. The first category is the kind that we usually think of when we speak of a pun today; it is made possible by the existence of two words of different origin and meaning that happen to be pronounced alike, and the punster chooses a context that will fit either word.

An example is the jest of the dying Mercutio: aske for me to morrow, and you shall find me a grave man. (RJ III.1.102). Other examples of homonymic puns occur in King Henry's dismissal of the angry Worcester: You have good leave to leave us (1H4 1.3.20) and in Falstaff's quibble: were it heere apparant, that thou art Heire apparant. (1H4 1.2.62). The present-day practice of distinguishing between some pairs of homophones by using consistently different spellings for the two words was not followed in Elizabethan times, and occasional spellings can help to give an indication which words were homophones.

Dialectal or vulgar pronunciations sometimes form the basis of puns, as do the mispronunciations of foreigners, and there are bilingual puns in *The Merry Wives of Windsor* (Latin-English) and *King Henry V* (French-English). The lesson which Evans gives to William (MWW IV.1.) abounds in echoes of the Latin grammars used in schools at the time. Such scenes tell us something of the kind of audience for which Shakespeare wrote; the grammatical terms had to be familiar to the audience for Nell Quickly's misunderstanding of them to have any point.

A semantic pun arises from the use of a word in two different senses within a single sentence. The word may be a very common one, such as 'by' when Antony says that he would like to die 'heere by *Cæsar*, and by you cut off,' (JC III.1.162). It is not uncommon to find one character using a word in one of its senses while another deliberately understands it in a different sense. Benvolio says to Romeo: Tell me in sadnesse, who is that you love? Romeo replies: What shall I grone and tell thee? (RJ I.1.207). Benvolio is using *sadnesse* in the sense 'seriousness', but Romeo chooses to understand it in the sense 'misery'. Silence, remembering Shallow's youth, says: You were call'd lustie *Shallow* then (Cousin). (2H4 III.2.15). *Lusty* has two common senses: 'lively' and 'lascivious'. Either or both of these senses may be intended here. Both senses provide a contrast between Shallow as he is now and as he may have been as a young man.

410. For Shakespeare a pun was not necessarily a joke; it could, like any other figure of speech, be a solemn and dignified way of adding point to a statement. Famous examples of Shakespearian puns in serious contexts are Gratiano's retort Not on thy soale: but on thy soule harsh Jew Thou mak'st thy knife keene: (Merch. IV.1.123); and Lady Macbeth's Ile guild the Faces of the Groomes withall, For it must seeme their Guilt. (Macb. II.2.55).

411. Shakespeare was fond of bawdy puns. It is not only characters like Mercutio or Mistress Quickly who indulge in them; women of fashion like Rosalind and Celia shared the taste. This fact has its significance in textual interpretation; we must not start with the assumption that a lady would not say such things. Bawdy puns are often unsuspected by a modern reader because of changes in pronunciation or word-meanings, but their presence can be inferred from their effect on other characters. Jaques. reporting Touchstone, says:

> And so from houre to houre, we ripe, and ripe,
> And then from houre to houre, we rot, and rot,
> And thereby hangs a tale.   (AYL II.7.26)

This causes Jaques to 'laugh, sans intermission An houre by his diall', and a reader of today is liable to think that Jaques is very easily amused. Kökeritz, however, points out (p. 59) that *houre* was pronounced like *whore*, that there were two verbs *ripe*, one meaning 'ripen' and the other 'search', and that *tale* is a pun on *tail*. An hour's laughter still seems excessive, but there is an ingenious threefold bawdy pun. Other examples of bawdy puns are Nell Quickly's malapropism *fartuous – virtuous* (MWW II.2.101), the equivocal broken English of Evans and Dr Caius, and the mock-Latin examination in *The Merry Wives of Windsor* (II.1).

412. Many Shakespearian puns have been concealed by changes in pronunciation that have taken place since his time, and we are sometimes uncertain whether a pun was intended. Henry Bradley (*Shakespeare's England* II.541) rejected the possibility of a pun on

night and *knight* in the reference to 'Squires of the Nights bodie' (1H4 1.2.24), saying that the initial *k* in *knight* was pronounced, but Dover Wilson pointed to the probable pun on *nave* and *knave* in 2H4 11.4.277. The explanation of many such uncertainties lies in the likelihood that variant pronunciations were used side by side, and when a pun adds point to a passage we can often assume that it was intended even though the required pronunciation was occasional rather than usual. There are unsolved mysteries in the text of Shakespeare which may be due to a play on words; such may be the explanation of 'M,O,A,I' in the letter written to Malvolio in *Twelfth Night* (11.5.118). Sometimes there may be a slight obstacle to the understanding of a pun which restricts its enjoyment to the more sophisticated members of the audience. Only those spectators who knew the etymology of *capricious* would enjoy the quibbling on *goat* and *capricious* in AYL 111.3.6.

413. Allied to the pun is the jingle, which arises from the partial resemblance in pronunciation of two words used together, as in 'Who dotes, yet doubts' (Oth. 111.3.170). Another kind of jingle is provided when a short word is identical with a part of a longer word used in the same sentence, as in 'O take the sence sweet, of my innocence,' (MND 11.2.45).

414. Two important figures of speech point out likenesses between things superficially dissimilar: simile and metaphor. Sustained similes were common in the academic epics of Shakespeare's predecessors, and they are sometimes to be found in Shakespeare, as in the player's speeches in *Hamlet* 11.2.498, but they have an old-fashioned and artificial air. The most common image is that found when a simile is condensed into a metaphor, and in Shakespeare the condensation became more marked as his literary career progressed. It is condensation of thought which accounts for the much derided mixed metaphor. The author's mind passes rapidly from one comparison to another within a single sentence, and the reader whose mind moves less quickly is liable to describe as mixed what is really a rapid succession of metaphors. We thus get passages like Lady Macbeth's reproach:

> Was the hope drunke,
> Wherein you drest your selfe? Hath it slept since?
> And wakes it now to looke so greene, and pale,
> At what it did so freely? (Macb. 1.7.35)

A metaphor may be combined with another figure of speech, such as metonymy, as when Bertram describes himself as 'the for-horse to a smocke', i.e. 'the leader in a team of horses driven by a woman', (AWW II.1.30).

The most famous study of Shakespeare's use of metaphor is Caroline Spurgeon's *Shakespeare's Imagery and What It Tells Us* (CUP, 1935), and this book provides valuable evidence of the sort of topics and sensations to which Shakespeare was sensitive. The author points out, for example, that, in contrast with some of his contemporaries, Shakespeare was interested in nature and gardening but not in the life of towns; he drew images from everyday domestic life rather than from literature. He was sensitive to offensive smells, especially to unwashed humanity or decaying corpses; to make clear the offensiveness of sin he described it as having a bad smell. On the other hand, he could derive pleasure from the variations in the sound of the human voice. Cordelia's voice 'was ever soft, Gentle, and low, an excellent thing in woman' (Lear V.3.272), and Miss Spurgeon (p. 71) quotes many other references to the quality of the voice of characters in the plays. It is of especial interest to see how certain groups of images seem to dominate particular plays. In *Romeo and Juliet* the dominant images are those of light and darkness (Spurgeon p. 213); in *Hamlet* they are of disease, in *King Lear* they refer to animals. Certain images are recurrently associated with other images. The associations that are most interesting are those where the linked images are disparate. There is nothing surprising in the association of kingship with flattery, but the imagery of dreaming is often introduced as well. Death and vaults are natural associates, but it is remarkable to find eyes often mentioned in the same sentence. A very frequent group of images is that which links flattery with a dog licking and fawning or with sugar melting (Spurgeon p. 195).

Vickers[1] calls attention to Shakespeare's sensitivity to the way in which a character will react to the images used by another character. A quick-witted character will catch up the metaphor and reply, preserving the imagery:

> *Maria* Will you hoyst sayle sir, here is your way.
> *Viola* No good swabber, I am to hull here a little longer.
>
> (TN I.5.220)

1. Brian Vickers, *The Artistry of Shakespeare's Prose* (Methuen, 1968), p. 226.

If the person addressed is hostile or dull-witted, he will either pretend not to understand the imagery or will in fact be baffled:

Sir Toby Taste your legges sir, put them to motion.
Viola My legges do better understand me sir, then I understand what you meane by bidding me taste my legges.
(TN III.1.89)

415. Critics have not been slow to point out that the painstaking listing and classification of Shakespeare's images does not go to the heart of the matter in the study of his figurative language, but it is a useful beginning. The important question is not from what sources did he draw his images but how did he use them. The answer to this question demands a close study of the text of each play.

It is dangerous to assume on the basis of one or two contexts that Shakespeare regarded a particular image as humorous. We might assume on the basis of Don Armado's 'the *posteriors* of this day, which the rude multitude call the after-noone' (LLL V.1.94), or the reference by Menenius to 'the Buttocke of the night' (Cor. II.1.55), that Shakespeare regarded this image as one suitable only for satirical or light-hearted use, but it is found elsewhere in a quite serious context. King Henry IV says:

O *Westmerland*, thou art a Summer Bird,
Which ever in the haunch of Winter sings
The lifting up of day. (2H4 IV.4.91)

There may be a difference between Elizabethan and modern ideas about what imagery is to be taken seriously. Today the comparison of tears to rain, if used at all, would be light-hearted or flippant; it would not be used in speaking to someone suffering from real grief. It is in line with the Elizabethan willingness to play on words on serious occasions that Prince Hal can greet his brothers, watching their dying father: How now? Raine within doores, and none abroad? (2H4 IV.5.9)

CHAPTER 9

Dialects, Registers and Idiolects

🕮🕮🕮🕮🕮🕮

REGIONAL DIALECTS

416. When Shakespeare uses dialect in his plays, he does not use that of his native Warwickshire but is content with the conventional stage Southern dialect. Modern dialects can often help in the interpretation of passages from the plays, but the help that they give is usually due to the survival in dialect of words and meanings that were in Shakespeare's time features of standard English. The influence of regional dialects is to be found in Shakespeare's plays in vocabulary and pronunciation, and to a much less extent in syntax and semantics. The features of the conventional stage dialect that he used are today found chiefly in the South-West, but they were originally found in most of the dialects south of the Thames. They included such characteristics as the voicing of initial [f] and [s], the change of initial [θr] to [dr], and the use of *ich* for the pronoun *I*, with the consequent use of the contracted forms *cham* 'I am' and *chill* 'I will'. Some of the variants used by low-life characters are not necessarily dialectal. Peter Quince's *shrike* (MND 1.2.78) is used by King Richard II (R2 III.3.183); Pistol's *erne* (H5 II.3.2) has its parallel in *earnes* (JC II.2.129). Occasional dialectal forms are liable to occur in any of the plays. Gobbo's *philhorse* (Merch. II.2.101) is an example of the use of [f] for [θ] that we now think of as a feature of Cockney dialect, though it is much more widespread. Launcelot's *fia* for *via* (Merch. II.2.10) is an inverted form made possible by the voicing of initial [f] in Southern dialects.[1] Shakespeare's use of dialect is sketchy and conventional, consisting of a few hints to the actor. When he chooses a special language for his low-life characters, he generally uses malapropisms with coarse word-play. His foreigners either speak normal English or, for comic effect, butcher the English language, often with bawdy puns.

1. See H. Kökeritz, *Shakespeare's Pronunciation* (Yale University Press, 1953), p. 323.

417. The best example of conventional stage dialect is in the exchanges between Edgar and Oswald in *King Lear* (IV.6.237–50). The First Folio text has more dialectal forms than the First Quarto, although there is an exception in the Quarto reading *cagion*, compared with Folio *casion*. The First Folio version shows voicing of initial *f* and *s* in *vurther, vor, volke, vortnight* (but not in the loanword *foynes*); *Zir, ʒo, ʒwagger'd*. In *che vor'ye* (l.47) [ə] has developed between *ch* (for *ich* 'I') and a following consonant. *Vor* may stand for *warn*, or possibly *warrant*; in either case the spelling with *o* shows that the rounding influence of *w* had already become effective in Southern dialects. The use of *ice* for *I shall* in the same line is usually said to be Northern, but it is found in modern South-Western dialects.

418. A number of dialectal forms occur in *The Merry Wives of Windsor* and in the two parts of *King Henry IV* and *King Henry V*. The local pronunciation of *Cotswold* is reflected in *Cotsall* (MWW I.1.91). The initial Y in *Yead Miller* for *Edward* (MWW I.1.161) has a parallel in *Yedward* (1H4 I.2.149). This is found in a number of Midland dialects. Silence describes his daughter as 'a blacke Ouzell' (2H4 III.2.7), and Q reads *woosel*, a spelling which may reflect Silence's rustic pronunciation. OED records *Woosell* as a sixteenth- and seventeenth-century spelling. Bottom (MND III.1.128) refers to 'The Woosell cocke, so blacke of hew'. In *2 King Henry IV* Bardolph as drill sergeant, giving orders to his recruits, says: 'Hold *Wart*, Traverse: thus, thus, thus; (III.2.292). This is the Folio reading; in the Quarto the last three words are spelled 'thas, thas, thas'. Ridley[1] suggests as a special reason for the unusual spelling that this may be a parody of a drill-sergeant's pronunciation. To speakers of standard English many dialect speakers seem to omit the definite article freely. In fact the impression is often a mistaken one, the definite article being reduced to a glottal stop or a pause which can easily be detected by dialect speakers though not by unaccustomed ears. It may be that some such development underlies the language of *1 King Henry IV* where we should expect an article in standard English: Poore fellow never joy'd since the price of oats rose, (II.1.11).

419. Northern dialects are represented in *King Henry V* III.2, where the Scottish Captain Jamy appears, together with the

1. Quoted by A. R. Humphreys in the New Arden edition of the play (Methuen, 1967), p. 110.

Welshman Fluellen and the Irishman Macmorris. Jamy's *gud* may stand for [gʌd] or [gy:d]. *Grund* is for [grund] with a short vowel before a consonant group that has caused lengthening in standard English. *Bath* 'both' is from a Northern form without ME rounding of *ā*. The Scottish diphthongization of ME *ī* to [ei] is reflected in *ayle* beside *Ile* 'I'll'. The *ei* in *feith* points to a close vowel [e:]. *De* 'do' may be an unaccented form. An [e] has been lowered in *vary*. *Mes* 'Mass' is said to be chiefly Scottish and Northern (OED s.v. Mass sb.). *Wad* 'would' shows unrounding of the vowel. *Captens* has *e* to represent an unaccented vowel. *Breff* seems to have a short vowel. Initial *sh* appears as *s* in *sall*, and *lig* 'lie' is still found in Northern dialects. Jamy omits the auxiliary *have* in *I wad full faine heard* (l.26), a feature not confined to Scotland.

420. Costard says *vara* for 'very' (LLL v.2.488). He has metathesis of *re* in *pursents* for *presents*, i.e. 'represents' (v.2.489). These dialectal pronunciations led Dover Wilson to conjecture[1] that when Costard comments on the dancing of Rosaline and Boyet: *how both did fit it!* (IV.1.131), *fit* may be his pronunciation of *foot*.

421. In considering the extent to which Shakespeare uses dialect vocabulary, we have to remember that dialect words do not necessarily remain dialectal for the whole of their history. Today we think of *lass* as a north-country word, but it is not certain that it was so regarded by Shakespeare. It is in accordance with modern usage that Stephano should speak of Miranda as 'a Lasse' (Temp. III.2.111) but not that Cleopatra should be 'A lasse unparalell'd' (Ant. v.2.319). Iris, introducing the masque in *The Tempest*, uses the compound *lasse-lorne* 'forsaken by one's sweetheart' (IV.1.68), and the vocabulary of the whole speech is appropriately rustic, including such words as *Leas, Fetches, Pease, Stover, pioned, twilled, broome-groves, pole-clipt, grasse-plot*. It is sometimes said that *Barne* 'child' (WT III.3.71) is a northernism, because today *bairn* is especially northern, but the word was formerly current all over England. Shakespeare uses it in AW 1.3.28 and Ado III.4.49. On the other hand, Costard's *where-untill* (LLL v.2.501) is probably a northernism.

422. A few idiomatic phrases used by Shakespeare are preserved in dialects. 'Go on wheeles' is used in the sense 'to pursue a course of ease and self-indulgence' (Ant. II.7.100). The phrase is used in Warwickshire of a clock that goes fast. Iago urges Othello

1. In the New Shakespeare edition of the play (Second edition, CUP, 1962), p. 155.

to 'Speake within doore' (Oth. IV.2.144), meaning 'Do not talk so loud'. Bradley (*Shakespeare's England* II.572) reports the use of 'speak within the house' in the same sense in Birmingham.

423. Much information about Shakespeare's dialect vocabulary is included by C. T. Onions in *A Shakespeare Glossary* (1911), and in the Preface to that work (p. iv) he includes a list of words used by Shakespeare that are also found in Midland dialects, especially those of Warwickshire. The list includes such words as *ballow* 'cudgel', *batlet* 'club', *blood-bolter'd* 'having the hair matted with blood', *bum-baily* 'sheriff's officer', *elder-gun* 'pop-gun', *gallow* 'to frighten', *potch* 'to thrust at', *tarre* 'to provoke'. The list could be extended. *Frame* is used by Gower in *Pericles* (I, Prol. 32) in the sense 'to direct one's steps, go' and this sense survives in Yorkshire dialects. Sir Andrew says of Sir Toby: if he had not beene in drinke, hee would have tickel'd you other gates than he did. (TN V.1.204). *Other gates* 'in another way' presents no difficulty to a northerner familiar with *gate* in the sense 'way', as in 'Get aht o't gate'. In the Boar's Head Tavern Francis describes a trick which the Prince and Poins are to play on Falstaff. The comment of the First Drawer is: Then here will be old Utis; it will be an excellent stratagem. (2H4 II.4.23). The second half of this speech does not seem to be quite in character and it is certainly not typical lower-class speech, but the first half is more convincing. *Old* has the common Elizabethan sense 'great, plentiful, abundant', and something of this sense remains today in the phrase which A. R. Humphreys uses to gloss *old utis*: 'a high old time'.[1] *Utis* may be a variant of *utas* (from *octave*) 'jollification, period of festivity' (OED Utas 1c) and this may be the same word as that quoted in EDD from Worcestershire: '*Utis* "noise, confusion, din".' Parallels from modern dialects can be quoted to the Shakespearean uses of some very common words, for example *as* used as a relative is a feature of Elizabethan syntax that survives in dialects. Sir Hugh Evans says:

> But those as sleepe and thinke not on their sins,
> Pinch them, armes, legs, backes, shoulders, sides, & shins.

(MWW V.5.57)

This use is paralleled by the modern dialectal 'Let 'em gnash 'em as 'as 'em'.

1. In the New Arden edition of the play (Methuen, 1967), p. 63.

CLASS DIALECTS

424. The conception of class dialect is one that has acquired importance since the time of Shakespeare, but we find in his plays the beginnings of a feeling for the differences between upper- and lower-class speech. Prince Hal boasts that he 'can drinke with any Tinker in his owne Language' (1H4 II.4.20), and he obviously enjoys the role of field-worker in the study of the language of the drawers at the Boar's Head Tavern. He reports that they call him 'a Corinthian, a lad of mettle, a good boy' (l.11), and he makes a note of some of the phrases that they use:

> They call drinking deepe dying Scarlet and when you breath in your watering, then they cry hem, and bid you play it off. (l.15)

Certain words are used in the plays wholly or mainly by low-life characters. Idioms are less easy to identify as substandard, but *come* with expressions of time to indicate something that is to happen in the future seems to be used in Shakespeare, as it is today, chiefly by substandard speakers:

> I have knowne thee these twentie nine yeeres, come Pescod-time: (2H4 II.4.412, Mrs Quickly)

> his Childe is a yeere and a quarter olde come *Philip* and *Jacob*: (Meas. III.2.213, Mrs Overdone)

Low-life characters are constantly getting into trouble for reasons that they do not fully understand. They try to avert some of this trouble by apologetic parentheses. When Launcelot Gobbo says that Shylock is a kind of devil he says 'God blesse the marke' (Merch. II.2.26), and OED describes this (s.v. Mark sb. 18) as a formula to divert an evil omen. In the same speech Launcelot mentions the devil again, this time with the apologetic parenthesis 'saving your reverence' (l.38). Since the speech is a soliloquy, it is clear that these words have become a mere tag, and they are so used by Gobbo, who says in recommending his son to Bassanio: His Maister and he (saving your worships reverence) are scarce catercosins. (Merch. II.2.138). Gobbo's oaths are substandard: Be Gods sonties (II.2.42). When Launcelot speaks to his father he puts on airs, using the logical term 'ergo' and an off-hand elevated style: according to fates and destinies, and such odde sayings, the

sisters three, & such branches of learning (II.2.65). This is super-
ficial showing off. When he speaks of himself as 'deceased', he
patronizingly translates the word for his father's benefit: or as you
would say in plaine tearmes, gone to heaven. (l.67).

The form *a leuen* for 'eleven' is used chiefly by low-life characters. Examples are: Costard (LLL III.1.172); Launcelot (Merch.
II.2.171); and the Clown in *The Winter's Tale* (IV.3.33). Today the
clipped form is found chiefly in Northern and East Anglian
dialects.

Love of detail is a traditional feature of the language of low-life
characters. Launcelot Gobbo says:

> I will not say you shall see a Maske, but if you doe, then it was
> not for nothing that my nose fell a bleeding on blacke monday
> last, at six a clocke ith morning, falling out that yeere on
> ashwensday was foure yeere in th'afternoone.   (Merch. II.5.23)

425. We find in *As You Like It* the beginnings of a feeling for
class dialect, when Orlando comments on Rosalind's speech:

Orlando   Your accent is something finer, then you could pur-
          chase in so removed a dwelling.
Rosalind I have been told so of many: but indeed, an olde
          religious Unckle of mine taught me to speake, who
          was in his youth an inland man,   (III.2.360)

It has been suggested that the dialect which Rosalind has acquired
is a regional one, but there is a clear suggestion that the dialects of
remote places are less 'fine' than those spoken by educated people.
As often today, a regional dialect has become one of class. Similarly
in *King Lear* Gloucester notices the improvement in the speech of
the disguised Edgar:

> Me thinkes thy voyce is alter'd, and thou speak'st
> In better phrase, and matter then thou did'st.   (IV.6.7)

Later in the play Edmund is willing to accept the challenge of
Edgar, giving as one of his reasons: that thy tongue (some say) of
breeding breathes, (V.3.143).

426. We tend to think of class dialect as being only a question
of the speech of social classes considered as a number of horizontal
layers, but any group of people who use the same variety of a
language can be regarded as speaking a class dialect, provided that

the link joining them together is not a regional one. In Shake-speare such groups are old men, affected courtiers, foreigners with an imperfect command of English, the logic-chopping clowns in the early plays, and many others. The everyday speech of the artisans in *A Midsummer Night's Dream* when they are talking to one another is different from that which they use in their play within the play, where Shakespeare burlesques the inflated langu-age used seriously by other dramatists. Within the groups charac-ters are individualized in fairly simple ways. The recruits in *2 King Henry IV* (III.2) are all low-life characters, but Bullcalf has his own favourite phrase 'for mine owne part', and Feeble has his conso-latory proverbs. Euphuistic devices are commonly found in the speech of minor characters who act as messengers or describe events that have taken place off-stage. Such characters are Osric and the nameless gentleman in *King Lear* (III.1.4). But not all messengers talk in this way; The messenger from Antony to Brutus in *Julius Cæsar* (III.1.122) speaks quite differently. Another variety of speech used by minor characters is that of the gardeners in *King Richard II* (III.4.29), with their application of gardening similes to politics.

427. The most noticeable characteristic of the speech of Shake-speare's old men is that they speak in short, jerky sentences, as though out of breath. The old shepherd in *The Winter's Tale* says:

> 'Mercy on's, a Barne? A very pretty barne; A boy, or a Childe
> I wonder? (A pretty one, a verie prettie one) sure some Scape;
> Though I am not bookish, yet I can reade Waiting-Gentle-
> woman in the scape.'   (III.3.69)

They have individual habits as well. Shallow, for example, is fond of repeating his short sentences. He has not many ideas and he makes up for their lack by saying what he has to say several times. In reply to Falstaff's 'You must excuse me, M. *Robert Shallow*' he says:

> I will not excuse you: you shall not be excused. Excuses shall
> not be admitted: there is no excuse shall serve: you shall not be
> excus'd.   (2H4 v.1.4)

He attaches importance to titles, including his own: he is '*Robert Shallow* Esquire' and Dr Caius is 'Mr. Doctor *Caius*' (MWW 1.1.110 and 11.3.19). He is patronizing in his forms of address: 'good

Master *Page*' and 'My merry Host' (MWW II.1.202, 211), and his greetings are pompous and fulsome: 'Good-even and twenty' (MWW II.1.202). His vocabulary is old-fashioned: a fight is a 'fray' (MWW II.1.206). One of his characteristics is 'the pride that apes humility'. He describes himself as 'a poore Esquire of this Countrie' (2H4 III.2.63), and in reply to Falstaff's praise of his house he says 'Barren, barren, barren; Beggers all, beggers all Sir *John*: Marry, good ayre' (2H4 V.3.6). He is feeble-witted and too appreciative of Falstaff's very elementary humour:

> Ha, ha, ha, most excellent. Things that are mouldie lacke use: very singular good, Well saide Sir *John*, very well said.
>
> (2H4 III.2.119)

One of the reasons for speaking of oneself in the third person is self-importance. Shallow, like Dickens's Major Bagstock, does this: beleeve me, *Robert Shallow* Esquire, saith he is wronged. (MWW I.1.109). He jerks from one subject to another and back again, mixing the serious and the trivial. He accepts Silence's reminder that all men must die:

> *Shallow* Certaine: 'tis certaine: very sure, very sure: Death is certaine to all, all shall dye. How a good Yoke of Bullocks at Stamford Fayre?
> *Silence* Truly Cousin, I was not there.
> *Shallow* Death is certaine. (2H4 III.2.40)

The idiom *my name is called* is used chiefly by old men: My name is call'd *Vincentio*, (Shrew IV.5.55). Ægeon asks: Is not your name sir call'd *Antipholus*? (Err. V.1.286). Pistol uses the idiom: My name is *Pistol* call'd (H5 IV.1.62), but Miss Cusack is no doubt right in suggesting that he is using an idiom associated with old-fashioned speakers.[1]

428. One of the best satirical portraits in the plays of Shakespeare is that of a character who never appears: Hotspur's description of the lord who comes on behalf of the king to demand his prisoners. This lord, who belongs to the school of Osric and Le Beau, seems to have annoyed Hotspur by his speech-habits as well as by his other affectations: With many Holiday and Lady tearme He question'd me: (1H4 I.3.46). It annoys Hotspur

1. Bridget Cusack 'Shakespeare and the Tune of the Time' in *Shakespeare Survey* 23 (CUP, 1970), p. 5.

that the lord should 'talke so like a Waiting-Gentlewoman' (l.55), and he dislikes 'This bald, unjoynted Chat of his' (l.65).

REGISTERS

429. Register is the name given to a variety of language which depends not on the speaker but on the occasion when that variety is used. Recognition of the appropriate register has a good deal to do with our appreciation of a play or a novel. It is instructive to see how the register may change many times in the course of a single scene; the entrance of a new character may change the atmosphere from friendly to hostile and this change is reflected in the language. Among registers we may include the different kinds of repartee, greetings and oaths, and the ways in which characters modify their speech according to their opinion of the persons they are addressing.

430. Repartee takes many different forms. One type is the deliberately uninformative reply, like that of Malvolio when he is questioned by Olivia about Viola: 'What kinde o' man is he?' 'Why of mankinde.' (TN 1.5.160), and Hamlet's reply to Polonius's question 'What do you read my Lord?': 'Words, words, words.' (Ham. II.2.191). Another way of expressing resentment is to seize upon one word of a question and to hurl it back, often with a syntactic function that it does nor normally bear (see § 63). Sometimes the word thus scornfully repeated has been used only in the imagination of the speaker. Falstaff, after robbing the travellers, chooses to assume that they have claimed to be grand-jurors: 'you are Grand Jurers, are ye? Wee'l jure ye, ifaith.' (1H4 II.2.96). A character may take up the last word used by another speaker and use it in a different sense. Hermione says, with admirable restraint, that Leontes is mistaken in calling her an adultress. Leontes replies: You have mistooke (my Lady) *Polixenes* for *Leontes*: (WT II.1.81). Sir Toby Belch resorts to this trick twice in replying to Maria:

Maria Your Cosin, my Lady, takes great exceptions to your ill houres.
Toby Why let her except, before excepted.
Maria I, but you must confine your selfe within the modest limits of order.

Toby   Confine? Ile confine my selfe no finer then I am: these cloathes are good enough to drinke in, and so bee these boots too: (TN I.2.4)

The most common kind of repartee is that found when a character deliberately misunderstands a word used by another character, and replies with a pun or by polysemy, giving to a word a meaning different from that intended by the speaker. Glendower claims that he has repulsed King Henry:

> thrice from the Banks of Wye,
> And sandy-bottom'd Severne, have I sent him
> Bootlesse home, and Weather-beaten backe.

Hotspur   Home without Bootes,
> And in foul weather too,
> How scapes he Agues in the Devils name?

(1H4 III.1.64)

The speaker's object is not to convince but to confuse or amuse his hearer.

Desdemona expresses her horror of adultery without convincing Emilia:

Des.   Would'st thou do such a deed for all the world?
Æmil.   Why, would not you?
Des.   No, by this Heavenly light.
Æmil.   Nor I neither, by this Heavenly light:
> I might doo't as well i'th'darke.   (Oth IV.3.64)

Emilia's readiness to jest on such a subject emphasizes Desdemona's purity by contrast. The device is often used by a sophisticated character in teasing a simple one. Touchstone undertakes to prove that Corin is damned for not having been at court:

Why, if thou never was't at Court, thou never saw'st good manners: if thou never saw'st good maners, then thy manners must be wicked, and wickednes is sin, and sinne is damnation:
(AYL III.2.39)

Most of these examples of misunderstanding are deliberate, but a fairly frequent comic situation arises when a character fails to understand the words used by himself or someone else. The Clown in *The Winter's Tale*, having got some new clothes, boasts that he is now 'a Gentleman borne' and has been 'any time these foure houres'. He hammers home the point of the joke by saying: 'but I was a Gentleman borne before my Father' (WT v.2.147).

The Clown provides another example of humour arising from misunderstanding when Autolycus uses the word 'advocate', baffling the Clown and his father until the Clown explains: Advocate's the Court-word for a Pheazant: (IV.4.764). This type of humour is old.

A less common form of deliberate misunderstanding is to pretend to mistake a word for another that slightly resembles it, as when Olivia says to Sir Toby: 'how have you come so earely by this Lethargie?' and he replies 'Letcherie, I defie Letchery:' (TN 1.5.131).

One form of repartee is simple vituperation, as practised by Thersites in *Troilus and Cressida*. In his encounter with Oswald in *King Lear* Kent begins by using the obstructive repartee that we associate with the Clowns in the early plays, but this soon gives way to eloquent vituperation:

> A Knave, a Rascall, an eater of broken meates, a base, proud, shallow, beggerly, three-suited-hundred pound, filthy woosted-stocking knave, a Lilly-livered, action-taking, whoreson glasse-gazing super-serviceable finicall Rogue, one Trunke-inheriting slave, one that would'st be a Baud in way of good service, and art nothing but the composition of a Knave, Begger, Coward, Pandar, and the Sonne and Heire of a Mungrill Bitch, one whom I will beate into clamours whining, if thou deny'st the least sillable of thy addition. (Lear II.2.15)

A man skilled in repartee shows how to escape blame by making it appear that he is the injured party. Prince Hal's admission that it was he who picked Falstaff's pocket makes it clear that the charge against Mistress Quickly is completely without foundation, but the discovery produces no apology: Hostesse, I forgive thee: . . . Thou seest, I am pacified still. Nay I prethee be gone. (1H4 III.3.191). Even the normally loquacious Hostess has no reply. Sometimes action, or proposed action, provides the deflation that is the purpose of repartee; it can be used to suggest that the speaker finds the discussion unprofitable. Of this kind is Celia's remark to Rosalind after hearing the eloquent confession of her love for Orlando: And Ile sleepe. (AYL IV.1.224). Sleep is a comment. Another example is Hotspur's brief reply to Glendower's eloquent boast that he is not in the roll of common men:

I thinke there's no man speakes better Welsh: Ile to Dinner.

(1H4 III.1.50)

We often find that one character makes a direct comment on the wit of another. Hamlet says of the gravedigger: How absolute the knave is? wee must speake by the Carde, or equivocation will undoe us: (v.1.150). The Clowns sometimes excite comments of admiration, like Viola's 'This fellow is wise enough to play the foole' (TN III.1.67) but more often the reaction is exasperation, as when Lorenzo tires of Launcelot's quibbles: How everie foole can play upon the word, I thinke the best grace of witte will shortly turne into silence, and discourse grow commendable in none onely but Parrats: (Merch. III.5.49). The language of this protest is too involved to be effective, and Lorenzo gets better results from a more direct protest: I pray thee understand a plaine man in his plaine meaning (l.59).

431. The technical terms of logic are frequently used in the plays, as when Falstaff says 'I deny your *Major*' (1H4 II.4.545). A frequent source of humour among Shakespeare's clowns is the use of the outward forms of logic to conceal a fallacy. Fallacious reasoning is often based upon a play on words. To get up early in the morning is often assumed to be virtuous, and it is an easy step for Sir Toby to assume that 'to get up' means the same as 'to be up'. Hence he assures Sir Andrew that 'to go to bed after midnight, is to goe to bed betimes.' (TN II.3.8).

In Shakespeare's plays arguments are frequent. Clowns are expected to be skilful in argument, as when Feste shows his worth by proving Olivia a fool (TN I.5.64). The gravediggers in *Hamlet* are skilled disputants. Every educated Elizabethan would have a knowledge of the forms and processes of argument, and Shakespeare adapts these devices to many different dramatic purposes. In *Twelfth Night, As You Like It* and *Much Ado About Nothing* the argument is light and playful. Rosalind, Benedick and Beatrice, and Cressida are skilful at fencing with words and are never at a loss for a reply. Richard III and Iago argue skilfully, though sometimes fallaciously, in support of their plotting. Hamlet's soliloquies are full of argument.

432. There is satire of the art of conversation expressed by both

description and example. Hamlet, swearing his friends to secrecy, gives a good imitation of people who give the impression that they know a lot that they do not choose to put into words:

That you at such time seeing me, never shall
With Armes encombred thus, or thus, head shake;
Or by pronouncing of some doubtfull Phrase;
As well, we know, or we could and if we would,
Or if we list to speake; or there be and if there might,
Or such ambiguous giving out to note,
That you know ought of me;   (1.5.172)

Iago provides examples of the use of tricks of behaviour to influence a hearer without words that can be quoted (Oth. iv.1). His starts, his hesitation and his feigned reluctance to speak can be inferred from Othello's comments and demands for explicitness. Iago begins by asking an apparently unimportant question and then attaches great importance to the answer: 'Indeed?' He makes it clear that he is holding something back by echoing Othello's questions instead of answering them. There is an illustration in the behaviour of Parolles (AW ii.3.1–45) of a slight unmeritable man pushing into a conversation by agreeing with everything that is said.

Some phrases are used as stop-gaps when conversation flags or when awkward questions call for a reply. Such is 'O Lord sir' used inappropriately by the Clown four times in speaking to the Countess (AW ii.2.47–54), causing her to comment on it. The same exclamation is much used by Costard (LLL v.2.485, 497, 500).

433. Certain conventional set pieces are incorporated in some of the plays. The best-known example of the 'advice to a son' is Polonius's advice to Laertes with its succession of short, pithy sentences; but the Countess of Rousillon provides another example in her advice to Bertram (AW i.1.67), and the theme was well established in Elizabethan times. Another favourite set piece is that where one character chooses a framework of similar questions to which another character is expected to give witty replies. Desdemona and Emilia play this game with Iago, asking how he would praise a woman who was black and witty, fair and foolish, and so forth (Oth. ii.1.117–161). Rosalind poses her own questions in saying with whom time ambles, trots, gallops and stands still (AYL iii.2.327), and the same approach is found in a less

stylized form in the conversation between Helena and Parolles on virginity (AW 1.1.117–178), where Helena acts as a 'feed' to encourage Parolles to be witty.

One type of set piece that we find in Shakespeare is that which enables a simple-minded character to sum up his views on life in a series of brief commonplaces expressed in simple language:

Touchstone Has't any Philosophie in thee shepheard?

Corin No more, but that I know the more one sickens, the worse at ease he is, and that hee that wants money, meanes, and content, is without three good frends. That the propertie of raine is to wet, and fire to burne: That good pasture makes fat sheepe; and that a great cause of the night, is lacke of the Sunne: That hee that hath learned no wit by Nature, nor Art, may complaine of good breeding, or comes of a very dull kindred. (AYL III.2.21)

Later in the scene Corin returns to his creed:

Sir, I am a true Labourer, I earne that I eate; get that I weare; owe no man hate, envie no mans happinesse: glad of other mens good content with my harme: and the greatest of my pride, is to see my Ewes graze, & my Lambes sucke. (l.78)

434. Greetings are sometimes deliberately fantastic:

Bragart Men of peace well incountred.

Pedant Most millitarie sir salutation. (LLL V.1.37)

More normal greetings are *Good morrow*, *(God) save you* and *How now?* In the two parts of *King Henry IV* the greetings between Hal and his associates at the Boar's Head Tavern vary with the characters and with their mood at the moment. Hal is fairly formal with Poins and Peto, and they are respectful ('good my Lord'). Falstaff is more familiar and on one occasion this familiarity is contrasted with a much more formal greeting to Westmorland, who is with Hal:

Prince How now blowne *Jack*? how now Quilt?

Falstaff What *Hal*? How now mad Wag, what a Devill do'st thou in Warwickshire? My good Lord of Westmerland, I cry you mercy, I thought your Honour had already beene at Shrewsbury. (1H4 IV.2.53)

435. There were several ways of avoiding the charge of blasphemy in the use of oaths. One was to substitute the pronoun *me* for the name of God, as when Menenius says: Fore me, this Fellow speakes, (Cor. 1.1.125). Another was to change *God* into some word of similar sound, as in 'Cockes passion' (Shrew IV.1.122); 'By goggs woones' (Shrew III.2.162); 'By Cocke and Pye' (2H4 V.1.1). A third way was to allow characters to swear by the gods of classical mythology. It is reasonable that Coriolanus should swear by Jupiter (Cor. 1.9.90) but less so that Malvolio should say 'Jove, not I, is the doer of this', (TN III.4.90). The oath 'by mine honor' was sufficiently new for Touchstone's use of it to occasion comment from Rosalind (AYL 1.2.66), but it is clear that it has become a vogue phrase whose over-use on trivial occasions is a proper subject of satire, when Touchstone speaks of a knight who swore by his honour they were good pancakes and swore by his honour the mustard was naught. Rosalind makes fun of mild oaths when she begins a speech to Orlando:

> By my troth, and in good earnest, and so God mend mee, and
> by all pretty oathes that are not dangerous, (AYL IV.1.193)

Sir Andrew Aguecheek is fond of mild oaths like *by my troth, in sooth, faith, i'faith*.

436. Persuasion may assume various forms. In addressing the Roman plebeians, Brutus appeals to their reason but, as Sister Miriam Joseph says (p. 286), he fails to understand that assent to the truth of an argument is no guarantee of action. Antony takes much more trouble to make sure that his hearers are in the right frame of mind to act on his suggestions. The artistry and rhetorical balance are too obvious in Brutus's speech. They are contrasted with the less obvious, but no less skilful, rhetoric of Antony and their lack of human feeling accounts for the failure of Brutus.

437. One aspect of register is the modification of speech in exchanges between people of different social classes. Hamlet is uniformly courteous in addressing servants. Orsino is so courteous in dismissing Feste from his presence ('Give me now leave, to leave thee', TN II.4.74) that editors have quite unnecessarily suspected corruption of the text. On the other hand, Portia addresses servants with abrupt familiarity: How now, what newes? (Merch. 1.2.128; Q reading); sirra go before (1.2.145). Courtesy to servants is illustrated by the various ways of giving a tip. Olivia, dismissing

Viola at the end of her first visit, says: 'spend this for mee' (TN
1.5.303); and Viola, in her turn, disguises her payment to Feste
with a formula that has been found useful in more recent times:
'Hold there's expences for thee' (III.1.47). Orsino's 'There's for
thy paines' (II.4.70) is conventional, but Sebastian's temper is
obviously wearing thin when he gives money to Feste: 'there's
money for thee, if you tarry longer, I shall give worse paiment.'
(IV.1.21).

IDIOLECTS

438. The Elizabethan conception of decorum was that words
should reflect the character of the speaker, and Shakespeare usually
took great pains to devise a form of language suitable to each of
his characters; but when we examine the appropriateness of Shakespeare's language to his characters, it is well to begin by admitting
that sometimes there seems to be no appropriateness at all. Caliban
says to Prospero: You taught me Language (Temp. 1.2.363); and
the reader's reflection must be that he made a very good job of it,
for Caliban's speeches, like the one telling Stephano that the isle is
full of noises (III.2.144), show a poetic feeling out of character with
Caliban the monster. It is quite common for characters in the plays
to describe their own linguistic habits, but these descriptions are
not necessarily true. There is a not infrequent type of irony which
leads them sometimes to be the exact opposite of the truth. Polonius
says that he will be brief and the promise emphasizes his prolixity.
After a long speech full of literary artifices, he swears that he uses
no art at all (Ham. II.2.96). The most eloquent character in Shakespeare preludes a speech dealing with moving accidents by flood
and field by saying: Rude am I, in my speech, And little bless'd
with the soft phrase of Peace; (Oth. 1.3.81).

439. Perhaps because stock character-types tend to appear in
different plays, it is possible to find pairs of characters whose
linguistic characteristics are similar. Slender and Sir Andrew Aguecheek are such a pair. Sir Andrew has to rely on Sir Toby for
constant prompting:

Toby And thou let part so Sir *Andrew*, would thou mightst
never draw sword agen.

Andrew And you part so mistris, I would I might never draw
sword again: (TN 1.3.64)

In the same way, Slender has to rely on Shallow in his wooing of Anne Page:

> *Shallow* Mistris *Anne*, my Cozen loves you.
> *Slender* I that I do, as well as I love any woman in Glocester-
> shire. (MWW III.4.42)

Just as Sir Andrew does not know the meaning of 'accost' (TN 1.3.55), so Slender misunderstands Anne's courteous enquiry 'What is your will?' (MWW III.4.55). They use the same forms of asseveration: I had rather then forty shillings (MWW I.1.205, TN II.3.20), and Slender's 'or else I would I might be hang'd (la), (MWW 1.1.267, cf. V.5.193) is in line with Sir Andrew's frequent method of confirming the truth of a statement. Slender apparently expects even his simplest statements to be disbelieved unless he adds some catch-phrase: he's a Justice of Peace in his countrie, simple though I stand here.' (MWW 1.1.266); Sir Andrew praises Feste's singing: a mellifluous voyce, as I am true knight. (TN II.3.54).

440. A good example of an idiolect is provided by the language of Gower, who appears as prologue to each act of *Pericles*. It is distinctive chiefly by reason of the archaisms in vocabulary and word-forms. Unusual words in his speeches include *Ember eves* 'the vigil of an Ember day', *frame* 'direct one's course', *wight* 'person', *Iwis* 'certainly' or 'I know', *long's* 'belongs to', *each* 'eke out', *dearne* 'secret', *wel-a-neare* 'alas', *hight* 'was called', *sleded silke* 'untwisted silk', *vaile* 'do homage', *prest* 'ready', *Inckle* 'tape', *aye* 'always'. *Attent* is used in the sense 'attentive' at III.Prol.11, but this word occurs elsewhere in Shakespeare (Ham. 1.2.193).

Beside archaisms of vocabulary, there are archaic forms: *mine Authors*, *killen* inf., *perishen* 3 pl. pres. ind., *been* 3 pl. pres. ind., *eyne* sb. pl. 'eyes', *drouth*, *yslacked*, *can* pret. 'began', *neele*, an old and dialectal form of *needle*.

In syntax the chief feature of Gower's language is the frequency of functional shift, which allows one part of speech to be used for another: *old* adv. 'of old', *plaine* v. 'to make plain', *enquire* sb. 'inquiry', *dumb's* v. 'makes dumb', *sisters* v. 'provides sisters for'. Some verbs are used in a slightly unidiomatic way. We are familiar with the idiom 'doing good', but we find 'tir'd with doing bad' (II.Prol.37) rather unusual, as we do 'to give him glad' in the next line. *Oppresse* is used in the etymological sense 'crush', applied to a mutiny, and *if might* is used elliptically to mean 'if it is possible'.

441. Even such a minor character as the Host of the Garter has many individual characteristics. He likes to use high-sounding words without having much concern for their meaning. He assures Simple that Falstaff will 'speake like an Anthropophaginian' (IV. 5.10). He is fond of displaying his knowledge of the technical terms of fencing:

> To see thee fight, to see thee foigne, to see thee traverse, to see thee heere, to see thee there, to see thee pass thy puncto, thy stock, thy reverse, thy distance, thy montant: (MWW II.3.26)

In his choice of words he ranges widely. He uses Italianate formations like *varletto* (IV.5.68) and *Cavaleiro* (II.3.76) as well as archaisms like *eeke* (II.3.76). He grows fond of certain words and uses them repeatedly in senses of his own, like *wag* for 'go' in 'shall we wag?' (II.1.236). He is proud of his vocabulary and constantly appeals for praise: thou shall have egresse and regresse, (said I well?) (II.1.226). He is exuberant rather than precise in his choice of words. His exuberance is shown by his piling-up of phrases to ring the changes on a single idea:

> Is he dead, my Ethiopian? Is he dead, my Francisco? ha Bully? what saies my *Esculapius*? my *Galien*? my heart of Elder? ha? is he dead, bully-Stale? is he dead? (II.3.29)

His lack of precision is seen when he promises Dr Caius to be his 'adversary toward *Anne Page*' (II.3.98). He uses short, clipped sentences, and he tries to be impressive by adopting an eccentric word-order: speake from thy Lungs Military: (IV.5.16).

442. Some of the characters are concerned to deflate the pretentious language of others. In *2 King Henry IV* both Hotspur and Prince Hal have this function. The Prince deflates Falstaff; Hotspur deflates his wife and Glendower. When Glendower boasts that the frame and foundation of the earth shook at his nativity, Hotspur replies: Why so it would have done at the same season, if your Mothers Cat had but kitten'd, though your selfe had never beene borne (1H4 III.1.18). Prose and homely images are both used to the same end: deflation of Glendower's high-flown pretensions. Hotspur himself can speak in an exalted vein, and the deflation of this is provided, in his absence, by the Prince. Hotspur is: he that killes me some six or seaven dozen of Scots at a Breakfast, washes his

hands, and saies to his wife; Fie upon this quiet life, I want worke. (1H4 II.4.117).

443. Armado in *Love's Labour's Lost* is satirized for his affectation and old-fashioned vocabulary. Before he appears we are prepared for him by a long speech of the King. Armado is:

A man in all the worlds new fashion planted,
That hath a mint of phrases in his braine: (LLL 1.1.165)

and Berowne sums him up:

Armado is a most illustrious wight,
A man of fire, new words, fashions owne Knight, (1.1.178)

He is preceded by his portentous letter. In the last scene of the play the Princess calls attention to his linguistic eccentricities: He speak's not like a man of God's making. (v.2.528). The speech which has occasioned this comment shows Armado at his most precious. With exaggerated courtesy he addresses the King: Annointed, I implore so much expence of thy royall sweet breath, as will utter a brace of words (l.523). He goes on to address the King as 'my faire sweet honie Monarch'. He uses rare loan-words like *infamonize* 'to defame' (v.2.685), but he can also use native words in an unusual way: I have no shirt, I go woolward for penance. (v.2.717). To say that Moth is badly cast as Hercules he can use perfectly simple language: hee is not so big as the end of his Club; but not before he has expressed the same idea less simply: He is not quantitie enough for that Worthies thumb, (v.1.134).

Even on trivial occasions Armado uses high-flown language, so it is natural that, when addressing the King of Navarre, he should let himself go:

Great Deputie, the Welkins Vicegerent, and sole dominator of Navar, my soules earths God, and bodies fostring patrone:

(I.1.222)

He achieves prolixity by insisting that every noun should have its adjective:

So it is besieged with sable coloured melancholie I did commend the blacke oppressing humour to the most wholesome Physicke of thy health-giving ayre: (l.233)

Another method of amplification is one which he shares with

other characters in the play: the piling up of near-synonyms such as 'some delightfull ostentation, or show, or pageant, or anticke, or fire-worke:' (v.1.119); 'thou viewest, beholdest, survayest, or seest', (1.1.245); or '*Anthony Dull*, a man of good repute, carriage, bearing, & estimation.' (1.1.272). He is fond of the methodical approach. In narrating a trivial event he asks rhetorically when, where and upon which ground it took place and then answers each question in turn (1.1.237–48). There is similar pedantry in his fondness for needlessly long words, as in his explanation of his reason for calling Moth a 'tender juvenal':

> I spoke it, tender *Juvenall*, as a congruent apathaton, appertaining to thy young daies, which we may nominate tender.
>
> (1.2.14)

444. Mistress Quickly has very distinctive speech-habits. Some of the spellings may represent variant pronunciations current in Elizabethan English, but some of them seem to represent eccentricities of her own: *alligant* for *elegant*, *rushling* for *rustling*, *Exion* for *action*. Her *Allicholy* for *melancholy* is not a clear example, because *melancholy* had an early doublet *malencolie*. She often raises *e* to *i*, as in *Ginnys case* 'genitive case' and *tirrits* 'terrors'. Her *Lubbars head* for *Leopard's Head* (2H4 II.1.28) is an old-fashioned form. She changes *e* to *a* before *r* in *fartuous* 'virtuous' and *tashan* 'tertian', with loss of *r* before a consonant. She seems to have had a long vowel in *Wheeson* 'Whitsun'. Consonant changes include the use of *f* or *ph* for initial *v* in *Pheazar* 'vizier' and *fartuous* 'virtuous', the voicing of intervocalic *p* in *debuty* 'deputy' and the unvoicing of final *d* in *Lambert* 'Lombard'. She corrupts *quotidian* to *contigian* with assibilation of [dj] to [dʒ], as in Modern vulgar *ojus* 'odious', and with *c* for initial *qu*, as often in Romance loan-words. For *wilt* she says *woo't*, *wot*, combining it with unstressed *ta* in *wot ta*. She has *pulsidge* for *pulse* or *pulses*, anticipating Mrs Gamp. She has *beseeke* 'beseech'; Chaucer often has *beseke* beside *beseche*.

She is much addicted to malapropisms: *Hony-suckle* for *homicidal*, *hony-seed* for *homicide*, *conformities* for *infirmities*, *Canarie* for *quandary*, *detest* for *protest*, *infection* for *affection*, *courageous* for *outrageous*, *speciously* for *especially*. If the malformation of a word will produce something resembling a word with improper associations, so much the better: *fartuous* for *virtuous*, *erection* for *direction*, *Captaine Peesel* with a possible pun on *pizzle*.

She is an innovator in word-formation. *Temperalitie* i.e. 'temper' combines *temper* and *quality*. *Pulsidge* 'pulse' has an unnecessary suffix, and *extraordinarily* 'ordinarily' has a prefix which makes nonsense of the word. She produces effective compound words, such as *horne-mad* and *eye-winke*. John Rugby is 'no tel-tale, nor no breede-bate:'. She can mistake meanings as well as forms as when she uses *flegmaticke* to mean 'angry' or when she says 'aggravate your Choler'. She is fond of using an abstract noun in place of a related adjective: *absence* for *absent*, *jealousie-man* for *jealous man*. Sometimes she uses a concrete noun for a related abstract noun: *messenger* for *message*.

There are occasional vulgarisms in syntax. One of them has remained a vulgarism to the present day. She says: she do's so take on with her men; the modern equivalent is 'she takes on so'.

Accused of being a woman, she replies with two familiar kinds of substandard prevarication. Her immediate reply is 'Who I?'. Since Falstaff and Bardolph are the only other characters present, her question is simply a device to gain time to think that has been used by many a schoolboy down to the present day. Her next reply, 'I defie thee', is a frequent term of substandard repartee. She finally gets round to replying to the charge: I was never call'd so in mine owne house before.

She sometimes indulges in exuberant repetitions: I have borne and borne, and borne, and have bin fub'd off, and fub'd off from this day to that day, that it is a shame to be thought on. (2H4 II.1.32). The mention of Pistol provokes a torrent of references to swaggerers and swaggering (2H4 II.4.80).

Like Juliet's Nurse, Nell Quickly darts from one subject to another, and it is not always easy to follow her meaning. This obscurity is sometimes deliberate; she is fond of indulging in dark hints, suggesting that she could say very much more if she wished. She puzzles Fenton by her comments on the wart above his eye:

Wel, thereby hangs a tale: good faith, it is such another *Nan*; (but (I detest) an honest maid as ever broke bread: wee had an howres talke of that wart: I shall never laugh but in that maids company: but (indeed) shee is given too much to Allicholy and musing: but for you – well – goe too – (MWW I.4.154)

She has a love of proverbial wisdom: all is in his hands above (MWW I.4.150); what the good-jer (MWW I.4.124); Why that was well said: A good heart's worth Gold (2H4 II.4.32). Her reply to Fenton's question 'how dost thou?' is 'The better that it pleases your good Worship to aske?' (MWW 1.4.144). Anne Page is 'an honest maid as ever broke bread' (MWW 1.4.155).

Mistress Quickly has a power of remembering irrelevant details worthy of Mrs Gamp. This mass of detail illustrates the excellent memory developed by those who do not rely on books for their information. She reproaches Falstaff:

> Thou didst sweare to mee upon a parcell gilt Goblet, sitting in my Dolphin-chamber at the round table, by a sea-cole fire, on Wednesday in Whitson week, when the Prince broke thy head for lik'ning him to a singing man of Windsor; Thou didst sweare to me then (as I was washing thy wound) to marry me, and make mee my Lady thy wife. Canst thou deny it? Did not goodwife *Keech* the Butchers wife come in then, and cal me gossip Quickly? comming in to borrow a messe of Vinegar: telling us, she had a good dish of Prawnes: whereby thou didst desire to eat some: whereby I told thee they were ill for a greene wound? And didst not thou (when she was gone downe stairs) desire me to be no more familiar with such poore people, saying, that ere long they should call me Madam? And did'st thou not kisse me, and bid mee fetch thee 30.s? I put thee now to thy Book-oath, deny it if thou canst?   (2H4 II.1.94)

The circumstances are rather special, for she is bringing a formal accusation, and no doubt thinks that a large amount of detail will make her case more convincing.

In her account of Falstaff's death we find the habits of speech that we laughed at used with serious effect. Her fondness for detail heightens the pathos as she describes the trivial actions of a dying man: for after I saw him fumble with the Sheets, and play with Flowers, and smile upon his fingers end, I knew there was but one way (H5 II.2.16).

445. *Pistol.* The chief characteristic of Pistol's vocabulary is its hospitality to words from many different sources. Falstaff speaks of his 'red-lattice phrases' and his 'bold-beating-oaths' (MWW II.2.29). There is room for conjecture about the meaning of both phrases, but they probably mean 'language fit for an ale-house' and 'browbeating oaths'. Pistol mixes colloquial with rhetorical language:

The King's a Bawcock, and a Heart of Gold, a Lad of Life, an Impe of Fame, of Parents good, of Fist most valiant: I kisse his durtie shooe, and from heart-string I love the lovely bully.

(H5 IV. 1.44)

He uses dialect words like *Neaffe* 'fist' and *mickle* 'great' and tavern words like *Puncke* 'strumpet', side by side with poetic archaisms like *whelme* 'overwhelm' and *Ebon* 'black'. One of his archaisms is the free use of the title 'sir', and it is in keeping with his slapdash habits that he bestows the title improperly. Actæon is 'Sir *Acteon*' and Nym becomes 'sir Corporall Nim'. By the introduction of a single unusual adjective he can transform a commonplace question into a piece of high-flown rhetoric, as in: Trayl'st thou the puissant Pyke? (H5 IV.1.40).

He uses familiar words in unfamiliar ways: *foot* as a verb 'walk', *affects* 'loves', *Give me thy fist, thy fore-foote to me give*. Besides these there are unusual loan-words like *fracted* 'broken', *Bilboe* 'sword', *labras* 'lips', *fico* 'fig', *corroborate*, used with little meaning at H5 II.1.130, and scraps of maltreated foreign languages, like *Couple a gorge* 'Cut the throat' and *Caveto bee thy Counsailor* 'Take care', but he cannot understand his prisoner's French (H5 IV.4.17). In syntax he is fond of inverting the usual positions of verb and object: Tell him my fury shall abate, and I The Crownes will take. (H5 IV.4.48). Another common inversion is that of a noun and its adjective: *Tortures vilde, Vultures vil'de*. He uses many short imperative sentences: Die men, like Dogges; give Crownes like Pinnes: (2H4 II.4.188).

He is a lover of quotations. Where the source can be identified, his use of it is so inaccurate that it is an echo rather than a quotation. In Pistol's:

Shall Pack-Horses, and hollow-pamper'd Jades of Asia, which cannot goe but thirtie miles a day, compare with *Cæsar* and with Caniballs, and Trojan Greekes? (2H4 II.4.179)

there is an unmistakeable echo of a famous passage in Marlowe:

Holla, ye pampered jades of Asia!
What, can ye draw but twenty miles a day?

(2 *Tamburlaine* IV.3.1)

Pistol is proud of his quotations and repeats them, with variations. 'Have we(e) not *Hiren* here?' occurs at 2H4 II.4.170 and 189. '*Si*

fortune me tormente sperato me contente' occurs, with variations, at
2H4 II.4.193 and v.5.100. There are many high-sounding lines
which seem like quotations, though the exact source is not clear,
perhaps because they are from the underworld of drama, ranting
plays which were never printed or, if printed, have not survived.
Pistol's style is infectious; Falstaff addresses him in his own kind of
language: O base Assyrian Knight, what is thy newes? (2H4 v.3.
105). He likes alliteration: Die men, like Dogges; (2H4 II.4.188);
giddie Fortunes furious fickle Wheele, (H5 III.6.27). Pistol speaks
in verse, of a kind, in scenes where the other characters use colloquial prose. His verse is a kind of metrical prose which in the
early editions is written as prose. Vickers says that he uses 'a stiff,
strutting Cambises style made more aggressive by the ominous
pauses produced by an incomplete line'.[1] These short extra-metrical
lines are a marked feature of Pistol's speech.

Pistol's speech is so distinctive that it marks him out from the
other characters in any scene in which he appears, but it has been
pointed out that it is not completely homogeneous. S. Musgrove[2]
notes that Pistol's quotations from plays do not begin until *2 King
Henry IV* II.4.151, or forty-six lines after his first appearance. From
this point every speech of his is made up wholly of dramatic
fustian and he uses nothing but blank verse, though previously,
like the other characters he has used prose. Pistol's appearance is
prefaced by a long build-up (lines 65–104), designed to let the
audience know what to expect. He is described as a swaggerer, a
drunken military bully.

446. *Falstaff.* There is a clear difference between the behaviour
of Falstaff in the two parts of *Henry IV* and in *The Merry Wives of
Windsor*. In *Henry IV* he is in command of every situation, whereas
in *The Merry Wives* he is the butt, and this difference is reflected in
his language. Even within a single play there are differences. In
soliloquy he uses a more natural prose style than the symmetrical
syntax that he uses in talking to others. In the scene where he and
Prince Hal take it in turns to play the part of the King (1H4
II.4.428), he has a distinctive style, which is a deliberate parody of
Euphuism. The subject is appropriate because most of the long
speeches in *Euphues* are spoken by old men who are trying in vain
to reform dissolute young men. Euphuistic features parodied by
Falstaff in this scene include:

1. *op. cit.* p. 124.   2. 'The Birth of Pistol' *RES* NS. 10, (1959) 56–8.

(a) Similes from natural history: For though the Camomile, the more it is troden, the faster it growes;

(b) Affectation of recondite learning: this Pitch (as ancient Writers doe report) doth defile;

(c) Trite quotations: If then the Tree may be knowne by the Fruit, (Matt. xii.33);

(d) Rhetorical questions: Shall the blessed Sonne of Heaven prove a Micher, and eate Black-berryes?

(e) Antithesis: him keepe with, the rest banish;

(f) Alliteration: not in Words onely, but in Woes also.

From the first the Prince is critical of Falstaff, though in the early scenes of *1 King Henry IV* the criticism is so good-humoured that we do not take it seriously. He and Falstaff are playing a game of 'flyting' and they vie with each other in the piling up of comparisons. Falstaff declares that he is 'as Melancholly as a Gyb-Cat, or a lugg'd Beare' (1H4 1.2.76). The Prince adds 'Or an old Lyon, or a Lovers Lute'. It is now Falstaff's turn: Yea, or the Drone of a Lincolnshire Bagpipe. The Prince suggests two more: What say'st thou to a Hare, or the Melancholly of Moore-Ditch? but Falstaff is now tired of the game: Thou has the most unsavoury similes. When he is roused, he has a great power of invective: Away you Starveling, you Elfe-skin, you dried Neats tongue, Bulles-pissell, you stocke-fish (1H4 11.4.268). Falstaff is also a flatterer, and there is plenty of flattery of the Prince mixed up with his insults. Flattery is carried to the point where it becomes insolence when he calls the Lord Chief Justice 'your Lordship' five times in the space of four lines (2H4 1.2.108). When the Lord Chief Justice goes away, flattery gives way to insult, and this is Falstaff's usual practice. Part of his humour is that of making derogatory remarks about the other characters in their absence.

In matters of detail Falstaff has no respect for the truth, but his chief use of falsehood for the purpose of humour is to make statements that are not merely inaccurate but the exact opposite of the truth. He claims that it is the Prince who is leading him astray. He says that the travellers whom he robs are fat and that 'they hate us youth' (1H4 11.2.90). When told that there are eight or ten of them, he says 'Will they not rob us?' (1H4 11.2.68) and this shows a similar readiness to consider an inversion of roles. He is not afraid of exaggeration: if I fought not with fiftie of them, I am a bunch of Radish (1H4 11.4.200). In 1H4 111.3.33–51 he takes a subject,

Bardolph's face, and worries it like a dog worrying a bone, dealing with every aspect of the subject with humorous exaggeration. Falstaff's equivocations show ingenuity. Prince Hal challenges his claim that the Prince owes him a thousand pounds. Falstaff replies: A thousand pound *Hal*? A Million. Thy love is worth a Million: thou ow'st me thy love. (1H4 III.3.157). An equivocator takes pleasure in altering the form of words in order to avoid making a remark which might legitimately cause offence, while making it clear that his meaning is unchanged. Poins threatens to stab him if he calls him a coward. Falstaff replies:

> I call thee Coward? Ile see thee damn'd ere I call thee Coward: but I would give a thousand pound I could run as fast as thou canst. (1H4 II.4.158)

When Falstaff finds criticism unanswerable, he brushes it aside with a complete *non sequitur*. Sometimes he refuses even to reply, in however off-hand a manner, to what is said to him:

> *Chief Justice.* Sir *John*, I sent for you before your Expedition, to Shrewsburie.
> *Falstaff.* If it please your Lordship, I heare his Majestie is return'd with some discomfort from Wales.
> *Chief Justice.* I talke not of his Majesty: you would not come when I sent for you?
> *Falstaff.* And I heare moreover, his Highnesse is falne into this same whorson Apoplexie. (2H4 I.2.115)

His reply to Nell Quickly's charges of broken contracts heard before the Lord Chief Justice is: My Lord, this is a poore mad soule: and she sayes up & downe the town, that her eldest son is like you. The Lord Chief Justice's rebuke is well deserved:

> Sir *John*, sir *John*, I am well acquainted with your maner of wrenching the true cause, the false way. It is not a confident brow, nor the throng of wordes that come with such (more then impudent) sawcines from you, can thrust me from a levell consideration, (2H4 II.1.120)

One of Falstaff's tricks is deliberately to misunderstand what is said to him. Accosted by the Lord Chief Justice's servant, he says: What? A young knave and beg? Is there not wars? Is there not imployment? Doth not the K. lack subjects? (2H4 I.2.84). He indulges in one of the stock forms of repartee in wrongly identifying a word used by another person in speaking to him. The Lord Chief Justice tells him that his waste is great and he replies that he wishes that his waist were slenderer (2H4 1.2.159). When the Chief Justice complains that he lives in great infamy, he replies that a man of his size cannot live in less, as though infamy were a garment (l.157). He is conscious of his role as a sort of court jester to Prince Hal with the duty of keeping his patron in constant good humour. His jests are planned and his comment on Shallow is 'I will devise matter enough out of this *Shallow,* to keepe Prince *Harry* in continuall Laughter, the wearing out of six Fashions' (2H4 v.1.86).

Perhaps from his constant association with Mistress Quickly, Falstaff recognizes the value of unimportant detail in adding to the interest of a narrative or argument. In his soliloquy on honour he reflects: What is that word Honour? Ayre: A trim reckoning. Who hath it? He that dy'de a Wednesday (1H4 v.1.138). The mention of the day of the week when the death took place makes the answer much more interesting.

Falstaff has a favourite type of asseveration which expresses the hope that something disastrous or ludicrous may happen if what he asserts is untrue:

Do'st thou thinke Ile feare thee, as I feare thy Father? nay if I do, let my Girdle breake. (1H4 III.3.170)

if it bee a hot day, if I brandish any thing but my Bottle, would I might never spit white againe: (2H4 1.2.234)

If thou get'st any leave of me, hang me: (2H4 1.2.104)

If I do, fillop me with a three-man-Beetle. (2H4 1.2.256)

A conversation with Bardolph illustrates one of Falstaff's comic methods. After an apparently moderate statement he adds a word that completely changes the meaning of what has gone before: dic'd not above seven times a weeke; went to a Bawdy-house not above once in a quarter of an houre, (1H4 III.3.14).

Nell Quickly produces a fitting epitaph for Falstaff which is completely in harmony with her normal speech habits (H5 II.2.9), but the really scathing epitaph comes later, when Fluellen says:

Harry Monmouth being in his right wittes, and his good judgements, turn'd away the fat Knight with the great belly doublet:

he was full of jests, and gypes, and knaveries, and mockes, I have forgot his name. (H5 IV.7.47)

FOREIGNERS

447. As a rule the setting of a Shakespearean play has little effect on the language used. Whether the scene is ancient Rome, Verona or Illyria, the language is Elizabethan English. There are occasional examples of the use of foreign languages to give local colour, as in the opening of *King Henry V* IV.2, where the Dauphin and Orleans use scraps of French to remind us that the scene is laid in the French Camp. Act III.4 of the same play is written almost entirely in French with scraps of English to illustrate Katharine's difficulty in learning English and to raise a laugh by introducing a number of bawdy bilingual puns. We see which English sounds cause difficulty to foreigners. Katharine has trouble with [ʃ], [tʃ], and [ð]; *sould* 'should', *sall* 'shall'; *sin* 'chin', *de* 'the', *dat* 'that', *den* 'then'. It looks as though English short *e* seemed a close vowel to French ears, since *neck* becomes *nick* and *elbow* becomes *ilbow*. Alice's *Anglish* is a blend of *Anglais* and *English*, and Katharine's *me understand well* shows an imperfect mastery of the cases of the English pronoun. The comic foreigner was a frequent figure of fun in Elizabethan and Jacobean plays, and he might be a character whose mother tongue was not English or a native of Wales, Scotland or Ireland, whose native dialects had acquired the status of national languages. The two plays in which such characters play a prominent part are *King Henry V* and *The Merry Wives of Windsor*, though there are occasional characters in other plays. Jespersen has shown, for example,[1] that Shylock has his own special linguistic characteristics to emphasize his difference from most of the other characters in *The Merchant of Venice*.

448. *Dr Caius*. Before Dr Caius makes his first appearance in *The Merry Wives of Windsor*, we are warned that his use of the English language is eccentric. Mistress Quickly asks John Rugby to go to the casement to see if Doctor Caius is coming. She goes on: if he doe (I'faith) and finde any body in the house; here will be an old abusing of Gods patience, and the Kings English. (1.4.3).

The most obvious indication of his foreign origin is his habit of slipping into French, of a sort. Sometimes he uses a French phrase

1. *Growth and Structure of the English Language* (Blackwell, fifth edition, 1927) § 221.

and then translates it: unboyteene verd; a Box, a greene-a-Box; oon Garsoon, a boy; oon pesant. Sometimes the French is not translated and sometimes there is a mixture of French and English: Ouy mette le au mon pocket, de-peech quickly. The mixture of French words adds to the complications of the editor's task. At 1.4.92 the Folios have *ballow*, but the emendation to *baille* or *baillez* is generally accepted, and at 1.4.71 *La-roone* of the Folios is read by modern editors as *larron* 'thief'. The spelling conventions of the early texts make Caius's English seem even more difficult than it is. At 1.4.45 the Folios have *des toys* for the *dese toys* of modern editions.

The following are the chief characteristics of Caius's use of English:

(a) Initial *th*, when voiced, often appears as *d*: *dese, dat, dere, de, den*. When the *th* is voiceless it sometimes appears as *t*, whether initial or final, and occasionally as *d*: *trot* 'troth', *troat* 'throat', *tree* 'three', *turd* 'third', *tank* beside *dank* 'thank'.

(b) Initial *w* or *wh* appears as *v* or occasionally *vh*: *varld* 'world', *vell, vill, vitness, Mock-vater, vat, vere, vherefore*. His use of *van* for *one* shows that the dialectal pronunciation with initial [w], which survives in Standard English today, was already in current use.

(c) Initial *f* is voiced to v in *vetch, vor, ver* 'for'.

(d) Words ending in a consonant often take a final vowel -*a*: *greene-a, take-a, content-a, peace-a, speake-a, send-a, littell-a, give-a, matter-a, tell-a, procure-a, let-a, meet-a, love-a, nursh-a*.

(e) Final -*d* in past participles and preterites often disappears: *he has save, he has pray, me have stay, have I not stay, he deceive me, he promise to bring me*.

(f) *Sh* is used for *ch* and *J* for *G*: *shallenge, mush; Jarteer, Jarteere* 'Garter', *Jamanie* 'Germany'.

(g) Caius has stolen a feature of Evans's idiolect in the unvoicing of initial *b* in *Pible* 'Bible'.

(h) The objective case of the first personal pronoun is often used for the subjective: *beare witnesse, that me have stay, me doe looke, me vill have it, me tanck you, me dank you, me vill kill de Priest, mee vill cut his eares*.

(i) He is full of strange oaths. His favourite is *By Gar!* but he also uses *Od's me!* and *By my trot!*

(j) Common idiomatic phrases are often given a foreign flavour by the omission of a few words: *Vat is you sing?* 'What is it that you sing?' (1.4.45), *do intend vat I speake?* 'Do you attend to what I say?'

(1.4.47), *it is not good you tarry here* 'it is not good for you to tarry here'. (1.4.116), *follow my heeles* 'Follow at my heels' (1.4.136), with a variant *come after my heele* (1.4.61).

(k) Like Mistress Quickly and many other characters in literature, Caius confuses one word with another of similar form: *intend* for *attend*, *villainy* for *villainous* and *villain*.

(l) The verb *is* is overworked. It is used with a plural subject in *dere is some simples* (1.4.65) and *there is no bodies* (III.3.228), and it is used for *does* in *he is not show his face* (II.3.33). We also have *it is tell-a me* 'I am told' and *is know* 'expects'.

449. The two chief Welsh speakers are Sir Hugh Evans in *The Merry Wives of Windsor* and Fluellen in *King Henry V*. Characteristics which they share include:

(a) Confusion between voiced and voiceless consonants, whether they occur initially, medially or finally. Initially the most common changes are the unvoicing of *b* and *v*: medially and finally voicing of unvoiced plosives is more common than the converse. Unvoicing is very common in the speech of both Evans and Fluellen; voicing is common only in that of Evans. Unvoicing by Evans occurs in: *fehemently, fery, fidelicet, focative, got, goot, ort* 'word', *pad, peard, peat, peaten, peds, pelly, petter, pid, pless, plessed, plessing, pold, pody, prain, preeches* 'breeched', *prief, prings, putter, py'r,* 'by our', *the tevil and the his tam, trempling,* 'trembling', *worts* 'words'; and by Fluellen: *aggriefed, Alexander the Pig, digt, falorous, gipes, offer't, pashful, pattle, peat, peseech, petter, the Plack Prince, pless, plood, ploody, plows, pody, porn, poys, pragging, prains, prave, prawls, pread, pridge, prings, Saint Tavy's day*. Voicing by Evans occurs in: *Hibocrates, cogscombs, taber* 'taper'; *Knog, laughing-stogs, vlouting-stog, hag, hang, hig, hog, sprag* 'sprack', *trib*.

(b) The loss of initial *w* before a back rounded vowel: Evans *'o-man, ork, orld, ort* 'word'; Fluellen *orld*.

(c) The treatment of sibilants is not quite the same in the two plays. Evans uses *s* for *ch* in *seese* 'cheese' and *pinse* 'pinch'; Fluellen uses *s* for *sh* in *silling*. It is not certain what pronunciation is intended by the spelling *aunchient*, which occurs several times in speeches by Fluellen; possibly *ch* represents [tʃ] while the usual spelling *c* represents [ʃ]. Other eccentric spellings involving sibilants in Fluellen's speeches are *voutsafe*, and *Jeshu* beside *Cheshu*.

(d) The addition of final *-s* to many different words. The largest group consists of abstract nouns, many of which are not generally used in the plural: Evans *affectations, attonements, behaviours, compremises, conjectures, discretions, disparagements, dispositions, drinkings, entertainments, fornications, jealousies, knaveries, likings, pleasures, possibilities, resurrections, starings, swearings, tattlings, understandings*; Fluellen *concavities, disciplines, reckonings, variations*. Examples of the addition of -*s* to other words are: Evans *a Christians* adj., *creatures* sg., *death's bed, desires* v. inf., *lunatics, metheglins, moneys, noddles* 'head', *'omans, peradventures, preeches* 'breeched', i.e. 'whipped'; Fluellen *being a little intoxicates.*

(e) The use of the singular number of the verb 'to be' with a plural subject: Evans *there is but three skirts for yourself, it is petter that friends is the sword, There is three umpires in this matter, the lips is parcel of the mouth, There is reasons and causes for it, This is fery fantastical humours, there is three cozen-germans*; Fluellen *the situations is both alike, if there is not better directions, there is gallant and prave passages, my fingers is, there is salmons in both.* The verb *is* is used for *has* in *What weapons is he?*

(f) The use of one part of speech for another. Evans uses *discreetly* for *discretion* in the phrase *with as great discreetly as we can.* This can be regarded as a mixture of two constructions: *as discreetly as we can* and *with as great discretion as we can.* A noun is used for a verb in *I will description the matter* and *can you affection the 'o-man,* a noun for an adjective in *if you be capacity of it, You are a very simplicity o'man, I wil not be absence at the grace,* and *It is a fery discretion-answer,* and a noun for a past participle in *Ile bee judgement by mine Host of the Garter, to be revenge on this same scall-scurvy-cogging-companion,* and *you must be preeches*; Fluellen *she is turning, and inconstant, and mutability and variation, reasonable great.*

(g) The use of a different verbal form from the one that normal syntax would require: Evans *and her father is make her a petter penny; seven hundred pounds . . . is her grandsire . . . give, Master Slender is let the boys leave to play, It is spoke as a Christians ought to speak*; Fluellen *the glove which your majesty is take, I hope your majesty is pear me testimony, this is the glove of Alençon that your majesty is give me, when time is serve, If you would take the pains but to examine the wars of Pompey the great you shall find.*

(h) An uncertain grasp of English idioms: Evans *if you can carry-her your desires towards her, save the fall is in the 'ord, dissolutely, If there is one, I shall make two in the Companie, Peace, your tatlings, I am of the Church and will be glad to do my benevolence, 'Plesse you from his mercy-sake, If Sir* John Falstaffe *have committed disparagements;* Fluellen *you may discuss unto the duke, speak fewer, he is an ass as in the world, he is enforced to retire, the perdition* . . . *hath been very great.*

(i) The use of words and phrases frequently associated with Wales or Welsh speakers: Evans *looke you, 'Plesse my soule, Metheglins;* Fluellen *think you? look you. Pribbles and prabbles,* as an exuberant extension of *brabbles* 'quarrels', occurs twice in MWW (1.1.55 and v.5.168). Since *prabbles* occurs in Fluellen's dialect: keepe you out of prawles and prabbles (H5 IV.8.69), it may be intended as a Welsh characteristic. Another word used by both Evans and Fluellen is the abusive adjective *scall* 'diseased, scabby' (MWW III.1.125), which is no doubt the same word as *scauld* (H5 V.1.4, 32, 34). Other phrases are not especially Welsh but serve to make Evans's speech distinctive by their difference from the normal usage of the time: *take your viza-ments in that* 'make your minds up about that', *priefe* (for *brief* sb.) 'note, record', *motions* 'suggestions', *got's Lords, and his Ladies, There is* Anne Page, *which is daughter to Master* Thomas Page. The change of suffix in *possitable* for *positively* serves a similar purpose in making Evans's speech seem foreign without making it distinctively Welsh. Characteristics of the speech of Evans but not of Fluellen include the loss of initial *j* in *udge* 'judge', the use of an abstract noun *virginity* for *virgin* to describe Anne Page, and the excessive use of the auxiliary *do,* as in *I doe despise a lyer, as I doe despise one that is false.* Characteristics of Fluellen not shared by Evans include the use of *th* for *d* in *athversarie* and the piling up of synonyms.

Sir Hugh's linguistic eccentricities are the subject of comments which serve to make the reader even more conscious of them. In the first scene of the play his pronunciation *good worts* gives Falstaff the opportunity for a pun: Good worts? good Cabidge (1.1.124), and in the last scene he is provoked by Evans's mispronunciations to say: Have I liv'd to stand at the taunt of one that makes Fritters of English? (v.5.150). But Evans is just as active as a critic of the English spoken by other characters as he is in providing material for their criticism. When Pistol says 'He heares with eares', Evans says testily 'The Tevill and his Tam: what phrase is this? he heares with eare? why, it is affectations. (1.1.154), and later in the same scene Slender's misuse of the word *dissolutely* calls forth the rebuke: It is a fery discretion-answere; save the fall is in the 'ord, dissolutely, the ort is (according to our meaning) resolutely:

(1.1.263), Fluellen's name is evidence of his Welsh origin, and the spelling illustrates the Englishman's way of coping with the initial voiceless *l* of *Llewellyn* by putting a voiceless consonant before it in the hope that assimilation will achieve the required result. Beside its Welsh characteristics, his language has qualities of its own. As a lover of rhetoric, he is fond of symmetrical syntax and heaps up nouns, adjectives and parallel phrases: *you shall finde the Ceremonies of the Warres, and the Cares of it, and the Formes of it, and the Sobrietie of it, and the Modestie of it, to be otherwise* (H5 IV.1.71; other examples are at III.6.7, IV.7.37 and V.1.5). He is fond of comparisons to express his enthusiasm. The Duke of Exeter is 'as magnanimous as *Agamemnon*' (III.6.5), and Pistol is 'as valiant a man as *Marke Anthony*' (III.6.13), who 'utt'red as prave words at the Pridge, as you shall see in a Summers day' (III.6.64).

450. Irish speech is represented by MacMorris in *King Henry V*. Its chief characteristics are:

(a) The use of *sh* for *s* as in *Chrish, ish, tish* 'it is'.

(b) The unvoicing of [dʒ] in *beseeched* 'besieged'.

(c) The loss of final [v] in *so God sa' me, so Chrish sa' me*.

(d) Lack of concord between subject and verb: *there is throats to be cut and works to be done*. MacMorris seems to regard *trumpet* as a plural noun: *the trumpet call us, the trompet sound the retreat*.

(e) Unusual past participles: *the work ish give over, I would have blowed up the town*.

Select Bibliography

🐌🐌🐌🐌🐌🐌

ABBOTT, E. A., *A Shakespearian Grammar*. Third edition, Macmillan, 1870.

BAMBAS, RUDOLPH C., 'Verb Forms in -*s* and -*th* in Early Modern English Prose'. JEGP 46 (1947) 183–187.

BARBER, CHARLES, *Early Modern English*. Deutsch, 1976.

BRADLEY, HENRY, 'Shakespeare's English' in *Shakespeare's England*. OUP, 1916, II, 539–574.

BROOK, G. L., *A History of the English Language*. Deutsch, 1958.

BROOK, G. L., *English Dialects*. Deutsch, 1963.

BYRNE, M. St CLARE, 'The Foundations of Elizabethan Language' in *Shakespeare Survey* 17 (1964) 223–39.

CLEMEN, W. H., *The Development of Shakespeare's Imagery*. Methuen, 1951.

CRANE, MILTON, *Shakespeare's Prose*. University of Chicago Press, 1951.

CUSACK, BRIDGET, 'Shakespeare and the Tune of the Time' in *Shakespeare Survey*. 23 (1970) 1–12.

DAHL, LIISA, *Nominal Style in the Shakespearean Soliloquy*. Turku, 1969.

DOBSON, E. J., *English Pronunciation 1500–1700*. Second edition, OUP, 1968.

FRANZ, WILHELM, *Die Sprache Shakespeares in Vers und Prosa* (Fourth edition of *Shakespeare-Grammatik*). Halle, Max Niemeyer, 1939.

HART, ALFRED, 'Vocabularies of Shakespeare's Plays' RES 19 (1943) 128–40.

HUDSON, KENNETH, 'Shakespeare's Use of Colloquial Language' in *Shakespeare Survey* 23 (1970) 39–48.

HULME, HILDA M., *Explorations in Shakespeare's Language*. Longman, 1962.

HULME, HILDA M., 'Shakespeare's Language' in *Shakespeare's World*, ed. by James Sutherland and Joel Hurstfield. Edward Arnold, 1964, pp. 136–155.

JONES, RICHARD FOSTER, *The Triumph of the English Language*. Stanford University Press, 1953.

JOSEPH, SISTER MIRIAM, *Shakespeare's Use of the Arts of Language*. New York, 1947.

KÖKERITZ, HELGE, *Shakespeare's Pronunciation*. New Haven, Yale University Press, 1953.

MCINTOSH, ANGUS, '*As You Like It*: A Grammatical Clue to Character', *Review of English Literature* 4 (1963) 68–81.

MACKIE, W. S., 'Shakespeare's English: and how far it can be investigated with the help of the "New English Dictionary"'. *Modern Language Review* 31 (1936) 1–10.

MAHOOD, M. M., *Shakespeare's Wordplay*, Methuen, 1957.

MATTHEWS, WILLIAM, 'Language in "Love's Labour's Lost"' in *Essays and Studies* 1964, John Murray, for the English Association, pp. 1–11.

MILLWARD, CELIA, 'Pronominal Case in Shakespearian Imperatives'. *Language* 42 (1966) 10–17.

MUIR, KENNETH, 'Shakespeare's Imagery – Then and Now' in *Shakespeare Survey* 18 (1965) 46–57.

MULHOLLAND, JOAN, '"Thou" and "You" in Shakespeare: a study in the second personal pronoun'. *English Studies* 48 (1967) 34–43.

ONIONS, C. T., *A Shakespeare Glossary*. Second edition, OUP, 1919.

PARTRIDGE, A. C., *Orthography in Shakespeare and Elizabethan Drama*. Edward Arnold, 1964.

PARTRIDGE, A. C., *The Language of Renaissance Poetry*. Deutsch, 1971.

PARTRIDGE, ERIC, *Shakespeare's Bawdy*. Routledge and Kegan Paul, 1947.

PUTTENHAM, GEORGE, *The Arte of English Poesie*, ed. by Gladys Doidge Willcock and Alice Walker. CUP, 1936.

QUIRK, RANDOLPH, 'Shakespeare and the English Language' in *A New Companion to Shakespeare Studies*, ed. Kenneth Muir and S. Schoenbaum. CUP, 1971, pp. 67–82.

SALMON, VIVIAN, 'Sentence Structures in Colloquial Shakespearian English' in *Transactions of the Philological Society* (1965) 105–140.

SALMON, VIVIAN, 'Elizabethan Colloquial English in the Falstaff Plays' in *Leeds Studies in English*, New series 1 (1967) 37–70.

SALMON, VIVIAN, 'Some Functions of Shakespearian Word-formation' in *Shakespeare Survey* 23 (1970) 13–26.

SCHMIDT, A., *Shakespeare-Lexicon*, Fourth edition, revised by G. Sarrazin, Berlin, 1923.

SHAKESPEARE, WILLIAM, *The Complete Works Reprinted from the First Folio*. Edited by Charlotte Porter and H. A. Clarke with an Introduction by John Churton Collins, (13 vols.) Harrap, 1906.

SIMPSON, PERCY, *Shakespearian Punctuation*. OUP, 1911.

SMITH, C. ALPHONSO, 'The Chief Differences between the First and Second Folios of Shakespeare' in *Englische Studien* 30 (1902) 1–20.

SMITH, G. GREGORY, ed. *Elizabethan Critical Essays*, (2 vols.) OUP, 1904.

SMITHERS, G. V., 'Guide-lines for Interpreting the Uses of the Suffix '-ed' in Shakespeare's English' in *Shakespeare Survey* 23 (1970) 27–37.

SPURGEON, CAROLINE F. E., 'Shakespeare's Iterative Imagery' in *Proceedings of the British Academy* 17 (1931) 147–178.

SPURGEON, CAROLINE F. E., *Shakespeare's Imagery and What It Tells Us*. CUP, 1935.

SUTHERLAND, JAMES, 'How the Characters Talk' in *Shakespeare's World* ed. by James Sutherland and Joel Hurstfield. Edward Arnold, 1964, pp. 116–135.

TREIP, MINDELE, *Milton's Punctuation and Changing English Usage 1582–1676*. Methuen, 1970.

VICKERS, BRIAN, *The Artistry of Shakespeare's Prose*. Methuen, 1968.

VICKERS, BRIAN, 'Shakespeare's Use of Rhetoric' in *A New Companion to Shakespeare Studies*, ed. Kenneth Muir and S. Schoenbaum. CUP, 1971, pp. 83–98.

VISSER, F. T., An Historical Syntax of the English Language. Volumes I to III (1), Leiden, 1963–69.

VISSER, F. T., Review of Wilhelm Franz's *Die Sprache Shakespeares in Vers und Prosa*. English Studies 26 (1944–45) 13–30.

WILLCOCK, GLADYS D. *Shakespeare as Critic of Language* in Shakespeare Association Papers 18 (1934).

WILLCOCK, GLADYS D. 'Shakespeare and Elizabethan English' in *A Companion to Shakespeare Studies* ed. Harley Granville-Barker and G. B. Harrison. CUP, 1934.

WILLCOCK, GLADYS D., 'Shakespeare and Rhetoric' in *Essays and Studies by Members of the English Association* 29 (1943) 50–61.

WILLCOCK, GLADYS D., 'Language and Poetry in Shakespeare's Early Plays' in *Proceedings of the British Academy* 40 (1954) 103–117.

WILSON, F. P., 'Shakespeare and the Diction of Common Life' in *Proceedings of the British Academy* 27 (1941) 167–197.

Subject Index

𝔊𝔊𝔊𝔊𝔊𝔊

Both indexes are selective. The Word Index is the more complete, but I have not thought it necessary to record every instance of such features as Fluellen's unvoicing of initial consonants or his plurals of abstract nouns. References are to pages.

Word Index

᠁᠁᠁᠁᠁᠁

217

appertainments 28
approbation 50
archerie 136
are 147
argal 64
argo 64
arise 143
arow 130
arrant 151
as 98, 100 f.
assassination 28
at 94
athwart 94
atone 50
attent 132, 193
audito(u)r 136
aught 82
aunchient 206
auncient 146
aunswer 146
aunt 57
away 90
aydant 133
aye 193
ayle 179
ayword 152
azur'd 134

bachelor 136
backe-returne 138
backward(s) 137
baille 205
baite 147
ballet 151
ballow 180
bankerout 129
banket 154
barefaced 28
barne 179
bath 179
batlet 180
battie-wings 135
bauk 152
bawcock 32

be 112, 125
bear 123
beautify 135
bedim 130
beefs 116
beetle 29
before-breach 138
before-time 88
beforetune 130
befriend 130
behaviour 117
behead 130
behowl 130
being 101
belike 91
belock 130
bemadam 130
bemock 130
bemoil 130
bemonster 130
berard 144
bereave 130
beseeke 196
besides 94
besot 130
bespeak 130
betime 88
betumbled 130
betwixt 94
bewhore 130
bewitchment 136
Biddy 32
big-boned 138
bight 153
bilboe 199
billet 134
bin 147
blasphemy 115
blastment 136
blended 125
blent 125
blood-bolter'd 180
bloud 148
bodement 28, 136

conflux 28
conformities 196
conscience 41
conspirant 133
conster 144
consult 133
contigian 196
convenient 61
convey 56
conveyances 153
coppy 157
coram 154
corpes 116
corroborate 199
cote 27
Cotsall 178
Cotsalman 144
countless 28
count'nance 145
countrey 144
courageous 196
courtcubbord 149
courtsey 156
courtship 28
coystrill 36
creato(u)r 136
credent 132
crescent 51
crop-ear 28
cross 94
cubbording 149
cuckoldly 128
cudgel 34
cullion 36
curl'd-pate 138
curphew 156
currence 150
curtsy 156
customer 57

dank 205
dare 125
darkling 136
dat 204

daughter 153
daunger 146
daylight 143
de, *art.* 204
de, *v.* 179
dead men's fingers 57
dearne 193
debile 42
debt 142, 150
debuty 149, 196
decimation 56
decrease 129
deep-contemplative 28
deep-fet 125
deer 53 f.
defect 129
defence 145
defend 51
defy 51, 197
deject 124
delay 143
demand 62
demerit 130 f.
den 204
depopulate 30
desartlesse 147
designe, *pp.* 151
desp'rate 144
destroy 149
detest 129, 196
dexteriously 133, 136
Dickens 36
die 156
diligence 115
disbench 131
disburthen 131
discandy 131
discovery 131
dismes 120
dispise 144
disquantity 131
dissolutely 129
dissolved 129
ditch-delivered 138

gallowes 170
galowses 116
gamester 137
gamouth 151
Gar 147, 205
gardon 44
gates 116, 180
ging 27
ginnys 196
girded 125
glory 117
go 56
goblet 134
golden 134
gondilo 144
gout 29
gozemore 153
grasse-plot 179
gratulate 134
great 15
greater 148
great-sized 138
greenesord 154
grim-looked 138
grow 45
grund 179
gud 179
gyrt 125

habit 47
half 142, 146
half-witted 137
handywork 130
hansomely 151
happily 54, 91
hardiment 27
harkee 107
harlotry 58
hath 122
haught 132
have 113, 125 f.
haviour 145
havoc 129
headlong 136

heady-rash 138
heat 30
heave 62
heighth 152
heir 134
help 121
hempen 134
hence 90
hence-departure 28
herb-woman 57
here-approach 28
here-remain 28
hers 78
hie 27, 153
hight 27, 126, 193
hilding 36
his 117 f.
hit 117
hitherto 90
hoist 124
hold-door 138
homeward(s) 137
honorificabilitudinitatibus 25
honyseed 196
honysuckle 196
hope 54 f.
horne-mad 197
houre 148
how 91
howbeit 102 f.
however 102 f.
howsoever 102 f.
howsome'er 102 f.
hoys'd, *p.p.* 150
hugger-mugger 28
humble 135
humour 29, 48
hundreth 151
hungerly 136
huswife 57, 148

ice 'I shall' 145, 178
ignomy 145
ilbow 204

mystery 51

naught 82
naughty 61 f.
nay 86
Nazarite 135
ne 99
neaffe 199
near 119
neele 193
neglection 133
neighbour 153
neither 99
never 86
news 50, 116
next 119
nick 'neck' 204
nigh 119
night 142, 153
nimble-footed 138
no 86
noble 31
nor 99
nosthrill 151
not 86
nothing 86
notwithstanding 103
nowadays 63
noyance 145
nunckle 152
nuthook 36

oak-cleaving 137
obay 149
occasion 152
occupy 63
odd-even 138
oeillades 43
of 95 f.
oft 88
often 89
ojus 196
old 'old' 35, 180
old 'wold' 154

'oman 206
on 96 f.
once 62
one 82, 84, 148
operant 30
oppress 193
or 99, 103
orchard 55
ore 150
ork 206
orld 206
orphants 151
ort 'word' 206
other 79
othergates 91
other where 90
otherwhiles 89, 136
Ottamittes 135
ought 126
out 91
out-Herod 131
outlawry 136
out-night 131
out-paramour 131
out-tongue 131
ouzell 178
over-night 138
owe 51 f.

pagan 57
Palentine 152
parlous 145, 147
parmacity 147, 153
parson 15, 146
passing 87
patience 144
peaceable 133
pear, *v.* 145
pease 179
penyworths 154
peradventure 91
perdie 35
perdy 27
peregrinate 21, 30

toward(s) 97 f.
traitorly 136
trap 36
tree 'three' 205
tributary 53
tristful 27
triumph 56
triumpherate 128
troat 205
tropically 41, 147
trot 'troth' 205
turbonds 151
turd 'third' 205
twain 119 f.
twelfe 120, 151
twenty 120
twiggen-bottle 134
twilled 179
two 119 f.
two-legged 138

umberella 144
unbonnetted 53
unbuild 132
uncapable 132
uncertain 132
uncharge 132
unchild 132
uncivil 132
undeaf 69
underhand 60 f.
undertaker 53
unexpressive 56, 135
unfair 69
unfirme 132
unfoole 132
ungenitured 28
unhair 132
unheedy 135
unkind 143
unless 98
unlucky 41
unplausive 28
unpossible 132

unrest 132
unrung 154
unsex 132
unshout 132
unthrift 132
unvalewed 134
unwound 132
upfill 132
upon 96 f.
uprous'd 132
use 114
utis 180

vade 150
vaile 193
van 'one' 205
vara 146, 179
varld 205
varletto 194
vary 179
vastidity 28
vasty 28
vell 205
vengeance 88
vent 19
venter 144
ver 205
vere 205
very 63
vetch 205
vherefore 205
vilde 151
vill 205
villager 134
villain 61
villainy 206
visitings 135
vitness 205
volke 178
vor 178, 205
vortnight 178
votarist 135
vouchsafe 24
voutsafe 206

vurther 178

wad 179
wafter 137
wag 64, 194
waighty 149
walk 146
wanion 32
warp 55
was 146
weepings 135
weird 29, 155
Wensday 151
what 81, 89
Wheeson 196
whelme 199
when 89, 104
wher(e) 'whether' 151
where 104
where-untill 179
whether 81
which 80
while(s) 104
whipster 137
whitster 137
who 79 f.
whom 80
whoreson 34
wight 27, 193
wilful-negligent 28
wilful-opposite 138
will 114, 126
willing 62
with 98
withal 98
without 98, 104
wittingly 127
wittolly 128

wives 150
woe 73
wolvish 150
womanish 135
wondrous 88, 145
wont 127
woollen 134
woolward 195
woosell 178
woosted-stocking 152
woo't 196
wot 127, 196
would 114, 152
wrastler 146
wretch 61
wring 123

yare 27
yclad 125
ycleped 115
yea 15
yead 178
Yedward 158, 178
yerewhile 154
yesternight 89
yet 89
ynchmeale 136
yon 77
yond 77
yonder 77
you 75 f.
youngster 137
your 79

zir 178
zo 178
zounds 35, 153 f.
zwagger'd 178